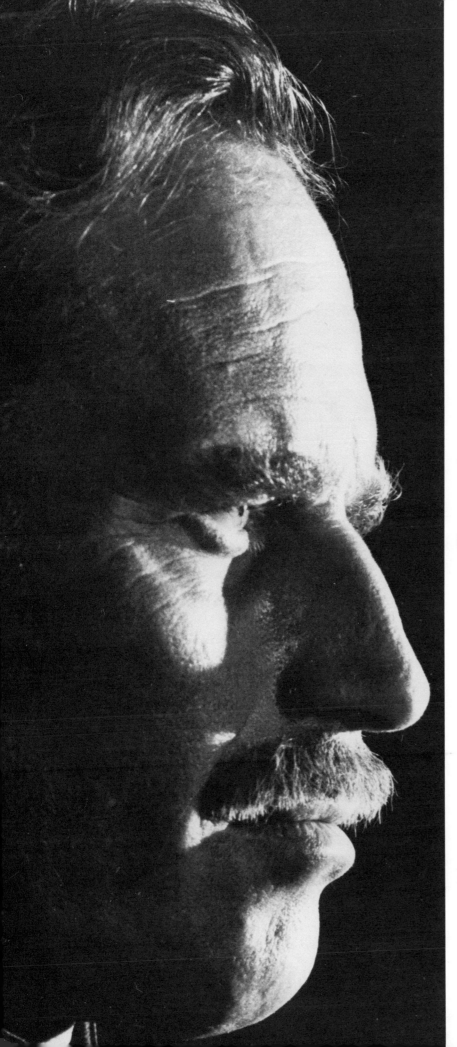

*The
Films
of*
**CHARLTON
HESTON**

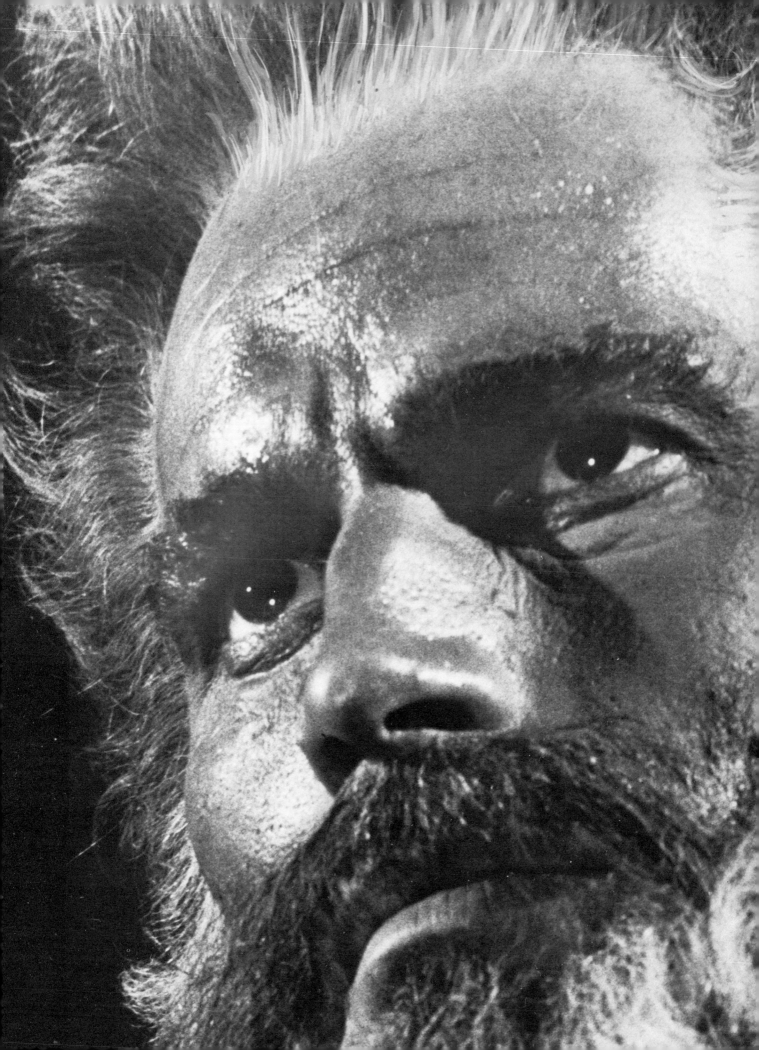

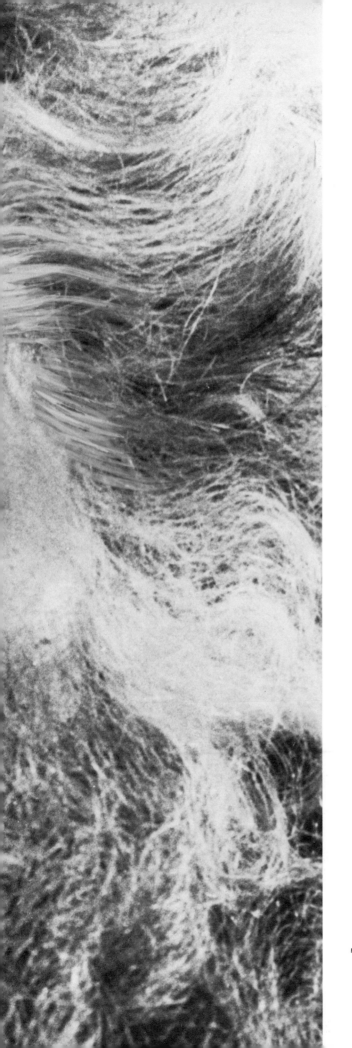

JEFF ROVIN

The Films
of
CHARLTON
HESTON

The Citadel Press   Secaucus, N. J.

First edition Copyright © 1977 by Jeff Rovin
All rights reserved. Published by Citadel Press
A division of Lyle Stuart, Inc. 120 Enterprise Ave., Secaucus, N.J. 07094
In Canada: George J. McLeod Limited 73 Bathurst St., Toronto, Ont.
Manufactured in the United States of America by Halliday Lithograph Corp., West Hanover, Mass.   Designed by Peretz Kaminsky

Library of Congress
Cataloging in Publication Data

Rovin, Jeff.
    The films of Charlton Heston.

    1. Heston, Charlton. I. Title.
PN2287.H47R6   791.43′028′0924   [B]   77–3398
ISBN 0-8065-0561-3

to Rose Rovinsky, who didn't laugh at a young boy playing Ben-Hur in

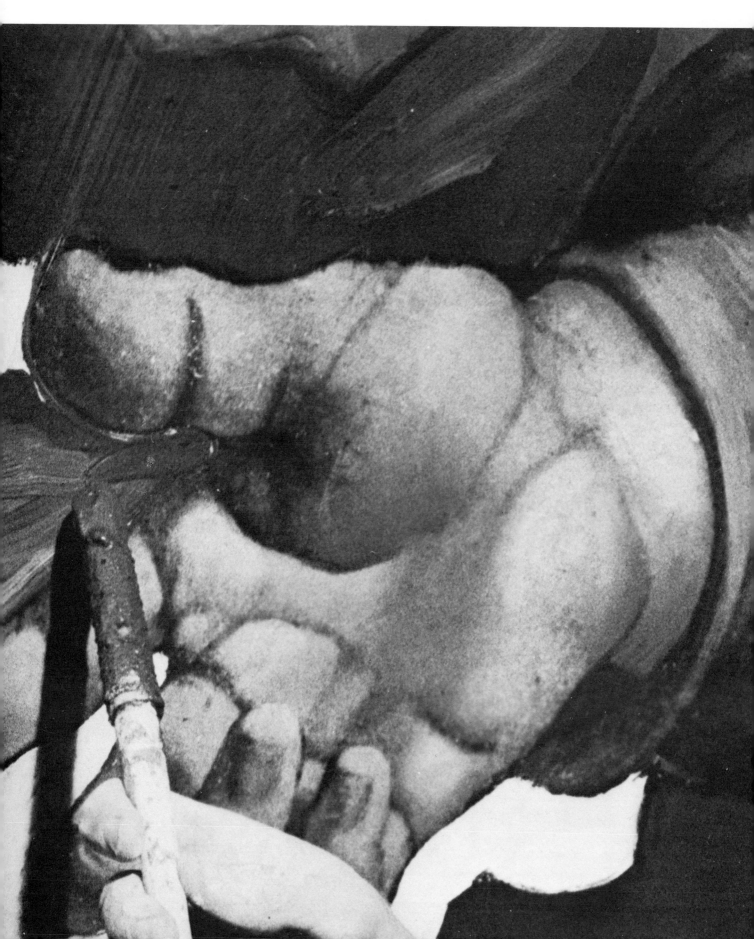

his backyard, or an older boy playing Ben-Hur behind a typewriter

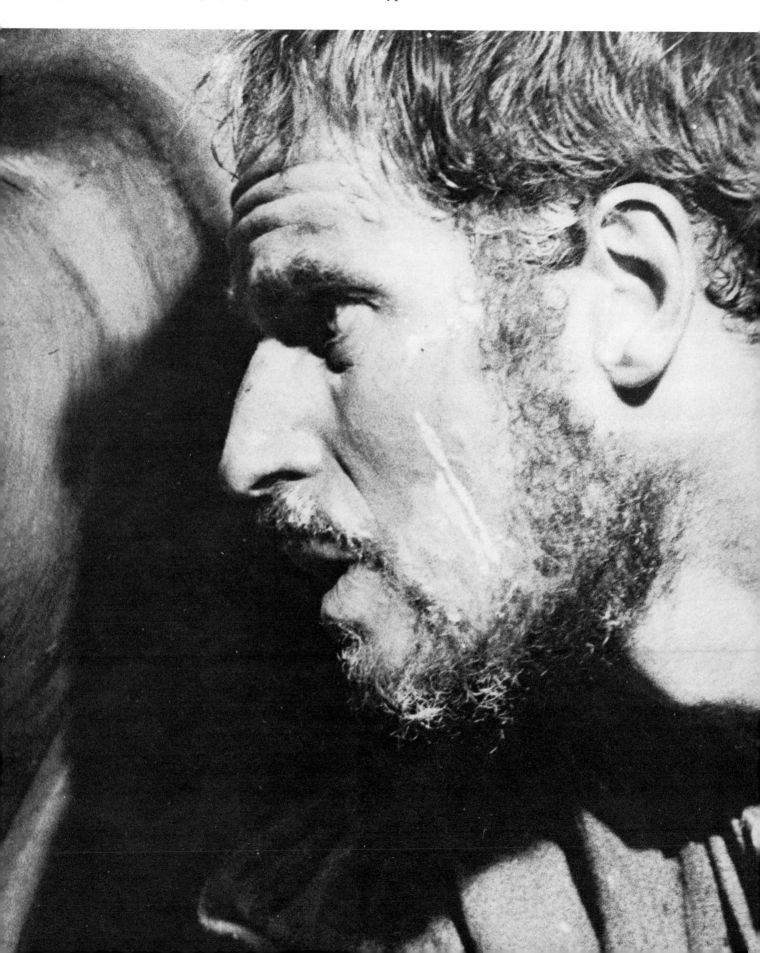

Acknowledgments

The author would like to express his grateful appreciation to the following for their help in assembling this book:

GEORGE THOMAS, for supplying biographical information and a generous number of photographs. . . .

DICK SIEGEL, for assistance in tracking a number of rare photographs. . . .

RICHARD MEYERS, for researching some of the lesser-known Heston films. . . .

ALLAN ASHERMAN, for making available portions of his private Heston collection and for sharing an interpretation of *The Big Country*. . . .

DAVID BRADLEY, for stills from *Peer Gynt*. . . .

LESLIE ROVIN, for holding the author together. . . .

and

CHARLTON HESTON, for his complete and thorough cooperation, interest and faith in this project.

The author would also like to thank the following for their cooperation: Metro-Goldwyn-Mayer, Paramount Pictures, Warner Brothers, Universal Pictures, United Artists, Allied Artists, 20th Century-Fox Film Corporation, and Columbia Pictures.

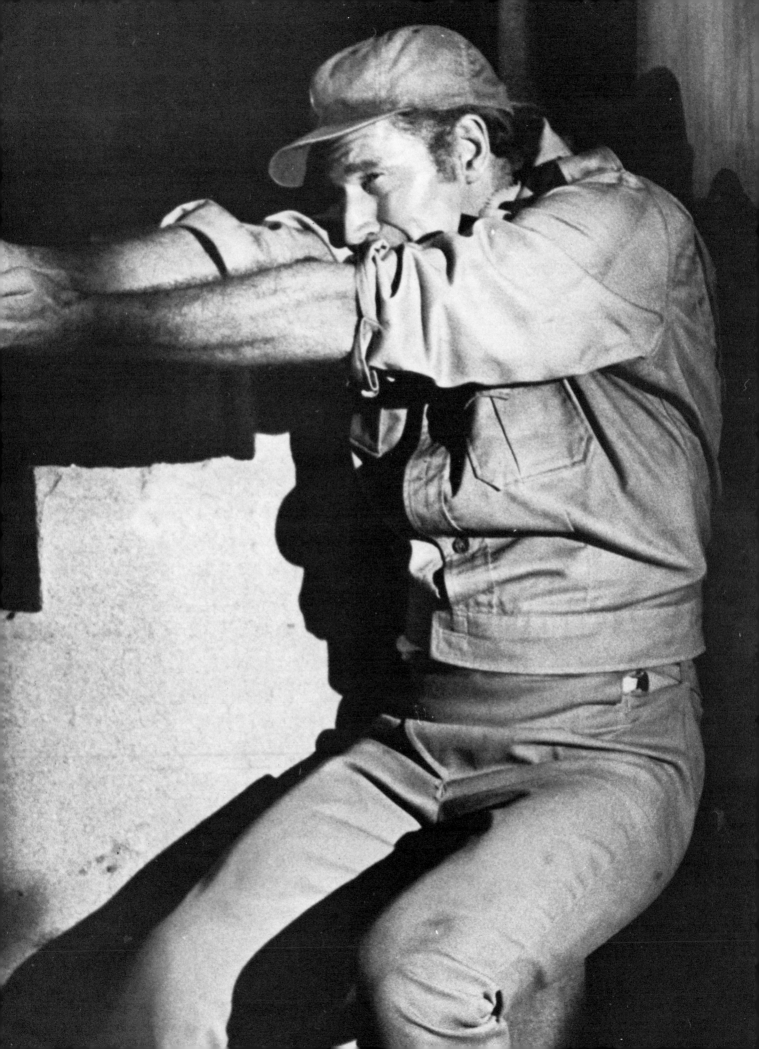

Contents

CHARLTON HESTON

Introduction to the Man

Peer Gynt, starring the seventeen-year-old Heston.

Charlton Carter was born in Evanston Hospital in Evanston, Illinois, on October 4, 1923, the son of Lilla and Russell Whitford Carter.

While the boy was still young, Mrs. Carter, whose maiden name was Charlton, and her son took the surname of Lilla's second husband, Heston. A mill-operator, Mr. Heston moved his family to St. Helens, a town in the upper Michigan woods. Years later, his stepson would note, "I loved it up there. I did all my schooling in a one-room schoolhouse." There, he picked up the acting bug. There was little companionship in this Michigan town, a community of a hundred-odd people, so Chuck learned to amuse himself by acting out the stories his father read to him. He did his first job of public acting in a school play at the age of five, playing Santa Claus. "Since it was a one-room schoolhouse with an enrollment of thirteen, landing the role was hardly due to unusual talent on my part."

After almost ten years of isolation in the "sticks," the Hestons returned to the big city, to Winnetka, Illinois, a Chicago suburb, where he attended New Trier High School. "I was very unhappy," Heston admits. "It was so remote in Michigan that when I first returned I remember actually being scared to death of the automobile traffic and the noise and everything else that goes with a big city."

Speaking of his new home, Heston continues, "I now went to a social kind of school, and I had never even learned to dance. And kids are the most conventional people in the world. It is more important than anything else for them to conform, and I was a kind of oddball. I was driven into being independent. I was very, very unhappy." Too, Heston was small for his age until he was sixteen, when he shot to six-foot-two.

After graduating from high school, Heston won a scholarship to Northwestern University, where he majored in speech and theatre, and played leads in many of the shows presented by the school's famous theatre department. "I knew then that this was what I wanted," he says, "and I've never wanted anything else."

During his free time, Heston worked a local radio program in Chicago.

Toward the end of his college career, Heston married fellow student Lydia Clarke (later the star of such films as *Atomic City*) on March 17, 1944. But getting her to the altar hadn't been all that easy. "I proposed to her on a weekly basis for an awful long time," Heston says, "and then, when I was about to go overseas and had just about given up all hope, I got a wire from her that said, 'Have decided to accept your proposal.' We solemnized it immediately."

While his new bride continued at Northwestern, Heston served three years with the Eleventh Air Force in the Aleutians, mostly as a radio operator in B-25s.

In 1947, after his discharge, Heston and his wife served as co-directors and performers in the Thomas Wolfe Memorial Theatre in Asheville, North Carolina.

"We went there to do one play, earn a little money, and then return to New York," he states. "And it was a pleasant thing, after having been thrown out of countless offices and having doors slammed in my face, to go somewhere and find that an opinion was respected and you could work!" So instead of one play, the Hestons did six, including *State of the Union, The Glass Menagerie,* and *Kiss and Tell.*

Returning to New York in 1948, the couple moved into a $40.00-a-month flat, a Hell's Kitchen tenement, because the rent was cheap and it was near the theatrical district. Heston made the rounds of the agencies, Lydia modeling to support them. "We never starved," Heston recalls, "but we weren't far from it, occasionally." He finally landed a job with Katharine Cornell's company, at the Martin Beck Theatre on Broadway as Proculeius in *Antony and Cleopatra* and in *Cockadoodle Doo*. "I'm sure I got the job because I'm over six feet. Miss Cornell was a tall woman and liked tall actors around."

During the seven-month run of *Antony and Cleopatra*, history was made. Television came of age, and Heston became one of the first Broadway actors to achieve success in the new medium, playing leads in "Studio One" and other dramatic programs. Among his many roles were as Rochester in *Jane Eyre* (1948), Heathcliff in *Wuthering Heights* (1949), Petruchio in the *Taming of the Shrew* (1949), Macbeth in *Macbeth* (1950), opposite Judith Anderson, and many others.

"When I started to do television," Heston says, "theatrical actors of any reputation wouldn't do it because it didn't pay anything, and film actors were contractually prohibited from doing TV. So I was competing with actors in my own category." In 1949, Heston did the short-lived (five performances) *Leaf and Bough*, and *Design for a Stained Glass Window*, opposite Martha Scott. The Hestons also did a series of plays in summer stock at the Mt. Gretna Straw Hat Theatre in Pennsylvania.

As an aside, it is interesting to note that before being discovered by Hollywood—specifically, Hal Wallis, for *Dark City* in 1951—Heston had already appeared in two films, although these are generally unknown, semi-professional productions. *Peer Gynt* offered Heston his movie "debut" at the age of sixteen, although he drew more wide-spread attention as Marc Antony in David Bradley's widely acclaimed 16mm, $11,000 film version of *Julius Caesar* (1950).

Heston does not like popular music much. He prefers symphonies, although he also enjoys Frank Sinatra. His favorite actress was Katharine Cornell; his favorite actor, Laurence Olivier. He reads novels and biographies by the score, and reads newspapers from front page to last, including the comics. He is a fanatic tennis player and horseman, as well as an excellent artist. His pen-and-ink drawings have been exhibited in galleries of New York, London, and Glasgow, not so much, he feels, because he poses a threat to Hal Foster, but because he is Charlton Heston.

He retains his love for the Michigan woods, and has a small place amid 1,400 acres of forest, which he bought with the first money he earned in Hollywood. He spends much of his free winter-time at this home.

When his schedule permits, Heston appears on stage "to renew my passport." His most auspicious ventures into theatrical plays were as Macbeth in Ber-

muda (1954) and Ann Arbor, Michigan (1959), as Mister Roberts (1954) at Palm Beach, as Kell in *The Tumbler* (1960), as Sir Thomas More in a tour of Robert Bolt's *A Man For All Seasons* (1965), which he performed in Chicago, Los Angeles, and Miami, breaking records and drawing critical praise in each city; as John Proctor in Arthur Miller's *The Crucible*, for a highly successful six-week run in 1972 at the Ahmanson Theatre, in Los Angeles, during the winter of 1972-73, and again as Macbeth, in Los Angeles (1975), opposite Vanessa Redgrave. His most recent television appearances have been as Thomas Jefferson in *The Patriots* (1963), and as the Earl of Essex in *Elizabeth the Queen* (1967), opposite Judith Anderson.

In his capacity as a public person, Heston has toured for the State Department's Cultural Presentation Program, was a United States delegate to the Berlin Film Festival, and visited American troops fighting in Viet Nam. He also has the honor of serving on the panel of the National Council on the Arts, was five times elected president of the Screen Actors Guild, and is currently Chairman of the Board of Trustees of

Heston between takes on David Bradley's amateur film *Peer Gynt*. The 85-minute film was silent and based on the play by Ibsen. A musical soundtrack was added in the 1965 augmented version using the music of Grieg.

Charlton Heston (age 17) as Peer Gynt.

the archival, student filmmaker apprenticeship organization, the American Film Institute.

The Hestons have two children: a son Fraser, born February 12, 1955, and a daughter, Holly Ann, born August 2, 1961.

It has been said that Charlton Heston is one of the most conscientious actors in the business. Yet many film personalities have panned Heston's abilities severely, calling him a star, and not an actor; referring to him as "stonefaced."

"Which," Heston believes, "is because I've played so many men of whom statues have been made."

Other critics have declared Heston a personal manifestation of his most popular characterization, that of Moses. When, for example, Heston played El Cid, a reviewer for *The New York Times* commented, "El Cid, played by Charlton Heston in his best marble-monumental style, is a figure of noble proportions who, of course, does no wrong, only right. The wrong is done by others around him who are moved by anger, envy, and greed. He just moves through a series of encounters, personal and martial, in which he usually wins. Charlton Heston marches through it all with the heroic swash of a man who has gained monumental stature and confidence in *Ben-Hur* which, of course, qualifies him immediately for the righteousness of *El Cid*."

Is this a just criticism? For one thing, it was not just in *Ben-Hur* or *The Ten Commandments* that Hes-

Seventeen-year-old Heston as Peer Gynt.

Heston and Solveig (Kathryne Elfstrom)

Heston and Ingrid (Betty Barton)

Heston posing as a prophet seduces Anitra (Rose Andrews) in *Peer Gynt*

Heston in Bradley's *Julius Caesar*.

Heston learns that Decius Brutus (Frederick Roscoe) has donned the hat of Brutus so that his commander can escape.

ton gained his "heroic swash." We will see how through films such as *Pony Express* and *Arrowhead*, Heston has always been the hero with larger-than-life dimensions.

"Of course," Heston admits, "I can't tell how I've been personally affected by playing men of this timbre. But everybody's life is the sum of his experiences. It's like picking up a fresh copy of the newspaper. Some of the ink comes off on your fingers. But you have to be careful about bringing home the character too much after work. This is a very iffy question for actors and different actors go about it in different ways. Most of us believe, and have been trained to work in terms of the idea that you can play a part best if you believe it. And that's what you're aiming for when you work. If you're playing a biographical character, there's the additional element of research involved, and exploring, as deeply as you can, into what the character actually was; what kind of man he really was. You have to develop a point of view about him. With many great figures, Andrew Jackson or Michelangelo, for an off-hand example, or Gordon of *Khartoum*, for that matter, there are different views of what he was. If you do your homework right, you read

biographies that reflect the different views. But still, you have to arrive at one view that you decide is the one you're going to use. You assimilate and choose from among them. Because, obviously, they present conflicting attitudes about the figures, as is frequently the case; certainly with all the men I've mentioned. And about the most recent biographical character I've played, Cardinal Richelieu (*The Three Musketeers*), this is also true. There's hardly been a major figure who's not been interpreted differently by his biographers. If there's been more than one biography, the two biographers will usually take a different stand. But you can't try and present a compendium of all of them. You have to find one view that you think is right. It has to do in part with not only your opinion of the character, intellectually, but also with the equipment you can bring to bear on him.

"You obviously choose a view of the man that will lend itself most readily to your own equipment. Not simply physical equipment, but emotional equipment as well. And all this process is a necessarily time-consuming and, to anyone else, a rather boring part of your work. Personally, I find it fascinating, and I talk about it very seriously. But it's the nuts and bolts of

Caesar's funeral oration, filmed on the steps of Chicago's Museum of Science and Industry.

the profession, just as an engineer's slide rule, and the way that works is for him. But it's quite properly of no real interest to an audience. All they're interested in is the end result."

The end result, for Heston, has been this type-casting as the heroic and incorruptible. From Moses to Ben-Hur to El Cid, he has become the prototype for the moral, upstanding savior-figure. And mention that Heston is himself just such a man, due solely to his having played these roles, and you'll get an argument.

"That's a dangerous claim to make," he warns. "You have to be careful, in my opinion, for it's very easy to get trapped in a character and become more and more involved in him. It's happened to me once or twice. I suppose it has certain creative dividends, but it also can be personally complicating; you know, working on a character, taking him home more and more every night. I think a certain amount of stand-offishness is necessary, not only in keeping your personal life and your own identity free, but also in supplying a certain objectivity which is a necessary part of the creative process in any art.

"Now you can get arguments on that from some actors; I can't challenge their convictions. But mine are slightly different. The question of seriousness is a large one, too. People are, I think, made uneasy by the idea of acting as a serious profession, and of actors as in any way intellectually complicated people. This is probably by and large correct. The favorite public view of actors is the one presented by Bob Mitchum who is, in fact, a very bright fellow; probably bright enough to have figured out that this is the ideal personna to present. But Mitchum, in interviews, never takes himself or his work seriously. He always puts down the work he's done and is doing, and, in consequence, enjoys a marvelous press. Journalists like this kind of attitude about acting. As I suggested, the most popular actors—and I don't mean in terms of their box office, but the actors that present the kind of personality that journalists and, indeed, almost everybody finds comfortable—are kind of skeptical idlers, which is kind of the image Mitchum presents. The lazy cynic who hastens to put down himself and his work, thus making it impossible for the interviewer to do it. Now, you can carry this one step further. For example, what Marlon Brando does is an even more acceptable point of view: The actor as the fatally flawed and gifted child.

"Actors are—public actors, a term I prefer to star; it's such a tatty phrase—public actors are, obviously, objects of envy because they get lots of girls and have lots of money, and they obviously make a living doing something they like doing; indeed, doing something that looks like fun, and on the evidence is something that often anybody can do. Therefore, they are proper targets of a great deal of resentment and envy, unless they can be discerned to be objects of pity and contempt; if they can be demonstrated to be drunks, or

Heston in Bradley's *Julius Caesar*.

Production shots from *Julius Caesar,* filmed in 16mm by David Bradley. The film cost under $15,000 and starred players from local Chicago theatre groups and radio stations. Heston returned from New York to play Marc Antony.

foolish irresponsibles, or, as with Marlon, 'deeply troubled' personalities, incapable of dealing properly with their problems, or absolutely incapable of a successful relationship with a woman—you know, wife after wife, and so on. That sort of thing. And I have come, over the years, to understand this syndrome.

"As for myself, I make, actually, fairly dull copy. Because I'm not a drunk, have had only one wife, and don't get into fights in nightclubs. Indeed, I seldom go to them; I find nightclubs smoky and difficult places in which to talk. I have to go to a good many parties professionally, and that satisfies whatever urge for gatherings I have. I prefer to stay with my family. So that leaves relatively little to say about me."

This public image aside, Heston returns to discussing this aspect of an actor taking his work seriously.

"An audience will best believe you if you believe yourself. Now, obviously, as an absolute, that's impossible. You cannot really believe, in the dagger speech in the first act of *Macbeth,* that you are trying to persuade yourself to kill a king, because if you really believe that, you will go off and stab a stagehand. Clearly, the belief is never total.

"Further, an actor is a prisoner of the parts he is offered. It's true that I have a certain opportunity to make pictures happen, but even there, that's a very limited option. It depends on the projects that are brought you, and while a few of us are in the position to, as they say, 'put films together,' that's not an infinite situation. You can put films together that appeal at a certain time to the people at the studios. So I don't think an actor can therefore plan his career goals. At least I don't understand how this can be. I'm very fortunate to be still offered a great many parts, and I shall continue to try and pick them as best I can."

"Of course, if you're six-foot-three and weigh 200 pounds, you'll never be cast as Hamlet or Uriah Heep. Nor is it likely you'll play a rebel. I accept those limitations."

Yet it is never talent alone that makes an actor a star. Or a "public actor," if you will. In Heston's case, for example, he believes it was his supreme good fortune to have landed a role in DeMille's *Greatest Show on Earth*.

"My first film was an unmemorable, although a professionally and efficiently made film for Hal Wallis, called *Dark City*. But my second film was the circus picture, *The Greatest Show on Earth*, which won the Academy Award as Best Picture and was seen by immense numbers of people. Indeed, it attracted more critical praise than any film DeMille made. I can't say what would have happened if the second film hadn't come when it did, but that secured my place as an important performer long enough for me to get a few turns at bat. And that's important. You have to stay in the line-up and in the first division, and that did it for me."

With this in mind, it is not difficult to see how any actor becomes intensely involved with his work. For acting, as painting, writing, or singing, is a chancy proposition. Heston's wife, for instance, had this to say.

"He is, after all, an actor, and there are times when he gets too tied up in his work for his own good. I remember hearing the Dead Sea Scrolls discussed at breakfast, the way other men might discuss baseball. And it's still a bit unnerving to see him tramp into the kitchen in chain mail or a suit of armor, or dressed like Michelangelo. I would like to see him work less and enjoy the success he has more. But he goes into each new film just as if it were his first."

Still, Heston is pragmatic about all.

"Of course my work intrudes enormously on my personal life, and takes time from my wife and from my children that I wish it didn't have to take. But they react with understanding. My work is the center of my life, and they understand that. We're quite cohesive about it."

Charlton Heston has few personal friends in the movie world. He has had only one wife—for over thirty-three years—and is, in fact, thought of as a rather pompous bonehead. One reason for this widely held attitude, as well as Heston's relative isolation, is the kind of characters he portrays on screen. A Hollywood agent put it this way: "If you had a party going, with lots of loose broads, plenty of booze, people with other people's wives, tell me, how would you feel if you looked across the room and saw Moses leaning on the mantelpiece, staring at you?"

True enough. But deeper than this superficial reaction is the man behind the image. Much of this

personna, of course, is based on how Heston views our world, as well as the people in it.

"I'm not very sanguine about the human condition," Heston admits. "My admiration for man is in terms of the extraordinary individual rather than man in the mass, who I think falls infinitely short of what God must have had in mind. Which has to be something better than us."

"Take, for example, this concept of the anti-hero which we were discussing before. Usually, in films and plays and novels—increasingly, of late—he is presented as a sympathetic protagonist, at least as I understand the term. An off-hand example would be Steve McQueen's part in *The Getaway*, or Warren Oates in *Dillinger*, or the Peter Fonda role in *Easy Rider*. I suppose that they are the victims of anti-humanistic concepts. But I am not so certain that they differ so much from the characters I've played; it's a question of the point of view of a filmmaker, playwright, or novelist. Any film or book or play has to have someone you're for. Now it can be someone like McQueen in *The Getaway*, who's a criminal, yet you're for him because he's against a lot of other criminals. Or the Fonda character in *Easy Rider*.

"Now this whole business of the anti-hero—and the other very fashionable phrase, the counter-culture point of view—is that society's *mores* are incorrect, that the man who challenges them and is destroyed by

Charlton Heston as James Otis in an early television appearance.

them in the purest form of that drama, is indeed the hero. Although anyone could find valid examples of that, basically I oppose it myself. I think we make an enormous mistake by challenging society. Because, in essence, we are challenging ourselves. And if there are no valid concepts—which is the ultimate view of the counter-culture, that nothing is valid, that nothing is worth being—then what are you living for? And indeed, this is the ultimate drop-out point of view.

"Now this is really not a new view; it's nihilism. Nothing is good, therefore nothing is worth doing or being. And I think this is basically destructive. Of course, a concept can be challenged; a commitment can be reexamined, but to say that there are no qualities of human nature that are, per se, admirable, that there are no points of view or ethical concepts that are simply of themselves good as opposed to other points of view, is futile. And it's impossible for a society so oriented to hold together. You have to have a commitment to an ethic. There's never been a society without it. Of course, there have been societies that have destructed before, and ours may be in the process of this, but I can't believe it.

"Which is why I involved myself in social and civic responsibilities. These are, you know, just things that everyone who is fortunate enough to have a successful career should undertake, in my opinion. But I don't consider them as more than a responsibility. I don't find them particularly attractive; they could never absorb me totally. Besides, I think it's strongly overestimated the kind, if not the amount, of influence an actor has to imagine that he can effectively change his world. He can, perhaps, provide a reasonable example of behavior or standards or goals to people who admire him, and to whom this may have some meaning. But I'm not certain that even a great political leader can make more than a ripple in the mainstream of history."

Beyond this overview of society, Heston targets superficial escapes from it as invalid. Drugs, for instance.

"I have never used marijuana or any of the hard drugs. To me, the remarkable thing about the controversy over marijuana is the attempt to justify it in metaphysical or poetic terms. I've never heard anyone defend alcohol in those terms. Besides, the most profound stimuli available to men are mental stimuli. Art, for example, ennobles mankind. I would simplify it even more. The experience of art is the most profound stimulation a man can have; and the satisfaction of art is one of the things that distinguishes man from the other animals. Beside this, the chemical stimuli fade to insignificance.

"But, as I've said, I have not used marijuana, so I cannot speak from personal experience. One of my closest friends is Chairman of the Department of Neuropsychiatry at UCLA and head of the Neuropsychiatric Institute, and he has done considerable research on not only marijuana, but on all the hallucinogenic drugs. So I'm more or less relying on his opinion when he says that the harmful effects of marijuana are, perhaps, not fully understood and until they are, nobody can categorically claim that marijuana is harmless. Especially the people who do, by the hundreds of thousands, without any hard information at all, use it. I see this as irresponsible in terms of their own personal lives, this question of society and its decline aside.

"Now, I use alcohol, but I don't pretend it does me any good. I don't pretend it enhances my performance any. And that, to me, is the amusing cop-out of the people who use marijuana. A lot of people eat too much, and let themselves get fat, and do a lot of things that are counter-productive to their lives. But only the people who use marijuana somehow claim that it's a good idea. The people who use alcohol don't make that point.

"Of course, this is an unfashionable opinion; I suppose I'm rather drawn to unfashionable opinions. But I can only think of a couple of first-rate artists who have used drugs; Coleridge is, indeed, the only example that comes immediately to mind. *Xanadu* was supposed to have been conceived under the influence of opium. And I think that, to my knowledge, is the only first-rate piece of art that is identified as having been conceived under the influence of narcotics. And it's an incomplete poem anyway. Poe, also, used alcohol a lot, and indeed was a drunk; he may well have used narcotics. I'm sure there have been others. Certainly a number of great actors; maybe a few painters. Toulouse Lautrec used absinthe, which is one of the most dangerous forms of alcohol; there have been half a dozen others. Among actors, Keane, Barrymore, and a number of contemporary English actors have been destroyed by alcohol. Robert Newton is a good example.

"Indeed, it's been argued—though I don't think you can justify this in terms of marijuana or narcotics—that alcohol does release the creative juices, and that somehow the spirit of Bohemian freedom is necessary for really first-rate, really classic creation. This is a fairly familiar point of view. But I doubt it. I really doubt it. I think almost all the artists, like Poe, like Keane, who were undeniably first rate, world class artists, and who have been drunks, would have been better off if they had not indulged. Almost all those men would have had far fuller, more productive careers if

they hadn't drunk. They were destroyed by alcohol. Keane may well have been the greatest actor who ever lived. Coleridge said to watch him act was to read Shakespeare by flashes of lightning, which has to be the classiest notice ever written. But he had a relatively short career, and at the end of it was a pathetic figure. Words chosen carefully: A pathetic figure. He was literally unable to learn a new part. And the last time he tried to learn a new part, he broke down fifteen minutes into the play and stumbled around the stage reciting bits from *Richard III* and *Othello*; not drunk, mind you, but gone. Crushed. The same thing was true of Barrymore, of course. If you want to include Errol Flynn, look at Flynn's last years. No, I couldn't buy that any artist, in his natural state, cannot lead a far more productive life without the use of artificial stimuli."

This is, of course, a rather stoic opinion that is anachronistic in our superficial society. Yet, paradoxically, Heston does not really feel himself obligated in any heroic way to his public.

"My only obligation to the public is to perform. And that's only an obligation to making a living. Society will survive without my performing. My obligation to them as a public person is to do my work and respond, in some way, to my public identity, and what their concept of their needs from it are. But I have rights as an individual to function on behalf of causes that seem interesting to me, or valid, or to which I want to commit myself. But that's certainly no part of my public responsibility."

One question that Heston observers have long pondered is Heston's view of God. He has, after all, communed with the Lord in movies; yet his thoughts surrounding this God are "nothing that I can communicate. I have, for example, no opinion of authority on the Bible save as a work of literature, in terms of the King James translation. But again, I believe in the individual. And I believe that whatever God is, and whatever His purpose is, He has more important things in mind than keeping track of all of us. It's a large universe, and we have to be a very small part of it. If He were following us more closely, we'd be doing better."

So this is the man in the flesh, a man who comes across the way he did in his film epics of yesteryear. Charlton Heston's a good man. A man who, when asked what is his cardinal rule of life, responded, "I think the best one man can do is to do his work and keep his promises." But what else would one expect from Charlton Heston—the man of whom comedian Dick Shawn said, "He is one of the few pure men left in the world. I feel very clean; very good next to him."

Heston and Ed Sullivan. One month after he won the *Ben-Hur* Best Actor Oscar, Heston made this, his second appearance on the Ed Sullivan show, to read from the Bible.

The Films
of
CHARLTON HESTON

DARK CITY

Paramount
1950

Produced by Hal Wallis. *Directed* by William Dieterle. *Script* by John Meredyth Lucas and Larry Marcus, from a story by Marcus. *Photography* by Victor Milner. *Music* by Franz Waxman. 97 minutes. *Starring* Charlton Heston (Danny Haley), Lizabeth Scott (Fran), Viveca Lindfors (Victoria Winant), Dean Jagger (Capt. Garvey), Don DeFore (Arthur Winant), Jack Webb (Augie), Ed Begley (Barney).

Dark City was Charlton Heston's first professional film. He made it for Hal Wallis who saw Heston on television and signed him to a contract.

Dark City is the story of a con game; specifically, a card game. It was made some twenty years before *The Sting,* but is not quite as lighthearted. Co-starring were Jack Webb and Henry Morgan—future *Dragnet* partners—with Lizabeth Scott as Heston's girl.

In the film, Heston and his card-shark friends allow an out of town business man to beat them during a night of poker. Knowing that the fellow is now confident, they ask him back for another game, aware that he carries a check in the sum of several thousand dollars. This is money he is turning over, as middleman, to another. The visitor, Mr. Winant, is, of course ignorant of the fact that he is being set up. The next night, they take him for all his money. As a result of losing the check, Winant kills himself.

Hearing of this, Winant's psychotic brother comes after the four men, planning to kill them one by one. Heston and Webb, the last living members of the game, start a two-man search for the killer to prevent their own demise. "We've got this guy on our tail," exclaims Heston at one point, "and we don't even know what he looks like!" To even up the odds somewhat, Heston poses as Mr. Branton, an insurance investigator, and visits Winant's widow. He dates her, searching for information, until Mrs. Winant learns that Heston is one of the men responsible for her husband's death.

A happy Chuck Heston punches in for work.

Meanwhile, Webb is killed. Shortly thereafter, Heston and the killer meet face to face and slug it out. Heston is victorious. He gets together with Frances, a singer who has been after Heston to settle down and marry her.

The plot is entirely mediocre. What is interesting is the Heston character, Danny, and his philosophy.

Danny is suffering from an emotional depression brought on by lack of direction after his military stint in World War II comes to an end. "No one can live without getting involved," Frances tells him at the picture's onset. "I can try, can't I?" Heston responds simply. He elaborates on this attitude later when she asks, "Don't you want to know what's going on in the world?" to which Heston responds, "What's going on in the world stinks." This gives Heston opportunity for brooding introspection, something he does well.

Heston, himself, is not particularly charitable about this film. "It's a special film, of course, but I don't think *Dark City* is a good film," he says. "It's not nearly as good a film as *Touch of Evil.* It's the kind of film that is not made nowadays. It's like *The Movie of the Week*—strictly a television movie. It has some interesting performances and is a competent enough suspense film, but in no way remarkable. It's never been clear to me why the impact I made in it was sufficient to boost my career. This is something an actor always has to consider. After you've done six or seven films, you can survive a mediocre one. But when a mediocre one is your first film, it's a little dicy.

"The character I played, Danny, is a cynical, rather amoral veteran. He is not a very interesting

Heston in a publicity still.

Jack Webb and Charlton Heston plan their strategy in defeating a homicidal killer.

Heston and Lizabeth Scott.

character really, and certainly he doesn't show much in the way of convictions. He is only mildly disturbed at the sleazy gambling racket he is engaged in, and finally is simply a victim, a fugitive trying to escape getting killed. Which is fair enough. But that's about all there is to the part. The only point of view he had was one of a rootless cynicism; skeptical because of his war experiences, although that was not explored very deeply. I recall this was a point of view I used in the part."

Until he becomes involved in the murders, Heston is concerned only with "having a good time," as he himself admits. He doesn't want or need companionship. Not Frances', not that of the Webb character, Augie. Pursued by Sid, Heston goes out of his way to note, "Look Augie, I don't like you any more than you like me. But as long as someone's trying to kill us both, we're forced into a partnership." But Heston is fair. He also avoids Frances. Whenever the girl sees him come into the bar where she sings, she croons such lines as, "You're the lover I have waited for," "I wish I didn't need your kiss," "I wish I didn't love you so," and so forth. Despite all this, when someone comes up to Heston and asks, "She your gal?" Heston responds laconically, "It's a free country. We go out." He is even cynical about his war years. Before enlisting, he sold insurance and "then my father got his wish. I signed up to be a hero."

Heston gives this role the detached sarcasm it needs. Everyone else is completely intense. Webb and Morgan are dead serious; Scott is starry-eyed. Mrs. Winant (Viveca Lindfors) waxes poetic. "The stars are the only things that never change," she says to Heston one night, "and that's only because we can't reach them." Heston, stepping out of character, dutifully asks, "What makes you think we can't?" Which is about the only romantic thing he says as he winds his less than idealistic way through the film.

Dark City is slick and well photographed. There is a strong sense of the lurking psychopathic menace throughout; Sid's determined swath of death is a fine counterpoint to Heston's nonchalance, which dissipates only when he is faced with the prospect of death.

THE GREATEST SHOW ON EARTH

Paramount
1952

Charlton Heston and Jimmy Stewart.

Produced and *Directed* by Cecil B. DeMille. *Script* by Fredric M. Frank, Barre Lyndon, Theodore St. John, from a story by Frank, St. John, and Frank Cavett. *Photography* by George Barnes. *Music* by Victor Young. 154 minutes. *Starring* Betty Hutton (Holly), Charlton Heston (Brad), Cornel Wilde (Sebastian), Dorothy Lamour (Phyllis), Gloria Grahame (Angel), James Stewart (Buttons).

To date, this was DeMille's most successful film, both critically and in the public view. It won the Oscar as Best Picture of 1952.

The Greatest Show on Earth is big and impressive. The producer paid Ringling Brothers $250,000 for the use of their name, their talent, and their equipment, and the magnificent circus backgrounds served as a properly gaudy vehicle for the film.

Holly, the great circus aerialist, is in love with Heston who runs the show. Heston's entire life, however, revolves around the circus. He has no time for women or love. He imports a great French acrobat, Sebastian, who gets center ring, replacing Holly. The girl resents this and protests to Heston, but she is nonetheless intrigued by the newcomer. She competes with him for the spotlight by performing dangerous stunts.

Angel, the elephant girl, also is in love with Heston. Her boss, the manager Klaus, is jealous and comes to hate Heston even more when he is fired. Klaus plans to rob the circus train. Unfortunately, during the robbery, his car gets stuck on the tracks. The train rams into it, killing Klaus and wrecking the railroad. During the crash, Heston is seriously injured. At this, Buttons, a clown, reveals himself to be not an entertainer, but a doctor wanted for murder. He saves Heston's life. He is disclosed and taken into custody by the FBI. Meanwhile, Heston clinches with Holly, Sebastian falls in love with Angel, and the show goes on.

The film is garish, tinsel-eyed, as are most De-Mille epics, but here it all works. For what else is the circus but loud and splashy color? Of course, some critics were not so lenient. *Time Magazine* said, "By sprinkling his footage with shots of circus audiences munching tidbits at the refreshment stand, DeMille tightens his claim to yet another distinction: *The Greatest Show on Earth* is likely to sell more popcorn than any movie ever made." Other reviews felt it was unnecessary for DeMille to schmaltz up the circus with a silly love story. *The New York Times* countered with, "The romantic story is reflective of the daily romance of circus reality."

The film would have been better without the hoke. The circus is properly meretricious as is. But the

The Greatest Show on Earth comes to town. Note plug on theatre marquee for DeMille's previous production.

Heston gets tough with a ringmaster.

Cornel Wilde complains to whomever will listen about the terrible accident which led to his becoming a cripple.

A cameo appearance by two innocuous looking circus goers.

soap-opera theatrics were important as a means of getting people into the theatre, and one cannot knock *The Greatest Show on Earth* in terms of box office.

The film was shot mostly on location and is an awesome technical achievement. It was the last picture DeMille made in three-strip technicolor. However, in terms of motion picture reality, it is an impressive footnote. A blimp on DeMille's camera was the size of a desk. "And boy," Heston remembers, "you're really undertaking something if you try and do a tracking shot with one of those babies."

DeMille's picture showcased the greatest train wreck this side of *How the West Was Won*. Although the western adventure used real trains as opposed to DeMille's miniature models, the effect here was no less impressive; a controlled and somewhat more stylized execution. One might almost say the circus smack-up was a triumph in destructive choreography!

The acting was uniformly overblown, as is true of most of the DeMille films of the 50s.

Heston and Betty Hutton on the set.

RUBY GENTRY

20th Century-Fox
1952

Produced by Joseph Bernhard and King Vidor. *Directed* by King Vidor. *Script* by Silvia Richards, from a story by Arthur Fitz-Richard. *Photography* by Russell Harlan. *Music* by Heinz Roemheld. 82 minutes. *Starring* Jennifer Jones (Ruby Gentry), Charlton Heston (Boake Tackman), Karl Malden (Jim Gentry), Tom Tully (Jud Corey), Bernard Phillips (Dr. Saul Manfred).

Ruby Gentry is a weak and rambling narrative of love and social intrigue. Heston plays the son of an aristocratic family, lately fallen to ruin. His great dream is to reclaim the swamplands, restore his family's good name, and develop the town in which he lives. "A man and his work are the same thing," is his philosophy.

Heston finds none of the local businessmen willing to finance his elaborate plans. Hence, he sets out to marry a rich society girl. In doing so, he sacrifices his love for Ruby Corey. She is a tomboy, has no money, and cannot serve Heston's more important purpose. Spitefully, Ruby marries Jim Gentry, one of the businessmen who had rejected Heston. This occurs right after the death of Gentry's invalid wife Laetitia.

Jim is killed in a yachting accident and everyone assumes that Ruby was responsible. Ruby discovers that, coincidentally, most of these people owe her husband money. She sets out to ruin them all, Heston included. She has Heston's land flooded, and he, in turn, rapes her. Despite these happenings, romance blossoms again between them. Ruby's brother Jewel, a religious fanatic, won't allow his sister to marry Heston. He kills Heston, and Ruby, in turn, shoots and kills her brother. With Heston dead, Ruby returns to her yacht, and all ends, if not happily, then with justice having been served.

Ruby Gentry is an absurd, trite story, with equally trite performances. For one thing, the plot contrivances are studied. Conveniently, Laetitia dies for Jim; Jim dies for Ruby. This renders Ruby from poor to rich in a matter of minutes. Too, everything is seen in black and white. Revenge. Immorality. Morality. Debt. Wealth. There is little grey in the scheme of things. Heston represents pride; Ruby, its victim. Jim is money; Jewel is morality. All the pieces fit too tightly, without complication or depth, which makes *Ruby Gentry* just another pointless melodrama of the 50s.

In the film's favor, however, the swamp sets are magnificent. The murk and the mud are more carefully delineated than the characters.

Heston, Jennifer Jones, and Karl Malden.

Heston and crew member between takes.

Heston and his wife behind-the-scenes.

THE SAVAGE

Paramount
1952

Produced by Mel Epstein. *Directed* by George Marshall. *Script* by Sydney Boehm, based on the novel by L. L. Foreman. *Photography* by John F. Seitz. *Music* by Paul Sawtell. 96 minutes. *Starring* Charlton Heston (War Bonnet/Jim Ahern), Susan Morrow (Tally Hathersall), Peter Hanson (Lt. Weston Hathersall), Joan Taylor (Luta), Richard Rober (Capt. Arnold Vaugant), Don Porter (Running Dog).

This is one of Heston's poorest films, although it needn't have been. Backed by a sturdy cast and strong direction (George Marshall), *The Savage* lacked only a sensible script.

Photographed in the Black Hills of South Dakota, the film is a sympathetic look at the Indian, one of the few Hollywood efforts to present the native Americans as people.

The Savage opens with a wagon train attacked in Sioux territory by the aggressive Crow Indians. All, save young Heston, are massacred. Sioux warriors arrive in the nick of time to scatter the Crows, and Heston is spared. But his bravery has been noted by Yellow Eagle, chief of this Miniconju branch of the Sioux, and Heston is adopted into the tribe and given the name, War Bonnet.

Time passes and the boy grows to manhood. But he is the constant object of criticism, railed at by his fellow braves. War will soon break out between the Sioux and the encroaching white man; on whose side will Heston fight, they gibe.

Meanwhile, love interest develops. A squaw named Luta has fallen in love with Heston, but he sees her only as "Little Sister." She reacts by calling him a "Man of stone . . . man who sees no woman . . . blind one!"

The time soon arrives for a summit among all the Indian tribes affected by the westward movement. "The meeting will be a big one," one native comments. Another responds, "No bigger than the one fifteen years ago. I was there," he offers reassuringly. At the meeting, the question of Heston's divided loyalty is broached. In conclusion, though, all his father will say is, "My son: I ask only one thing. Do not bring disgrace to my name." Heston assures him he will not. "Is it the pigment of a man's skin," he begins before the assembled warriors, "which makes him a Miniconju? The color of his eyes? Neither of these things. No, it is the beating within his body." One suspicious warrior notes, "He speaks with the smoothness of a white man!"

But Heston must prove himself. He will go to the camp of the soldiers, infiltrate the fort, and learn when

Heston murders a fellow brave.

Warbonnet (Heston) and Luta (Joan Taylor).

33

Heston and a compatriot prepare to rescue the kidnapped Luta from a rival tribe

Heston (third from right) listens to his father speak

34

Speared for being a traitor, Heston is turned over to pale-face soldiers who have become his friends.

the palefaces plan to move the Sioux to reservations. He has two moons to procure this information.

On his way to the fort, Heston encounters a party of soldiers surrounded by the Crow Indians. He picks off the offending warriors, which earns him the gratitude of the Colonel in command.

Posing as scout Jim Ahern, Heston, still in braids, is taken to the fort. There, once again, the savage is suspect. As a dinner place is set for him, Heston overhears one soldier comment, "Do you think we can trust him with one of these?" indicating a table knife. Heston walks in the door, and the soldier fumbles for verbal cover. "Civilized people don't listen in on other people's conversations," he says. To which Heston responds, "Savages speak their insults to a man's face." A fight is narrowly averted.

The next day, as Heston rides out with the soldiers, he sees a smoke signal. Luta has been kidnapped by the Crow. Quickly, he returns to the Indian encampment and, with three other braves, rides to the rescue. Heston and one Indian ford a river to enter Crow territory; the other two Indians, fearful for their lives, flee. Still, the rescue is effected, and Heston, Luta, and their companion ride off. Meanwhile, their cowardly brothers return to camp and report all three Indians dead.

Unfortunately, the soldiers left by Heston find three of their men in the forest, dead. When they see Heston, his aide, and Luta riding toward them, they see only faceless Indians. They fire, and Luta is killed. Heston and the other Indian ride off. They return to the Indian settlement and Heston is angered beyond words. "From this day forth," he decrees, "let no man call me white." The two braves who deserted him are killed ("He who has lived without honor shall die without honor," notes Yellow Eagle), and a plan of action is formulated.

It is decided that Heston should return to the fort and lead the trusting soldiers between two cliffs, into an ambush. The men do indeed ride out, but there is a hitch. They are assigned to join a wagon train and see

them to safety. If Heston allows the ambush to go through, innocent men, women, and children will be killed. A half-mile before the ambush, he warns the soldiers that he 'sees' Indians in the hills. Before the caravan enters the gorge, it breaks and the palefaces run for it, leaving the waiting Indians stunned.

After this, Heston rides into the Indian camp, knowing what awaits him. Before the inevitable, however, he addresses his people. "My heart no longer quickly grows hot with anger," he admits. "For all whites are not killers." Heston is reminded again that "He who has lived without honor shall die without honor." So he knows he must die. "But I say this final thing," he offers. "More soldiers will come, as many as there are stars in the sky. And for every soldier you kill, ten will come. . . ." He pleads for peace. But his father is unimpressed. "I do not ask for sympathy," Heston confesses. "I am here to stop you from destroying yourselves." This doesn't stop Yellow Eagle from destroying Heston, or going through the motions of so doing. He plunges a spear into his adopted son's chest, as is the law. He must, he says, or his people will accuse, "There are laws for all except the chief of the Miniconju."

The thrust, however, is not fatal, and Heston is returned to the fort, to a woman with whom he has fallen in love. And when the two races part, it is with a semblance of peace in the air.

In *The Savage*, Heston plays one of his early martyr figures. Unfortunately, this script is so flat as to render ineffective any and all sincerity on the part of the players. It gives them nothing in the way of character dimension with which to work, particularly Heston, who is hopelessly wooden. The only sturdy performance comes from Milburn Stone, as a soldier whose down-to-earth philosophizing offers some enjoyable substance.

When we look at Heston's other savior-figures—such as El Cid—it will become obvious how these early efforts were planned as Grade-B material. At worst, they were silly; at best, unpretentious.

THE PRESIDENT'S LADY

20th Century-Fox
1953

Heston is shot and narrowly escapes death defending his wife's hon or.

Produced by Sol C. Siegel. *Directed* by Henry Levin. *Script* by John Patrick from a novel by Irving Stone. *Photography* by Leo Tover. *Music* by Alfred Newman. 97 minutes. *Starring* Susan Hayward (Rachel Jackson), Charlton Heston (Andrew Jackson), John McIntire (John Overton), Fay Bainter (Mrs. Donelson).

Heston goes to inspect his living quarters as Susan Hayward looks on.

Heston is one of the few actors who has had the opportunity to play two historical characters twice each. One was Marc Antony, whom he portrayed in *Julius Caesar* (1970) and *Antony and Cleopatra* (1972). The other was Andrew Jackson.

"I think I admired Andrew Jackson more than any of the other men of that genre I've played," Heston says. And his first contact with "Old Hickory" was in the film *The President's Lady*. "In preparation for this film, DeMille had let me see his 1938 version of *The Buccaneer* to study the character. He also let me look at some research materials. He was very kind about it. In fact, he loaned me a combination research item and good luck piece, a lovely little wax statuette of Jackson, about ten inches high, which I kept in my dressing room while we were shooting *The President's Lady*. Afterwards, I duly returned it to him.

"Five years later," Heston continues, "DeMille was planning to remake *The Buccaneer*. At the time I don't think it was settled to what extent he was planning to involve himself in the production. I still had one picture left on the contract that Paramount had purchased from Hal Wallis. I asked to play Jackson in a cameo role to use up the remaining commitment. He thought it was a fine idea. The intended cameo role, however, blossomed into a considerable part as the script developed. As additional recompense, he gave me the little wax statue of Jackson."

The President's Lady is a good little movie, largely overlooked as one of the more human historical efforts. The film opens with Jackson, then a lawyer, arriving at the backwoods home of his future bride. Unfortunately, she is already married. This proves inconsequential, as Rachel and her husband divorce soon thereafter. She marries Heston, but it is then revealed that the divorce wasn't finalized. The couple dodge rumor and scandal, and only after Heston nearly loses his life in a pistol duel, which he wins defending his wife's honor, do Jackson and Rachel know peace. Shortly thereafter, Old Hickory becomes the seventh President of the United States. Rachel, however, dies on the eve of his victory.

As a love story, the picture is moving. As an historical document, it is only fair. But the performances and characterizations are strong, and there is honest laughter during moments of lighthearted fun between the two, such as a ride down the Mississippi where Heston flees Indian arrows. There is drama; Heston's defending his wife from the harpy-like puritans who malign her marital escapades; and, of course, there is pathos. Mrs. Jackson is shown smoking a pipe at home quite casually, as history says she was wont to do. The actors, Heston and Susan Hayward, are perfectly at ease in every aspect of their roles.

Heston shows off his new bride, Susan Hayward.

Heston on the campaign trail.

Heston and Susan Hayward.

Susan Hayward dies on the eve of Heston's election to the presidency.

PONY EXPRESS

Paramount
1953

Produced by Nat Holt. *Directed* by Jerry Hopper. *Script* by Charles Marquis Warren, based on a story by Frank Gruber. *Photography* by Ray Rennahan. *Music* by Paul Sawtell. 101 minutes. *Starring* Charlton Heston (Buffalo Bill Cody), Rhonda Fleming (Evelyn Hastings), Jan Sterling (Denny Russell), Forrest Tucker (Wild Bill Hickok).

This is easily the most enjoyable of the Heston westerns, made in the 50s. It leaves all other historical dramas in the dust of its tongue-in-cheek heels.

Based on a story by Frank Gruber, *Pony Express* tells of what was involved in linking California with the rest of the Union. Heston portrays Buffalo Bill Cody; Forrest Tucker is Wild Bill Hickok. Together, the men face insurmountable odds and, so the picture makes it seem, create the mail route single-handedly.

The plot is insignificant. What really makes the film are the performances and interplay between Heston and Tucker. Through it all, Heston is the personification of cocky self-assurance.

In the beginning of the film, Heston flags down a stage-coach after losing his horse to plains Indians. "I'm Buffalo Bill Cody," he tells the driver. "Sure, and I'm Wild Bill Hickok!" the coachman responds. Heston laughs and boards the wagon. "Nope," he counters, "you're not that ugly!"

When he arrives in town, the flamboyant Heston finds himself the object of two young girls' envy. A passerby, noting this, asks what anyone sees in Heston. "Never could figure that out myself," Heston answers, "unless it's my looks and personality."

Soon thereafter, Heston and Tucker meet. They greet each other in most unusual fashion. Taking turns, bullet for bullet, they blow parts of each other's clothing away; plant lead between each other's feet, and so forth. "It's better'n shakin' hands," one of Heston's lady friends notes. Later, the two men, along with friends and antagonists Evelyn Hastings (Rhonda Fleming) and her brother, are trapped in a cabin by Indians. Yellow Hand, an obnoxious Indian leader, hopes to gain a name by killing Heston. The latter informs the Indian that he's a snake. Shocked, Tucker notes, "If he ever catches you, I hope you're not

In the opening minutes, Heston loses his horse in a vicious Indian encounter.

Heston accepts the challenge of, confronts, and beats an Indian who looked to gain a name by killing Buffalo Bill.

After killing Yellow Hand, Heston strides through a crowd of onlookers.

Jan Sterling has taken a bullet meant for Heston and dies in his arms.

Heston carries the dead Jan Sterling to her final resting place.

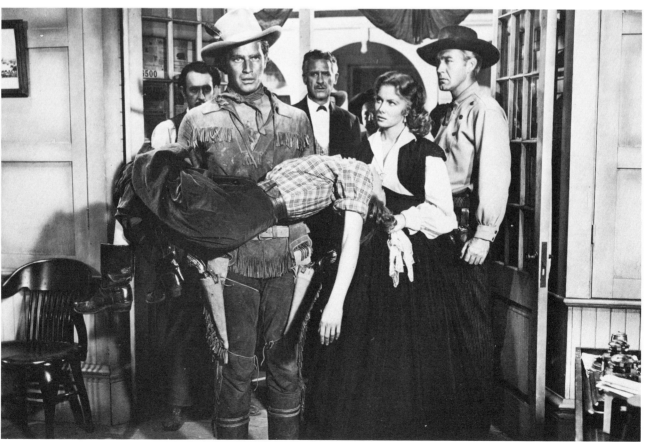

around." Nonetheless, to save the party, Heston must battle the brave. "Well, I'll see you later," he says without fear, adding, "Don't wait up for me." The fight concludes with Heston the victor, and upon Yellow Hand's pre-mortem promise, the palefaces are freed.

This entire hostile-Indian situation is, of course, fostered by Mr. Hastings, who stands to profit if the Express is not founded. For in that event, 'a foreign government' would get California and their agent Hastings would get rich. So he organizes the sale of rifles to the savages to sabotage the operation.

Anyway, before the film is through, Miss Hastings falls in love with Heston and betrays her brother; the Pony Express is established; California is linked with the Union and votes against slavery. What's great about *Pony Express* are the characterizations of Heston and Tucker. Heston is casual, rakish, and always at ease. Tucker is a little more stuffy, a little less interested in other people, and is more concerned with finding a viable store of whiskey than in anything that even hints at grand purpose.

Heston and Tucker are very active in a rip-roaring way. For instance, when express outposts are being blown to splinters, the men ride to undo the damage with a frenzy that is contagious. The film is worth watching if only to see them in action.

Still, the production qualities are no better than similar efforts. There is a sameness about it all that cannot be ignored. But the two stars are great, and that's what makes the movie fun.

Heston and Tucker track down their enemies

ARROWHEAD

Paramount
1953

Produced by Nat Holt. *Directed* by Charles Marquis Warren. *Script* by Charles Marquis Warren, based on the novel by W. R. Burnett. *Photography* by Ray Rennahan. *Music* by Paul Sawtell. 105 minutes. *Starring* Charlton Heston (Ed Bannon), Jack Palance (Toriano), Katy Jurado (Nita), Brian Keith (Capt. North).

Arrowhead used many of the sets, actors, and technicians from *The Savage*. But there's one major difference. *Arrowhead* is an excellent motion picture. Indeed, any film with Jack Palance as the villain can't be all bad. He is classic in this respect. And, of course, Heston is the perfect hero. Pit them against one another with a tight script, good directing, and a strong supporting cast, including Brian Keith and Milburn Stone, and you've got a winner.

The film is based on fact, the story of Al Sieber, an Indian scout who, according to the film's opening credits, "deserves to have his name ranked with Daniel Boone, Kit Carson, and William F. Cody." The commentary goes on to detail how he deserves the Congressional Medal of Honor for performance above and beyond the call of duty.

In the film, Sieber is Ed Bannon (Heston), chief of scouts for U.S. armed forces fighting Apaches in the post Civil War west. Our picture opens with Heston and Stone alone on the plains. Heston catches sight of Apaches. He orders Stone to stay behind and goes after the braves. Sneaking up behind them, he announces, "Turn around, dirt," and proceeds to massacre the warriors. The army, of course, disapproves of Heston's actions. They have a treaty with the Indians and Heston has broken it.

The men return to the fort where the Colonel chastises Heston for wearing Confederate colors. "I like grey," Heston informs him. "You like bein' ornery," the Colonel retaliates. And he's right. Heston's actions against the Apaches have caused the loss of soldiers' lives and earned him the indignation of the remaining soldiers. As a result, Heston promptly gets into a fist fight. An irate sergeant has insulted Heston and the latter takes him on. Needless to say, he beats the soldier to within an inch of his life. Afterwards, he

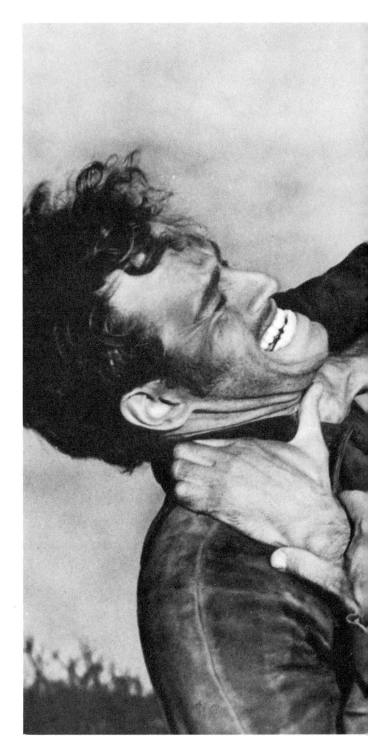

Heston (left) and Jack Palance in one of their many confrontations.

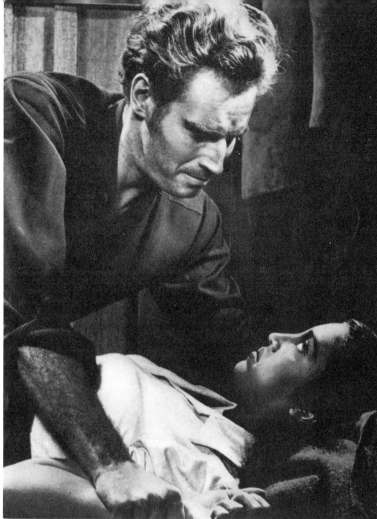

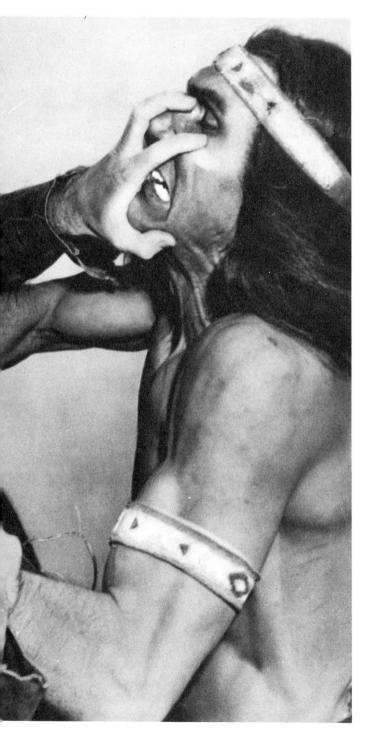

Heston prepares to beat Katy Jurado to within an inch of her traitorous life.

stoically says, "Made another enemy in the sergeant." Not surprisingly, Heston is relieved of his commission.

Meanwhile, a strong secondary plot has developed. The soldiers must prepare all Apaches for transport to a reservation in Florida. Simultaneously, Toriano (Palance), son of the strongest Apache chief, Chatez, returns west from an eastern college. Though Toriano cooperates with the soldiers, Heston doesn't trust him. Once before they had been at odds, and the white man had given Toriano a great scar on his neck. This, when the latter had tried to kill a crippled child by bashing in his skull. The Indian had sworn revenge.

Chatez seriously intends to make the move, but Heston knows that Toriano sees this as weakness. He warns the young brave that, although he is no longer an official arm of the militia, he is going to keep an eye on him. Toriano is unimpressed.

Heston's words prove true. The Indians are being catalogued, given collars with their names on them. These must be worn about their necks. The first brave is led to a tent where the register stands and is asked his name. He says nothing. Repeated questioning gets the soldiers nowhere. Heston watches the goings-on from a nearby position. After several minutes of this, Toriano says he objects to his people being herded like cattle. And they will not cooperate.

That night, realizing that something must be done, Heston, in a move that is both brave and against army orders, visits the Indian encampment which is surrounded by soldiers. Toriano moves to kill him, but cannot: Heston is unarmed. By law, an Indian cannot kill a man who comes unarmed into a settlement. Chatez, however, has to argue this point strongly to stop Toriano. After a lengthy discussion, Heston finds he is unable to learn Toriano's plans. He leaves, but he makes one final comment. "I will go," he begins in typical Heston style, swaggering the line through gritted teeth, "but I tell you this. I know the beat of your drums. I'll fight against you," he warns.

Now Heston, who has been given his old job of scout back, is frustrated. He confides in Anita, a young Indian girl who does the laundry at the fort. She is also Heston's lover. "I thought I knew every ritual in the Apache book," Heston admits to her as he listens to a far away drumbeat, but this one, inspired by Toriano through the Great Spirit, has him mystified.

Things begin to break in Toriano's favor. Heston and Stone are out on patrol when they are attacked by Anita's brother. Heston drowns the brother, but not before Toriano and his braves arrive in hot pursuit. Our heroes make it back to the fort. Heston confronts the Colonel who is about to ride out with his men to corral the Indians and take them to the trains that will carry them to Florida. Heston warns him not to go. The Colonel tells Heston to stay out of this. Insulted,

the scout says, "I don't care what happens to you as long as I know you were warned first." He leaves the men with a final note: "You were knee-high and learning math while I was learning how to slit a man's throat so it takes him an hour to die."

With this happy thought in his mind, the Colonel once again relieves Heston of his position, replacing him with Johnny August and Jim Eagle. The soldiers do not know, of course, that Jim Eagle works for Toriano. At this time, Heston discovers that Anita also works for Toriano when she tries to kill him. Failing to do this, Anita stabs herself. Dying, she gasps, "I failed to kill you, but my people will not." And, "I hated your hands against me." Heston is unmoved and calls for help. "There's a dead Apache in here," he tells a pair of soldiers. "Get it out!"

Later, he finds Toriano, surprises him from behind, and slits the man's wrist, pressing it to his own slit wrist; the two are now blood brothers. The only way to break it is for one of them to die. If another brave were to kill Heston, the bond would survive. This is something Toriano could never allow. Thus, the Indian leader announces to his braves, "There will be no more fighting until Bannon has met Toriano."

The two assign a time and place to meet and do battle. After an absolutely frenzied time, Heston kills Toriano. The Messiah lies, Christ-like, crucified in the dirt, his back broken. And, their leader gone, the Indians realize the futility of their position and return to their reservation and to their fate.

BAD FOR EACH OTHER

Columbia
1953

Produced by William Fadiman. *Directed* by Irving Rapper. *Script* by Irving Wallace and Horace McCoy, based on the novel by McCoy. *Photography* by Frank Planer. *Music* by Mischa Balaleinikoff. 82 minutes. *Starring* Charlton Heston (Dr. Tom Owen), Lizabeth Scott (Helen Curtis), Dianne Foster (Joan Lasher), Mildred Dunnock (Mrs. Owen), Arthur Franz (Dr. Jim Crowley).

Once again, Heston is a man-gone-wrong who finds final redemption. In *Bad For Each Other*, he plays Tom Owen, a soldier-medic who returns to the gritty Pittsburgh mining town in which he used to live before service in the Korean War. Since he is a doctor and has status, Heston is immediately snared by the spoiled Lizabeth Scott, whom one critic accurately labeled "a prowling debutante." Our hero must choose between the needs of poor miners who can certainly use his services and the lure of a swank society clientele. He picks money over altruism.

Heston is much criticized, but is blinded by infatuation and greed. Towards the end of the film, however, a mining explosion causes him to see the light, and Heston leaves Scott for one Nurse Lasher. With this renunciation comes new responsibility and a truly rewarding future.

This obscure effort is based on Horace McCoy's short story *Scalpel*. As for Heston's performance, it is simple-minded as he self-righteously pushes his way through society, casting a shadow of irresponsible naiveté that is not generic to his real-life-personality. As a result, the portrayal doesn't come off.

Heston's future is given direction by the seductive Lizabeth Scott; she lures him into the world of swanky clientele.

But Heston's better instincts win out, and his medical talents are put to use in a hospital where he meets lovely Dianne Foster.

An explosion in a local mine convinces Heston that human needs are more important than riches. With Arthur Franz and Dianne Foster.

THE NAKED JUNGLE

Paramount
1953

Produced by George Pal. *Directed* by Byron Haskin. *Script* by Philip Yordan and Ranald MacDougall, from the story *Leiningen vs. the Ants* by Carl Stephenson. *Photography* by Ernest Laszlo. *Music* by Daniele Amfitheatrof. 94 minutes. *Starring* Charlton Heston (Christopher Leiningen), Eleanor Parker (Joanna Leiningen), William Conrad (Commissioner).

The Naked Jungle is an exciting, unusual adventure film, and one that was unique for Heston. In it he plays an out-and-out heel with absolute conviction.

The film is set in the year 1901, on a plantation in South America. It is an empire that took Heston fifteen years to build, turning the swamps into acre upon acre of prosperous chocolate crop.

The story opens with pretty Joanna (Eleanor Parker) sailing on a tug down the Amazon River. She has just married Heston by proxy, i.e., they've never met. All arrangements and the ceremony were performed by Heston's brother in New Orleans.

The boat docks a day after entering Heston's property, so vast is the land. But Heston is not there to meet his wife. He sends, instead, his charming aide who apologizes for his master saying that he is away in the jungle.

By nightfall, Heston still hasn't arrived, and Joanna prepares for bed. As she sleeps the neigh of a horse awakens her. There are shouts. Heston has arrived. We first glimpse him from afar in the courtyard as he dismounts. Dressed in riding togs, he holds a horsewhip and wears a cocked white cowboy hat. He makes his way somberly to his wife's chamber. "Leiningen, ma'am," he announces from without. "I'll be right there," she answers. Joanna comes out in a nightgown. Heston is startled. "You're not dressed, madam. I'll come back another time." This, of course, takes Joanna by surprise, but she recovers and asks him to stay and talk. They get off to a very bad start. For Joanna kids Heston about some small point. "You have a sense of humor," he notes gruffly. Then, "I don't like humor in a woman." "I'm sorry," she apologizes quickly. "And you interrupt," Heston adds, annoyed. Things go downhill from there. He asks Joanna why she decided to come; she says it was because she was intrigued by Heston's letters to his brother. "I could tell how lonely you were. I could tell you needed me," she offers. Which is the wrong thing to say. "I don't need anyone," Heston slams right back.

The next day is even worse. At dinner, Joanna comments, "Dinner was wonderful. Very good chicken." "It was lizard," Heston answers politely. Joanna, looking slightly ill, continues trying to make conversation. "It isn't nearly as hot here as I thought it would be." Heston is brief. "This is winter," he responds. Silence. Then Heston asks Joanna to play the piano. "I'd like to hear it played before the termites get at it," he says without a touch of humor in his voice.

She begins to play, but an argument erupts between them. Joanna caps it by saying, annoyed, "You don't like a woman with a temper." But she is in for a surprise, for Heston announces, "I don't mind. I have a temper myself." But something is brewing in Heston's mind. Here is a cultured, good looking, intelligent woman. And she left her native New Orleans for the primitive jungle. Why? "You're looking for a fault in me," she reads his mind. "Something so that you can ignore me." She presents Heston her flaw on a silver platter. Joanna, it seems, had been married once before, something which crushes Heston completely. "How many others have there been, madam?" he yells. "You've seen my house. They laughed at me, up and down the river. I wanted to fill it with beautiful things. The only condition was that anything I brought up the river had to be new!" And Heston continues, he considers Joanna "used."

She is angered. "If you knew anything about music," she draws an analogy, "you'd know that the best piano is one that's been played." Not at all convinced by her metaphor, Heston storms out.

The next night, the Province Commissioner, Heston, and Joanna dine together. The girl plays the piano, but within moments cannot continue. She informs the Commissioner that Heston has asked her to leave, to return to New Orleans. Heston interrupts, saying Joanna doesn't like the country. But, she re-

Heston and Eleanor Parker.

torts, this isn't so. She loves the country. But Leiningen doesn't love her. With that, she retires, and the men talk.

"Each year, Mr. Leiningen, I've seen you get a little harder . . . a little more lonely," the Commissioner notes. "You're turning to stone." Heston gets upset. He changes the subject, asking the Commissioner what he found on his expedition up the Rio Negro River, the river from which Heston has raised his plantation. The Commissioner says that something is driving the animals out of the area. "What?" Heston inquires. The Commissioner is silent. Then, in reverent, understated tones, he says the one word.

Marabunda.

Heston closes the doors to the room. If the natives should hear this, they'd panic. "You really think it's that?" Heston asks. "Twenty-seven years ago was the last time," the Commissioner notes. "You sound frightened," Heston chides. "Not you, huh?" the Commissioner says, annoyed. "What does it take to frighten you, Leiningen?" "I haven't seen it yet," Heston boasts. "You haven't seen Marabunda," the Commissioner smirks.

The next day, Heston and the Commissioner take Joanna to the boat that will return her to civilization. Joanna wears a dress. "She's having a bad time of it," the Commissioner says, adding, "But not a single complaint." "Stubborn," Heston retorts.

Something wakes Joanna up that night. She runs from her lodgings to find Leiningen and the Commissioner up and about. Strangely enough, they were awakened by the silence. Heston fires five shots into the forest. Still not a creature stirs. "There's something out there," he says, "but it's not afraid of guns." The group move out immediately into an old village. The natives of this two-hundred-year-old settlement are nowhere to be found.

"There's no sign of a struggle," Heston observes. "They weren't forced out. They ran," he concludes. At this, Heston asks Joanna if she has courage. "Yes," she responds. "Lots of courage," he repeats. She says yes again. Whatever it is, Heston and Joanna decide to stick this thing out. The Commissioner protests. He claims Marabunda is too dangerous for Joanna; indeed, for both of them. But Joanna realizes if she leaves, Heston's servants will leave as well. That would leave him alone and surely beaten. To this, the Commissioner agrees reluctantly. And Heston is visibly proud of Joanna.

They climb to a high cliff, and there come face to face with their enemy. Marabunda. "Billions and billions of soldier ants on the march," Heston comments. "How do you stop them?" Joanna inquires. "You don't," the Commissioner says. "You get out of their way."

Traveling six miles a day, the ants near Heston's plantation. In preparation, he blows up the bridges that lead to his land and floods the rivers by opening several of the smaller dams. This puts a moat between his home and the ants. But it is not enough. The carnivorous ants shear leaves from trees and float across the water on 'rafts.' In response, Heston has brush set afire within and without the walls of the plantation. Still the monster army moves on.

Heston is exasperated. "You've given up!" his wife scolds. "No," he corrects. "I've been beaten. There's a difference. Now I've lost everything . . . except you." Still, he'll not give up. In a last desperate effort, Heston decides to blow up the big dam and flood all of his property. "I'm giving back everything I took from the river," he tells Joanna, while preparing to brave the menace without. Heston covers himself with grease, runs out into the maelstrom, and is beset upon almost immediately by ants. He struggles his way to the mighty wall and blows it up; the waters come rushing in, nearly drowning Heston, carrying trees, huts, and land with the torrent. Finally, the waters rush against the walls of Heston's home, and they hold! The mansion is saved; the ants are destroyed. And Heston, at long last, is a human being. Joanna stays, and they live happily ever after.

The Naked Jungle is a fine adventure film, with impressive special effects and fine acting. The script is a little hokey in spots, but the story is unique and Heston turns in a strong performance. He is cold and hard when we meet him, but softens visibly by the time the film has unreeled. Eleanor Parker is good, playing her role with tongue ever-so-slightly in cheek.

Technically, the film is incredible. Produced by George Pal and directed by Byron Haskin, the film had to be a visual tour-de-force. Pal is the man responsible for such special effects of science fiction and fantasy epics (Oscar winners for technical effects) as *The Time Machine, Tom Thumb, 7 Faces of Dr. Lao, and Destination Moon.* Together, he and Haskin did *War of the Worlds,* based on the H. G. Wells classic. And, accordingly, this film, based on the short story, *Leiningen vs. the Ants,* has a flood that looks frighteningly real, although done entirely with miniature models; exploding bridges, again miniatures, look entirely realistic and, of course, the army of ravaging ants is impressively rendered. There are long shots of the bugs blanketing the countryside; these are fair process shots. Better are the closer views, showing yards of ants in one glance, the ants really there and really moving.

The Naked Jungle is more than just another programmer. It's unique, and it's good. And one must admit this is due to Charlton Heston. For he took it and played it straight.

Heston as the stiff-necked plantation owner.

SECRET OF THE INCAS

Paramount
1954

Produced by Mel Epstein. *Directed* by Jerry Hopper. *Script* by Ranald MacDougall and Sydney Boehm. *Photography* by Lionel Lindon. *Music* by David Buttolph. 101 minutes. *Starring* Charlton Heston (Harry Steele), Robert Young (Dr. Stanley Moorehead), Nicole Maurey (Elena Antonescu), Yma Sumac (Kori Tica), Thomas Mitchell (Ed Morgan).

Two soldiers of fortune, Heston and Thomas Mitchell, are on the trail of the Incan Sunburst, a fantastic trinket weighing some thirty pounds and encrusted with over a hundred diamonds and other precious gems.

Accompanying the men on their journey is a Rumanian refugee who hopes to gain entrance to America without going through all the requisite legal complications.

This treasure-hunting troupe meets with another crew on the same mission, but for a different reason. Led by Robert Young, the others seek the Sunburst convinced that if found it will restore the lost Incan civilization to the natives.

At the tomb of four-hundred-year-old King Manca, the Heston organization grab the archaeological specimen, but there is a falling out between Heston and his partner. To add to the struggle, there is a com-

Heston and Nicole Maurey.

54

plication in the form of a girl, along for the ride, who is in love with Heston. After much to-do, our hero, not really the bastard he makes out to be, turns his bauble over to the natives, admits love for Nicole Maurey, and all ends happily.

Again, the film is an average action programmer, hardly extraordinary. This, however, is an appropriate time to discuss an aspect of many Heston roles. *The New York Times* made the analysis of his Harry Steele (note the surname) calling it 'laconic,' for he's a tough character, very precise and frugal with words. But, though restrained, this is not to be confused with the more rounded Heston performances of this sort.

In *Secret of the Incas*, Heston is made of granite, without depth or humanity. He is not of granite *will* as in *El Cid*, or of granite *determination* as in *Ben-Hur*, he is simply immobile, set upon a rugged path of his own selection.

Of course, that Heston is always thrust into such regal roles is an instance of the part being tailored to the man, rather than vice versa. Many critics feel this is a weakness in Heston's range, noting that actors should adapt to their characters, embellishing them with their own experience. But Heston does not play the average man. He cannot, really. Not the way Paul Newman, or Jack Lemmon, or Marlon Brando can. This is painfully evident in the popular but dismally acted *Earthquake*. However, Heston can bring to his more substantive roles (such as *Will Penny*, as an aging cowboy, or in *Khartoum*, as a British General) a sense of quiet dignity and self-worth that cannot be shaken. Perhaps in the eyes of critics this is a limitation; that Heston cannot play weak-willed individuals. But consider the inverse: even in a film as poor as *Secret of the Incas*, only Heston could have pulled off this kind of brick-hard characterization.

Heston watches Thomas Mitchell mishandle rare gems.

THE FAR HORIZONS — Paramount 1955

Heston in a publicity still.

Produced by William H. Pine and William C. Thomas. *Directed* by Rudolph Mate. *Script* by Winston Miller and Edmund H. North, from the novel *Sacajawea of the Shoshones*, by Della Gould Emmons. *Photography* by Daniel L. Fapp. *Music* by Hans Salter. 107 minutes. *Starring* Fred MacMurray (Merriwether Lewis), Charlton Heston (William Clark), Donna Reed (Sacajawea), Barbara Hale (Julia Hancock), William Demarest (Sgt. Gass), Alan Reed (Charboneau).

Once again, as with many Heston films, action is the star and, in this case, the sole positive grace of the film. *Far Horizons* tells the story of Lewis and Clark's expedition into our northwest. Heston is Clark; Fred MacMurray is Lewis.

The picture takes as many liberties with history as it does with good filmmaking. Initially, MacMurray finds Heston involved with his girl, which sets the expedition off on the wrong foot. Then, as the trip gets under way, their Indian guide Sacajawea falls in love with Heston, resulting in the further antagonism of MacMurray. Thus, between Indian attacks, ambushes, leaking boats, the scaling of cliffs, and similar adventures, the two men bicker and argue and, after scouting Jefferson's Louisiana territory purchase and clawing their way to the Pacific, they return to Washington. However, as Heston is about to marry Sacajawea, she decides she can't take civilization and returns to the wilderness.

Critics voiced approval of Heston's "terse nonchalance," a breath of fresh air as opposed to MacMurray's sullenness (*The New York Times*), while other critics found Heston's Clark merely a "likeable, adventurous sort of guy." (*Commonweal*)

Whatever, Heston had managed to survive yet *another* average film.

MacMurray, Reed, and Heston in *The Far Horizons.*

Donna Reed tries to act "civilized"

. . . But prefers her Indian ways, and returns west, after the expedition ends.

THE PRIVATE WAR
OF MAJOR BENSON

Universal
1955

Heston, his liquor bottle hidden behind him, greets Sister Redempta

Produced by Howard Pine. *Directed* by Jerry Hopper. *Script* by William Roberts and Richard Alan Simmons. *Photography* by Harold Lipstein. *Music* by Joseph Gershenson. 105 minutes. *Starring* Charlton Heston (Major Bernard Benson), Julie Adams (Dr. Kay Lambert), William Demarest (John), Tim Considine (Cadet Sgt. Hibler), Tim Hovey (Cadet Thomas 'Tiger' Flaherty), Sal Mineo (Cadet Col. Sylvester Dusik).

The Private War of Major Benson is one of Heston's two comedies, the story of a martinet major assigned to command a boy's military school.

The picture opens with adult military war games. Heston is busy observing his men and is visibly displeased. "Major, we've executed the maneuver twenty-seven times," an officer complains. "The men are tired." "They missed their objective," Heston barks. He calls them together. "This army is overfed and undertrained," Heston begins a practiced speech and notices that one soldier (David Janssen) has it memorized. When questioned, the Private admits he has heard it before and has, as well, just read a transcript of it in this week's *Newsweek*. Heston is shocked. "They ran that interview?" he inquires. The soldier nods affirmatively. Simultaneously, Heston receives orders to report to headquarters. General Ramsey (played by Milburn Stone) is unimpressed with Heston's constantly shooting off his mouth. Published comments such as "I'll turn milk drinking kids into whiskey drinking soldiers!" have brought the General much pressure from higher-ups to relieve Heston of his command. Ramsey gives the Major one last chance. Heston is to head the ROTC program at Sheridan Military Academy in Santa Barbara.

Arriving late at night, he is met by Joe, the caretaker, and by Dr. Lambert, a pretty young doctor. Heston feels awkward with the girl. He passes a remark about her being awfully young for this position. "I'm quite capable of doing my job," she retorts curtly.

The next morning after it has been discovered that Heston was drinking, he is dressed down by the school staff. William Demarest is second from the left; Julie Adams is on the right.

"And I hope we can say the same about you." She continues with "You see, most of our cadets drink milk."

Joe takes Heston to his room, leaves, and Sister Redempta comes to meet the Major. Heston had not realized that this school was run by nuns. She welcomes the soldier while he tries to conceal from her a bottle of liquor. When she finally departs, Heston settles down to drink. But he is unable to escape the piercing gaze of the founding nun's portrait, and eventually just pours the full bottle down the drain, tossing the empty jar out of the window.

The next morning Sister Redempta informs Heston that the institution is on probation. That unless the ROTC program is whipped into shape, the school will lose it and thus many students. Challenged, Heston is understandably anxious to meet the men. He trots onto the training field where he finds the "men" are sub-teenagers. One in particular, Tiger the "Pri-

Attending his first day of drilling the cadets, Heston is surprised to find they are kids; not adults. The boy is Tim Hovey, the Private.

Heston questions young Hibler (Tim Considine) about a stolen watch.

Because he has harassed the youths,
Heston finds strange things begin to happen to him.

vate," is unique. He is six years old and greets Heston with a lengthy soliloquy, the bottom line of which is "When I see a lot of blood, it makes me sick to my stomach." They had been discussing the boy's cut finger. Heston is shocked at the age of the group he must lead. He drills the kids hard and they grow to hate him.

After the drill, Heston speaks to Sister Redempta. He wants out. But she tells him to think of it as if he were the father of these three hundred boys. "I'll admit," Heston says, "I'm married to the army, but I didn't expect it to go this far!"

Through with the lecture, Heston visits Dr. Lambert—Lammy to the kids. He wants to ask her out but doesn't know how best to approach the girl. So he butters her up by reiterating and claiming as his own philosophy what the Sister had just explained to him. "I look upon this as a soul-shaping experience," Heston states. Lammy is sincerely impressed, unaware that he is soft-soaping her.

Meanwhile, the kids get together before going to bed. "Men," one of them begins, "we might as well face it. Major Benson's a creep." The other lads agree. Something, they decide, has got to be done. One of the boys, Gerald Hibler, decides he will get in touch with his parents who know people high-up in Washington and will get Benson out of the army.

That night, one of the older boys, Sylvester, comes to the Major's office for some advice. He doesn't know how to write a letter to this girl with whom he's infatuated. How can he make a good impression?

The Major tells him that all he needs to do is snow the girl. "Females are about 10% brains and 90% emotions," he tells him. However, during the course of their conversation, the boy notes that Heston is scheduled to be the coach of the school football team, something Heston had not known.

Practice is grueling, worse than drilling for the kids. And the boys resent it. One day, after telling a player to "hit the practice dummy," the boy accidentally tackles Heston. And to add insult to injury, Sylvester speaks again with his coach. This time to tell him he took Heston's advice on the letter to the girl. And Nancy had written back that it was the "soppiest" letter she had ever read. Heston is more than a little dismayed.

Practice continues, and on another occasion Heston is ganged up upon by the kids, his leg sprained in the process. Lammy looks at it, and while she is so doing, Heston asks her for a date. This time she accepts and tells him she'll pick him up at 7:00. To Heston's unhappiness, the Private goes along with them. When, in the theatre, she holds Heston's hand, the young boy gets jealous and complains about her not

Things get worse when Heston begins coaching the football team. . . .

. . . And finds himself the victim of severe tackling.

Nonetheless, the school wins the football trophy.

Heston treats the Private (Tim Hovey) to a hamburger after the fatherless boy runs away from the school.

Unfortunately, the Private makes himself visible even on Heston's dates with Julie Adams.

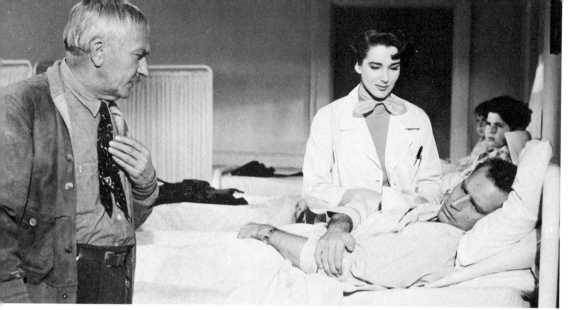

Heston abed with the measles.

holding his hand as well. Even when they kiss good-night, things go wrong. A nun walks by and Lammy becomes flustered, leaving Heston abruptly.

The boys have had it with Heston. They sign a petition and mail it to Washington, via the Hiblers. Simultaneously, Heston, upset by the football incident, leaves the school to return to Washington. Lammy chases him to the airport to tell him she loves him. Heston says, however, that he must go.

Meeting with Ramsey, the Major tells him he's learned his lesson. That he is ready to return to active duty in the adult army. But Ramsey is unconvinced. "You've handled yourself as gracefully as an elephant in an escalator," he shouts, telling Heston further that Sister Redempta, Ramsey's natural sister, has been sending him progress reports of the pitiful job Heston has done. Ramsey orders the Major to return to Sheridan with a new attitude.

The next day, Lammy's watch, a gift from the kids, is found to be missing. All that remains is a clue to its whereabouts, a boy's pin discovered in Lammy's office. Heston checks all the uniforms. Only Hibler's is missing the tack. Heston summons Hibler to his office. The boy explains how he just likes to take mechanical things apart, like the typewriter, and that's it. He intended to put the watch together again and return it. Heston doesn't yell at the lad, but is patient and understanding. He won't tell Hibler's parents, nor Lammy, nor any of the other students. Instead, Heston takes the pieces of the watch and dismisses Hibler who is overjoyed that he will not get into trouble.

When Hibler returns to his room, he is confronted by the other students, to whom he relates what has just happened, admitting that he took the timepiece. They are all surprised that Heston was so good to Gerald and regret having signed the petition—which, incidentally, has prompted a letter to Heston from Ramsey calling the Major back to Washington.

Saddened, Heston is to leave immediately. He goes to say goodbye to Lammy. While he is there,

Lammy says there are three boys who want to say goodbye to Heston. They are in the sick bay. Heston makes his farewells as, inexplicably, Lammy pushes him into a bed, telling Heston he has now been exposed to measles and must remain in quarantine.

Never having had the disease, Heston does, indeed, come down with measles. Ramsey tells him that since he will be laid up he might as well finish the semester until ROTC inspection. In his place his loyal friend Sylvester drills the boys.

On inspection day, before Ramsey and two other officers, the boys execute their maneuvers to perfection, impressing even Heston. They march to the cry of "Rah rah for Major Benson," something that both surprises and pleases the man. The school retains its rating, Heston is assigned battalion commander of Fort Dix, marries Lammy, and all ends happily.

In *Private War of Major Benson*, Heston is superb. The film shows he can play comedy, but it has to be the right kind of comedy—absurd and innocent. *Private War of Major Benson* is certainly absurd, with lines like the following: Heston and Sister Redempta pass through a hall and look at the picture of Sheridan's founder. She says, "He was canonized in 1853." To which Heston responds, in earnest, "I'm sorry to hear that." And, although he's a bit stiff, it all works. For Major Benson himself is tight. His strong-jawed naïveté is a fine pillar around which to construct a story such as this.

Julie Adams, fresh from a starring role in *Creature from the Black Lagoon*, portrays Lammy with emotional conviction that ranges from A to B. Contrarily, the supporting players are excellent. William Demarest, as Joe, the caretaker of the school, has all the good dialogue, and he delivers it under his breath with quiet, sagacious dignity. Milburn Stone, on the other hand, roars at the top of his lungs throughout the entire film. The perfect general.

But the important thing is that *Private War of Major Benson* serves to showcase Heston's versatility.

LUCY GALLANT   Paramount   1955

Heston and Jane Wyman.

Produced by William H. Pine and William C. Thomas: *Directed* by Robert Parrish. *Script* by John Lee Mahin and Winston Miller from the novel *The Life of Lucy Gallant* by Margaret Cousins. *Photography* by Lionel Lindon. *Music* by Van Cleve. 104 minutes. *Starring* Jane Wyman (Lucy Gallant), Charlton Heston (Casey Cole), Claire Trevor (Lady Macbeth), Thelma Ritter (Molly Besseman), William Demarest (Charley Madden).

How Heston got the reputation for being a biblical star is a curiosity. For here is yet another silly soap opera, also released as *Oil Town*.

Lucy Gallant, after being jilted at the altar, manages to turn her wedding gown into a multi-million-dollar department store in a Texas oil boom town. Heston is a well-to-do farmer who falls in love with her. However, Lucy's career interferes with their life together and he joins the army to get away from her. He becomes a hero in the process. As is standard in all these machine-lathed plots, Lucy discovers that her love is more important than financial success, and dumps it all for Heston. Who is himself rich, so it's no great sacrifice.

Again, reaction to the Heston performance was good, but his hard-headed Texan is not enough to withstand the silly plot line. The film was "Too much for the talents of even the longest suffering actors in the world," *The New York Times* was quick to assert.

Heston hears some fatherly advice from William Demarest in *Lucy Gallant.* That's Claire Trevor between them.

THE TEN COMMANDMENTS

Paramount
1956

"To transfer the Bible to the screen,
you cannot cheat. You have to believe."

Cecil B. DeMille

Charlton Heston
as Moses.

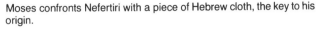
Moses confronts Nefertiri with a piece of Hebrew cloth, the key to his origin.

Produced and Directed by Cecil B. DeMille. *Script* by Aeneas MacKenzie, Jesse L. Lasky, Jr., Jack Gariss and Fredric M. Frank. *Photography* by Loyal Griggs. *Music* by Elmer Bernstein. 219 minutes. *Starring* Charlton Heston (Moses), Anne Baxter (Nefertiri), Yul Brynner (Ramses), John Derek (Joshua), Yvonne de Carlo (Sephora), Nina Foch (Bithia), Debra Paget (Lilia), Edward G. Robinson (Dathan), Sir Cedric Hardwicke (Sethi), Vincent Price (Baka).

The Ten Commandments remains one of the world's all-time top-grossing motion pictures, and it was the last film Cecil DeMille made.

Initial critical reaction to the production varied. *Time* declared the picture, "Something roughly comparable to an eight-foot chorus girl; pretty well put together, but much too big and much too flashy." *Variety* noted, "While DeMille has broken new ground in terms of size, he has remained conventional with the motion picture as an art form. Emphasis on physical dimension has rendered neither awesome nor profound the story of Moses."

Cecil DeMille was a religious man, and one to whom the story of the giving of man's greatest Laws was very personal. For years fans the world over begged the filmmaker to reshoot his original silent classic (1923), and with the phenomenal success of *Samson and Delilah* behind him, DeMille went ahead with the project. He had an incredible eight-million-dollar budget supporting him, but before the producer/director was through, he would run the tab to a then record thirteen million dollars.

The Ten Commandments was directed personally by DeMille himself. At the age of 78, this was no mean task. He was in no condition to go bouncing around Egyptian deserts or scaling mountain peaks to film a story as grand as that of Moses. But he assumed and executed the task with the same dedicated professionalism that marked his entire career. Indeed, during the shooting of a desert scene, DeMille suffered a massive heart attack, but was back on set the next day. This perseverance does not, in itself, make the movie great. But it does serve to underline DeMille's phe-

Moses, Joshua, and Sephora first spy the Burning Bush.

Moses arrives in Egypt after conquering Ethiopia.

Moses enters the palace of Sethi upon returning from Ethiopia.

nomenal regard for the subject and its undertaking. And this sincerity comes through, eviscerating the more mundane aspects of the film, the elements that are "pure Hollywood."

Yet DeMille was not the only participant whose thorough devotion to the film is legend. Charlton Heston gave this one all he had. And with good reason. First, *The Ten Commandments* was a trailblazer of the big, widescreen movies produced to meet the rising competition of small home television screens. Secondly, it was the making of Charlton Heston. He says in retrospect, "If you can't make a career out of two DeMilles, *The Greatest Show on Earth* and *The Ten Commandments*, you'll never make it." Accordingly, Heston worked at a furious pace. He refused to use doubles for lighting tests, and redid scene after scene until both he and DeMille were satisfied with the results. Biblical authenticity was of tantamount importance; for one scene, Heston went so far as to walk

barefoot across the sharp rocks of Mt. Sinai. In his spare time, Heston would delve into the psyche of Moses, memorizing vast sections of the Old Testament to aid his understanding of the Lawgiver. "Heston wanted to talk about Moses' id," one of the crew members recalls, "but we were only trying to find out how the hell to get cold beer in Egypt."

Of the actor's absolute consumption by the role, DeMille, in his autobiography, wrote, "before each of the big scenes, he would go off by himself for a half hour, in costume, and walk up and down in solitary thought. I never asked him what he was thinking at those times, but when he came back to the set and walked through the crowd of Arab extras, their eyes followed him, and they murmured reverently, 'Moussa! Moussa!' To them, Moslems all, he was the Prophet Moses."

The story of *The Ten Commandments*:

An edict from Ramses I details that all first-born

After hearing the Word of God, Moses returns to confront the Pharaoh in Egypt; "Let my people go," he commands.

Pharoah will not heed Moses' order, so the Prophet turns the Nile to blood.

Moses comforts Bithia, his Egyptian mother, when the Angel of Death strikes all the Egyptian first-born.

Hebrew male children be killed to prevent one of them becoming the prophesied Deliverer of an enslaved Hebrew people. One woman, Yochabel, sets her son adrift in a basket on the Nile. It floats to where the Pharaoh's sister is bathing. Bithia accepts the infant, this gift from the Nile God, as her own. Wrapped in its Levite cloth, the child is taken to the Egyptian court, where he is raised as an adopted son and heir to the throne.

Moses grows to be the Pharaoh Sethi's great right arm, earning the jealousy of the Pharaoh's real son, Ramses. For one of them must succeed Sethi upon his death.

One day, in a fit of rage, Moses kills Baka, an Egyptian master builder, as the latter is about to murder Joshua, a Hebrew slave. Moses' deed, and the truth of his origin, are revealed to Ramses by his Hebrew spy Dathan, and the Prince is banished.

After his cleansing on the hellish crucible of the twin wilderness Shur and Zin, Moses is ready for his Maker's Hand. And his first stop is the camp of Midian shepherd Jethro. When Moses fells three Amalakite nomads who attack the old man's seven daughters, the Egyptian refugee is honored by Jethro and, eventually, marries his eldest daughter Sephora.

Years pass, and one day while tending the family flock, Moses finds Joshua hiding amongst the rocks of Sinai. He has escaped his bondage and pleads that Moses return to Egypt and help his people. Joshua is convinced that Moses is the Deliverer. Moses is in a quandary. If God does not heed the people's cry, why should, or how can *he*? Just then, Moses sees a bush burning on the jagged cliffs of Sinai. He ascends to get a closer look. Through the bush, God speaks to Moses; tells him to return to Egypt and, in His name, free the Hebrews from bondage. With the might of God behind him, Moses does indeed liberate the people, albeit after ten plagues and much delay. He leads them into the desert and to Mt. Sinai, where God will give them His "Laws of life, and right, and good, and evil."

But before they reach their destination, camped against the Red Sea, the Hebrews are besieged by the Egyptian army led by Pharaoh, who has had a change of heart. As the pursuing chariots near, Moses bars their way with a pillar of fire; simultaneously, he parts the sea and leads his people through it.

As the Hebrews near the waters' far side, the pillar of fire dies, and Pharaoh's men rush into the sea. Moses brings the water down upon them; only Pharaoh survives the holocaust. Moses next leads the people to Sinai where he climbs the peak to receive God's Commandments. But he is gone for forty days, and the people become fearful. Led by Dathan, the Hebrews build and worship a Golden Calf. Moses returns in time to witness this pagan fête. He smashes the tablets against the idol, destroying Dathan and his followers.

As punishment for their sacrilege, the people are

Moses stands before the liberated Hebrews and prepares to lead them to the promised land.

made to wander in the wilderness for forty years, until all those who had sinned in the sight of God were consumed. Then, from atop Mt. Nebo, Moses watches his people cross the River Jordan into the Promised Land. He charges and bids Joshua lead the people thereafter; Moses must go to his God. Bathed in a glorious light, Moses becomes legend.

This, as here retold, is more or less the story as written in the Book of Books. But there is, of course, more to the DeMille story into which we must look, such as the absurd love triangle between Moses, Nefertiri, and Ramses.

Promised to Sethi's successor is Nefertiri, she through whom the throne is passed. She is not to be confused with Nefertiti, the princess pre-dating DeMille's by a century.

Nefertiri is a seductress who honestly loves Moses. For him she lies, kills, and, in the end, betrays her husband. She is selfish in life and, most certainly, in love.

Moses is portrayed as a humble man. In the beginning of *The Ten Commandments*, for example, he conquers Ethiopia, but does not strip her of dignity. Later, he gives the Hebrew slaves one day in seven to rest. Moses is a just man; a good man, and is, credibly, never represented as anything other than a servant of God. Had it been otherwise, acting the role would have been impossible.

These, then, are the characters; this is the story. But just how good is the film?

Personally, I find it awesome, not only in scope but in majesty as well. For all the picture's failings, only a hardened cynic can fail to be swept away by its sheer presence.

Of course, there was criticism about just how devout the film really is. Reviewers remembered De-Mille's treatment of *Samson and Delilah*, with its schmaltzy love story and picture-book religion. That, however, is an entirely different case. The orientation is biblical, true. But it is no more majestic than an Hercules epic.

Heston points out that the reason for this is that *Samson and Delilah* is based on a very short passage in the Old Testament, and is not really a religious film, whereas a film about Moses, however it is done, is a seriously religious film.

Leaving *Samson* behind, despite the pressures placed squarely on the producer/director's shoulders, Heston ". . . found DeMille quite easy to work for; a rather formal, very intelligent man with an almost flawless instinct for public response. DeMille treated all of his films with meticulousness. I never worked for a director that prepared as elaborately as DeMille did. Even George Stevens, who is a most painstaking craftsman, I don't think prepared quite to the degree that DeMille did. I'm not so certain that this was nec-

73

The incredible Exodus from Egypt. This scene was peopled by 8,000 extras.

essarily good; it simply was his method. There must have been three years of preparation. I was not as informed and knowledgeable an observer of this kind of thing then as I am now. I had conversations, conferences with him over a period of, oh God, five months; at least five months before I even got the part!

"And it was a very gutsy piece of casting on his part. I was very young, only 28. I didn't have a remarkable film reputation. The only reputation I had was that created by the other DeMille picture. In essence, he put the most expensive picture he'd ever made on my shoulders, and I was not very firmly established. He did have one great advantage: He didn't need a really big name. His own name on a marquee meant as much as any actor's.

"Ultimately, *The Ten Commandments*, which was undeniably DeMille's greatest success, will have been seen by more people than any other film I've ever made, or probably will make. It was an enormous role, like Christ; unplayable, really. It was beyond my capa-

cities then, and it would be beyond my capacities now. I dare say it would be beyond Olivier's capacities. I could do a better job now than I could then, but any actor with the brains God gave geese would be able to say that about any role."

Apart from the actor's emotional involvement with the film, there is the almost frightening physical analogy.

"During his deliberation in casting the role," Heston says, "somebody brought to DeMille's attention the startling resemblance between my face and that of Michelangelo's Moses in the church of St. Peter in Chains in Rome. It's true. The resemblance is unmistakable. The nose is broken in the same place. The cheekbones are the same. It's really curious how my face seems to belong in any century but my own.

"DeMille studied many photos of Michelangelo's Moses. During the course of a visit to Rome, he made a special trip to the church to view it in person. It could well have been the clincher. Somebody quoted

The parting of the Red Sea.

Charlton Heston in a majestic pose, with dark clouds swirling behind him, prepares to part the Red Sea.

him as saying, "If it's good enough for Michelangelo, it's good enough for me."

As far as DeMille was concerned, "There had never been any doubt in my mind about who should play Moses. And my choice was strikingly affirmed when I had a sketch made of Chuck in a white beard and compared it to Michelangelo's famous statue. The resemblance was amazing. But it wasn't merely an external resemblance. Charlton Heston brought to the role a rapidly maturing skill as an actor and an earnest understanding of the human and spiritual quality of Moses."

These comments would serve to indicate that while DeMille prepared elaborately for all his films, one must believe that he took *The Ten Commandments* more seriously. In his own words at a luncheon held in his honor prior to the film's debut, DeMille said, "What I hope for our production of *The Ten Commandments* is that those who see it shall come from the theatre not only entertained and filled with the sight of big spectacle, but filled with the spirit of truth; that it will bring to its audience a better understanding of the real meaning of this pattern of life that God has set down for us to follow; that it will make vivid to the human mind its close relationship to the mind of God.

"That relationship between God and man is the greatest drama in the world. A drama in which we are the actors, and the outcome of it is of vital importance, for in the final analysis, we do not break the Commandments. They break us, if we disregard them.

"Moses is everyman. In his pride, his bitterness at God allowing evil to befall his people, and in his reluctance to do God's work. And our constant thought while we were making *The Ten Commandments* was 'Can we be worthy of this theme?'

"That demanded close adherence to the Bible and to facts. In our search for authenticity, we consulted some 1,900 books and periodicals, collected nearly 3,000 photographs, and used the facilities of thirty libraries and museums in North America, Europe, Africa, and Australia. So that the hundreds of millions who will see *The Ten Commandments* can make a pilgrimage over the very ground that Moses walked, we rolled our cameras from Goshen to the Red Sea, then across the Wilderness of Shur, down through the Wilderness of Zin, and up the steep, barren, majestic, awe-inspiring slopes of Mt. Sinai, to the holy ground where Moses stood to receive the law.

"Is it too much to hope that our production of *The Ten Commandments* might help to do what centuries of bloodshed and argument have failed to do? To remind the millions of adherents of the Jewish, Christian, and Moslem faiths that they all spring from a common source, and that they have in Moses a binding tie, a universal prophet, and in the Decalogue a universal law of brotherhood?"

But just how much of this spiritual wealth has come through in DeMille's monumental effort? For though the total effect is successful, many individual elements are not. First, the performances. It has become impossible to visualize any Moses without referring to the Heston interpretation. Heston *is* the part, and no one will ever take it from him. Perhaps, at times, his acting is a bit melodramatic; overdone rather than mellow. But Heston is a presence with which to be reckoned; a presence that befits the role.

Anne Baxter, as Nefertiri, is an overripe plum plucked from the DeMille school of silly sensuality. While Miss Baxter is convincingly conniving, the characterization is without depth.

Yul Brynner, as Ramses, is superb. His arrogance and swaggering snobbery are well represented, and Brynner intelligently plays his cynical role against that of the always stoic Heston. He has some difficult lines to speak, but these are lines through which all the players, at one time or another, must wade. For example, Moses returns to Egypt at the command of God and, to prove his might to Pharaoh, tosses his mystic staff before the throne. The assemblage gapes in wonder as the rod turns to a snake. Brynner, however, is unimpressed. "Moses, Moses," he smiles, "Are there no magicians in Egypt that you must return to turn sticks into serpents or make rabbits appear?" Tongue firmly in cheek, Brynner carries it off. The same cannot always be said of the other players. For example, Bithia, played by Nina Foch, discovers the basket in which Moses has just floated down the Nile. "Oh Memnet," she cries, "The answer to my prayers!" At which point, Memnet, her slave, queries straightfaced, "You prayed for a basket?"

And talk about falling out of character: When Moses refuses to abandon the mud pits of his people for the throne of Egypt, Nefertiri reprimands him with, "Moses! You stubborn, splendid, adorable fool!"

Then there is humor. When Heston grants the slaves one day in seven to rest, Brynner is aghast. Heston argues that, "When your horses tire, they're rested. When they hunger, they're fed." But Brynner doesn't see the justice of the analogy. "Slaves draw stone and brick," he makes light of the situation, "My horses draw the next Pharaoh."

Actually, a lot of Heston's dialogue is tacky at times. He pulls it off, but only because he is Charlton Heston and can *do* such things. A rough one to mutter, for instance, must have been this one. Moses informs Jethro that he will live in Midian: "I will dwell in this land," he declares with solemn finality. Not live or settle down, but dwell. Or later on, when Moses sees the Burning Bush: "'Tis on fire, but the bush does not burn. I will turn aside and see this great sight."

In addition to the fields of corn, there is understatement. When Moses returns from Mt. Sinai to find his people have fashioned a pagan idol, he informs them, "For this you shall drink bitter waters," at which

Moses receives the Ten Commandments from God.

point half of them are killed. Bitter indeed! And then there is overstatement. During the first Passover, the child Eliezar notes that death is outside the house in which they honor the occasion. Moses turns to him and says, for our benefit as well as that of the child, "Remember, Eliezar. On this night, he passed over your house."

As for being a prophet, the film shows it's not an easy life! Even as he stands on the threshold of freeing his people, Moses is confused. The tens of thousands of Hebrews assemble outside the gates of Ramses in Goshen, but Moses stands alone by a Sphinx. "There are so many," he says to God, "so many. How shall I find thy road through the Wilderness, Lord? How shall I find water in the desert for this multitude?" Here Joshua interrupts Moses' reverie. "Moses, the people are assembled." And, quickly covering all signs of doubt, the prophet replies, "Then let us go forth to the mountain of God that he may write His Command-

ments in our minds and upon our hearts forever." Moses pauses before the gathered populace. "Hear, O Israel. Remember this day when the strong hand of the Lord leads you out of bondage." The people shout, "The Lord is One!" many times over, and march into the desert. Filmed with a full complement of eight thousand extras, this, for Heston, was the most incredible scene in the film.

"The Exodus is the best thing in *The Ten Commandments*. It was quite moving; a marvelously exciting experience. Because there are all those people, and they are really moving. You're prepared to believe they're going to walk to the Promised Land."

Which leads us to the more technical aspects of *The Ten Commandments*. Specifically, the alleged highlight of the film, the parting of the Red Sea. It is an exciting, dramatic scene, one for which the audience has waited nearly three hours, and it builds very slowly. As the people march from Egypt, DeMille's voice intones, "And Moses brought forth the people with joy and gladness. He bore them out of Egypt as an eagle bears its young upon its wings." They march out, and as they do, Nefertiri chides Ramses. The long-gone rulers of Egypt laugh at Ramses from their tombs, she accuses. All she really wants, of course, is Moses back in Egypt. But Ramses is convinced that he has been a coward and sends for his charioteers.

By this time, the people are up in arms against Moses, as Pharaoh rides within range. They wish to surrender, and Ramses is pleased with the situation. To an aide he notes, "The God of Moses is a poor general to leave him no retreat." We, of course, know better.

At the encampment, Moses is angry with his people. Above him clouds begin churning black. The sea is choppy. There is something ominous in the wind. "Ten times you have seen the miracles of the Lord," Moses exhorts, "and still you have no faith!" "He's a false prophet who delivers you to death!" charges Dathan. "Was it because there were no graves in Egypt that you took us away to die in the Wilderness?" he screams. The people roar for Moses to surrender them to Pharaoh, but he will have none of it.

"Fear not!" he asserts, holding his staff high. "Stand still and see the salvation of the Lord!" With this the audience expects the sea to be parted. But De-Mille has not yet completely built his scene. Before the charging chariots, Moses forms a tremendous Pillar of Fire which bars the soldiers' way. And while the Egyptians are thus occupied, Moses orders the people, "Gather your families and your flocks. We must go with all speed." "Go where?" Dathan yells, amazed. "To drown in the sea? How long can the fire hold pharaoh back?" Again the people lose faith, and Moses delivers his *coup de grâce*. "After this day you will see his chariots no more!" Dathan remains unconvinced. "No! You'll be dead under them!" he warns. But clouds swarm above the sea, thick and with great por-

Moses descends Mt. Sinai with the Law.

Moses comes upon the Hebrews worshipping a Golden Idol. "You are not worthy to receive these Ten Commandments," he cries.

tent, casting a shadowed hue over all. Moses stands at the edge of the sea, wind blowing his robes about, his rod upraised. "The Lord of Hosts will do battle for us!" he declares. "Behold His Mighty Hand!" Stretching his arms wide, Moses holds his staff above the water. At this, the waters chop madly, and as they do, the clouds form a cyclonic funnel and pass into the waters. They churn beneath the sea until, in an awesome moment, they push the waters apart, leaving a dry path in their wake. "Lead them through the midst of the water," Moses orders Joshua. "His will be done," the stupefied aide replies.

Meanwhile, restrained by the Pillar of Fire, Pharaoh is amazed. His associates are rigid with fear and ask that they turn back. "Man cannot do battle with a God," the Pharaoh's charioteer, Abbas El Bougdadly, advises. But Pharaoh will not be deterred. "Better to die in battle with a God than to live in shame," he commands.

The Hebrews march through the parted sea and when they near the other side, the Pillar of Fire dies. Ramses' men flow into the water. They are not destined to recapture their slaves, however. For as soon as the Hebrews are safe, Moses cries, "Who shall withstand the power of God?" and closes the sea upon the pursuing Egyptians. The men, save for Pharaoh, are destroyed. Moses offers thanks unto God. An ethereal

light bathes his face. "Thou didst blow with thy winds and the sea covered them. Who is like unto thee, O Lord? From everlasting to everlasting, thou art God!"

So the sequence ends. A dramatic scene, certainly. But while an emotional success, it fails on many counts. Much of the trouble lies in the quality of John P. Fulton's special effects work. Fulton parted De-Mille's original sea back in the silent days. For this earlier version, the sea was actually gelatin, filmed a frame at a time in much the same fashion as an animated cartoon. The end result was interesting, although hardly convincing. For the remake, Fulton used real water. To achieve his effect, 300,000 gallons of sea was poured into a tank, photographed, and then simply projected in reverse. On top of this action was superimposed the Hebrews, and rather poorly at that.

The process used for this 'double exposure' is known as a matte, the technical term for the superimposition of one element over another element in film; in this case, the real people over the miniature sea. A matte is achieved by backing the foreground elements (Moses, et al) with a duplicate strip of these figures, but in black. This black 'matte' is combined with the foreground elements via an optical printer. Thus, when placed over the pre-filmed background, the black matte prevents the frontal images from looking transparent, as they would be without the interfilm.

Moses comes upon the Hebrews worshipping a Golden Idol. "You are not worthy to receive these Ten Commandments," he cries.

Behind-the-scenes on the Goshen set.

And the mattes in *The Ten Commandments* are sloppy, something of a puzzle considering the film's budget. Most of the mattes are too large and overlap the figures; irritating black outlines are visible around the people. Matte lines on the sea itself, because of all the water beads and spray, are improperly synchronized, thus diluting the overall effect.

Even Heston was not impressed with the Oscar-winning effects, an award undeserved over that year's awesome *Forbidden Planet* work. Even as drama, Heston finds it weak. It was shot partially in Egypt, partially in Hollywood, and was experienced by him over a period of many months. "So," he admits, "I had no concept of that scene. I never knew until I saw the film what it was going to be. It was just a mosaic piece. And there's almost no performance to it. My presence was a chemical contribution.

"Certainly, the Red Sea sequence is not as good as the Exodus, in my view, structurally or in its final result. Putting aside any consideration of the technical qualities of the process work, which is a difficult thing to do because a scene like that really either works or it doesn't work. It requires belief. You have to believe it. So I don't think you can dismiss a consideration of the technical problems of the parting of the sea, because that's what makes the scene stand or fall. And, I suppose, now it could be done better."

But DeMille somehow makes it work. Or rather, through the inertia he had built to that point, the scene carries itself regardless of a technical albatross or two.

Unfortunately, as it is the scene for which everyone has waited, they're ready now to go home. But the film is not yet over. You've still got to give man the Ten Commandments and get him to the Promised Land. So in order to hold our attention after this spectacular sequence, we are treated to an equally spectacular giving of the Commandments, high atop Sinai, by God, who is manifest in a blazing fireball. He sends flame screaming from His midst and into the mountain, so we do not doze. DeMille even gives us an orgy while Moses is gone. For in DeMille's own words, the Hebrews "were as the children of fools, and cast off their clothes. The wicked were like a troubled sea whose waters cast up fire and dirt. They sank from evil to evil, and were viler than the earth. And there was rioting and drunkenness. They had become servants of sin. There was manifest all manners of ungodliness and works of the flesh. Even adultery and lasciviousness, uncleanliness, idolatry and rioting, vanity and wrath. And they were filled with iniquity and vile in affections." Now we have both scriptural *and* visual overstatement.

DeMille similarly punctuates other crucial transition sequences. After Moses' exile from Egypt, DeMille continues: "Into the blistering Wilderness of Shur, the man who walked with kings now walks alone. Torn from the pinnacle of royal power, stripped of all rank and earthly wealth, a forsaken man without a country, without a hope. His soul is in turmoil like the hot winds and raging sands that lash him with the fury of a taskmaster's whip. He is driven forward, always forward, by a God unknown on a land unseen. Into the molten Wilderness of Zin, where granite sentinels stand as towers of living death to bar his way. Each night brings the black embrace of loneliness. In the mocking whisper of the wind, he hears the echoing voices of the dark. His tortured mind, wondering if they call the memory of past triumphs, or wail foreboding of disasters yet-to-come, or whether the desert's hot breath has melted his reason into madness. He cannot cool the burning kiss of thirst upon his lips, nor shade the scorching fury of the sun. All about is desolation. He can neither bless nor curse the power that moves him, for he does not know from where it comes. Learning that it can be more terrible to live than to die, he is driven out through the burning crucible of death, where holy man and prophets are cleansed and purged for God's great purpose. Until, at last, at the end of human strength, beaten into the dust from which he came, the metal is ready for the Maker's hand. And he found strength from a fruit-laden palm tree, and life-giving water flowing from the well of Midian."

All of which proves that if the picture isn't great, it is surely reverent. For DeMille cared about *The Ten Commandments*. Not, perhaps, to the intellectual degree another director might have, but this is an academic point. For *The Ten Commandments* is ultimately an inspiring film, heavy with religious sentiment, remarkable presence . . . and Charlton Heston.

The Ten Commandments was Heston's first "epic" role, although it was his fifteenth film. Of it he says, "It secured my place as an important performer long enough for me to get a few turns at bat, you know, and that's important. You have to stay in the line-up and in the first division, and that did it for me." If Heston had not landed the role, one critic suggests, ". . . he might have gone the way of all second-rate action stars."

Of course, the reviewer in question exhibits a vast ignorance of his subject. Heston *did* get the role, and not simply because he resembled the Michelangelo statue. It is because Heston is the fine, dedicated performer of whom we spoke earlier.

But *The Ten Commandments* did more than simply further Heston's career. It gave him his public image. Henceforth, he would be the very personification of Moses. Whether this was intentional or not, what the public wanted or what Heston himself wanted, is something that will become apparent in due course.

THREE VIOLENT PEOPLE

Paramount
1956

Produced by Hugh Brown. *Directed* by Rudolph Mate. *Script* by James Edward Grant from a story by Leonard Praskins and Barney Slater. *Photography* by Loyal Griggs. *Music* by Walter Scharf. 98 minutes. *Starring* Charlton Heston (Colt Saunders), Anne Baxter (Lorna Hunter Saunders), Gilbert Roland (Innocencio), Tom Tryon (Cinch Saunders), Bruce Bennett (Harrison), Forrest Tucker (Cable).

Heston and Miss Baxter take time out from their westward trek.

Publicity still of Heston and Anne Baxter.

The three violent people are Charlton Heston, Tom Tryon, and Anne Baxter. Heston plays Colt Saunders, a Confederate ex-captain, Tryon is his one-armed brother, and Baxter is Heston's wife, a one-time prostitute.

Striding outside a bar, Heston sees a Southern woman step from a newly arrived coach. Northern carpetbaggers toss wisecracks in her direction. Heston warns one of them, "You can't talk like that to a Southern lady." The man throws a punch, and Heston decks him. The man's buddies come to his defense and knock Heston unconscious. Running to his side, Lorna asks a lawman to take Heston to her room in the hotel.

When Heston awakens he asks Lorna to dinner. "First," she says, "I'd better prepare you. You see, I'm an emancipated woman; I attended schools with progressive ideas. I may shock you." Heston sneers, "I don't see how anyone can look so right and think so wrong. I've got no time to waste. I just spent four years losing a war and I've got a ranch to build up and a family to raise. I'm looking for a wife. Miss Hunter, do you want to get married?" Lorna is taken aback. "Why, of all the cold-blooded, unromantic. . . ." she begins, only to be interrupted by Heston's kiss.

She and Heston are married, and they travel to the Southern officer's Bar-S ranch in Texas. When they arrive, Heston takes her inside and introduces her to Innocencio, his Mexican right arm. The man's sons, too, work the ranch. "Hey, amigo," Heston greets him, "Couldn't anybody find a broom all the time I was gone? The bedroom looks like a family of packrats wintered there." While Lorna gets acquainted with the place, things start getting tacky. Heston's one-armed brother Cinch is upset with his older sibling. It seems the Bar-S was left to Heston with the understanding that he would give Cinch whatever he felt the younger fellow deserved. But Cinch wants his portion now, and in gold. He believes that the Provisional government will collapse and he suggests Heston sell part of the ranch to any Northerner in the area who has money. Cinch, of course, knows that Heston would never do this.

Lorna asks Heston about Cinch. "We were just

Heston proposes marriage to a surprised Anne Baxter.

kids when it happened," Heston begins. "We were horsing around on the windmill platform on the south range. Cinch got his arm caught in the gears of the windmill. I had to amputate his arm . . . carry him back. People made quite a fuss about it, as if I'd been a hero." "How terrible," Lorna exclaims, "For both of you." Heston is impressed. "You know, you're the first person who ever realized that I got hurt that day too."

Soon, a new set of antagonists joins the cast. "I'm Deputy Commissioner Cable," announces Forrest Tucker, as Heston and his wife arrive at the office of the Provisional government. "When a gentleman is introduced to my wife," Heston corrects him, "even when the gentleman does his own introducing, he stands up." Tucker doesn't take kindly to the criticism; an incident is avoided by the arrival of the Commissioner. He brings bad tidings for Heston. He and all his fellow ranchers are to be heavily taxed to pay for the war. Heston is unhappy about this and leaves. But as he and Lorna ride away, a Mr. Massey recognizes Lorna as a former prostitute. He attempts to greet her, but she pretends she does not know him. Turning to Cable, Massey asks, "Who was that?" "Oh," Cable replies, "Captain and Mrs. Saunders, flower of the old South. "Saunders?" the new arrival cries. "Oh man, I almost made the mistake of the century. I mistook Mrs. Saunders for a gal I used to play around with back in St. Louis. Lorna Hunter. Oh man, what a mistake!" Cable is suddenly alert. "That's no mistake, man," he shouts. "I just heard him call her Lorna. I wonder if he knows? I'll bet he doesn't. I'd love to see the look on his face when he finds out!"

The Commissioner, Cable, and their soldier cohorts begin to plan some action and intrigue. "What're you sweatin' for," Cable asks a man. "It ain't a hot day." "I ain't as sure as you are that this is gonna work," the man counters. "Of course it's gonna work," Gable protests. "You insult Saunder's wife, he draws on you, and I kill him. Saunders is tryin' to get these ranchers to make a fight. We can't have that."

After this is settled, the government men go to Bar-S in search of the taxable horses they know are there. Heston tells them to get lost. The Commissioner greets Lorna and introduces his new administrative assistant, Mr. Massey. "Mrs. Saunders and me," Massey says, "we already met. Back in St. Louis. You remember, Lorna." "No, I don't," Lorna answers. "Lorna," Massey entreats, "ya can't have forgotten." "I'm sorry," she insists, "I've never seen you before." Massey continues to argue, but Heston intercedes. "Mrs. Saunders has twice said she does not know you, sir. Do not press the point." But the man is persistent. "Lorna, ya gotta remember me! There was us fellas on General Butler's staff, and you and Flossy . . . from Ruby LaSalle's place." Hearing this, Heston is upset. He asks Massey to come inside.

"Now then, Mr. Massey," Heston announces coldly, "you will go on with what you were saying." Lorna enters. She admits to remembering the man. At this, Massey leaves Heston and Lorna alone. She confesses to having been a prostitute. Entirely calm and collected, Heston tells her, "I'll be rounding up strays for a few weeks. There's a stage leaving around the first of the month. Cinch will put you on it." Lorna is crushed. "I'd get down on my knees if I thought it would help," which it apparently would not. It is then Lorna tells Heston she is going to have his child. Heston remains unmoved.

Meanwhile, fighting breaks out as government meets ranchers on the field of battle. During one encounter, Lorna joins the fray, but Heston has her carried back to the ranch. After the combat is over, Cinch and Heston get into a fight. Heston warns his brother, "If you ever set foot on Bar-S again, I'll kill you."

Immediately after this, Heston gives Lorna the horses he has been keeping, those animals which the

Charlton Heston and Tom Tryon

Anne Baxter, Charlton Heston and Tom Tryon.

government is out to tax. They are valued at $3,000. "When I order music," he says, "I always pay the piper, whether I like the tune or not. As soon as the baby can be turned over to a nurse, you can leave with the horses. You can't make that much money in that length of time in any occupation you're trained for." Soon after, the baby is born. It's a male, and in the cabin after its birth Heston refuses to drink a toast to the child. Innocencio is upset by this. He says he will take Lorna to the stage himself, and then with all his sons return to Mexico. Heston says simply, goodbye.

Simultaneously, Cinch visits the Provisional government which is falling to ruin. He comes with a proposal: a plan to kill Heston. As this drama unfolds, Heston readies Lorna for her departure. She is nursing the child as he arrives to present her with the bill of sale for the horses. She will need this if she is to resell the animals. Lorna tells Heston she will not take the child. She wants him to have the Bar-S, which is more than she could ever give him. "But Colt," she warns, "when you're raising the boy, try to remember something. That people aren't perfect. They just aren't. They make mistakes. And when they do, they suffer. They pay. So when he makes his mistakes, try to find it in you to forgive him." Just then, Cinch arrives and taunts his brother, goading him into a showdown. Heston cannot draw his gun. And while the two play

One of the many confrontations between Heston and Tom Tryon, as Cinch. Heston, Tryon, and Gilbert Roland.

cat and mouse, the government soldiers arrive and battle Innocencio and Heston's men for possession of the ranch. During the strife, Cinch is killed, and the agents of illegality are routed. Lorna and Heston realize they are truly in love, Innocencio stays on, and all ends happily.

Three Violent People is an entertaining film, and the three stars, especially Heston, are very good. *The New York Times* said, "Heston makes a mighty distasteful pillar of piety as Colt," and this is so. It is one of the many "bastard" roles Heston has undertaken, and the second in which a "tarnished woman" offends

his dignity. Heston is utterly convinced of his moral sanctity, even if this is based on the exclusion of all human emotion. Only an actor of his recognized stature and image could have made the character credible.

Anne Baxter, Heston's co-star in *The Ten Commandments*, is guilty of overacting, but it plays well with Heston's inflexible bearing. Cinch, as played by Tom Tryon—star of Otto Preminger's *The Cardinal*, and the future author of *The Other*—is somewhere between the two. He is sensible, but devious and greedy. Together, the three make for an entertaining show.

TOUCH OF EVIL

Universal
1958

Produced by Albert Zugsmith. *Directed* by Orson Welles. *Script* by Orson Welles. *Photography* by Russell Metty. *Music* by Henry Mancini. 93 minutes. *Starring* Charlton Heston (Ramon Miguel Vargas), Janet Leigh (Susan Vargas), Orson Welles (Hank Quinlan), Joseph Calleia (Pete Menzies), Akim Tamiroff (Joe Grandi), with guest appearances by Zsa Zsa Gabor, Marlene Dietrich, and Joseph Cotten.

A car has just exploded, and Heston rushes to the scene.

Heston telephones his wife from a cigar stand.

Touch of Evil is one of Heston's most interesting films, which is in no small part due to the fact that it was directed by Orson Welles.

Initially, *Touch of Evil* was to have starred Heston and Welles and been directed by a Universal "house" director. Since Heston had assumed that Welles would direct, he was prepared to back out of the project. As a result, the picture's producer, Albert Zugsmith, unwilling to lose a major star, allowed Welles to rewrite and direct the picture.

The film spotlights an incredible battle of wits and wills between two men: Heston, as Mike Vargas, a Mexican justice department lawyer; and Welles, as Hank Quinlan, a corrupt American police inspector.

The film opens with the explosion of a car, behind the wheel of which was Rudy Lanniker and his mistress. Rudy was one of the richest men in town, and his death is a mystery.

"An hour ago Rudy Lanniker had this town in his pocket," an observer notes, "Now you can strain him through a sieve." At this point, Heston, on his honeymoon, and about to cross the border to show his wife Mexico, arrives on the scene. "Can you tell me who's in charge here?" he asks. "I can't even tell you what happened," a witness responds.

Meanwhile, Heston's wife is coerced into joining some young Mexicans who tell her they have something of interest for Heston. They lead her to Grandi, brother of the leader of the Grandi drug ring. He warns Mrs. Vargas that Heston had better lay off their operation.

Susan is freed and carries the warning to Heston. By now, Quinlan has arrived on the scene and he forms a dislike for Heston almost immediately. Heston assures the Captain, "You won't have any trouble with me." To which Quinlan responds, "You bet your sweet life I won't."

Tracking suspects, Quinlan and his men cross the border into Mexico. Someone tries to splash Heston with a pail of acid. His wife wants them to return to America. But, "This isn't the real Mexico," Heston pleads. "All border towns bring out the worst in a country." Still, he decides it would be safer for his wife to stay at a motel in the middle of nowhere. Heston agrees to fetch her when the case is closed. After she has gone, Heston joins Quinlan who has begun questioning suspects. He starts—and finishes—with one. The lover of Lanniker's daughter.

Orson Welles (left) is impervious to Sanchez's (Victor Millan) pleas as a sympathetic Heston looks on.

Heston and Eva Gabor on the set

Heston is on the scene as Quinlan gives the half-breed lover the third degree. We later learn that Quinlan's wife was killed by a halfbreed, which accounts for his prejudice.

"A lady on Main Street picked up a shoe," Quinlan tells Sanchez, "and that shoe had a foot in it. I'm gonna make you pay for that." To further intimidate the man, Quinlan tells him not to worry; during interrogation they will not touch his face. "Leaves too many marks."

Sanchez turns to Heston for sanctuary. "Can't

you do something to help me?" he begs the lawyer. Heston *does* try to help, and discovers that the boy is being framed. While searching the bathroom minutes before, the lawman had knocked an empty shoebox into the bathtub. Moments later, Quinlan pulls two sticks of dynamite—of the identical sort used to bomb the car—from the same shoebox.

Heston sets out to discredit Quinlan and prove him a liar. This is difficult since Heston is operating in America where the crime was committed.

While this is going on, Quinlan and Grandi meet in Mexico to frame Heston. First, they take over the motel in which Heston's wife is staying. They blanket her clothes with marijuana fumes and shoot her full of drugs. Next, they carry her, unconscious, to a Mexican brothel where her discovery will ruin Heston's career.

In the meanwhile, Heston tries feverishly to prove that the shoebox dynamite was, in fact, taken by Quinlan from a construction site. "What are you trying to do," one of Quinlan's sergeants asks Heston, "ruin him?" Heston is unmoved. "What about all those people he put in the death house? Save your tears for them."

Quinlan kills Grandi. He realizes that Grandi is a coward and a traitor, and he may give away their plot. This is something Quinlan cannot chance. Subsequently, Heston gets the bad news that his wife is in jail charged with possession of narcotics, prostitution, and the murder of the enormous Grandi. "Who the hell does Quinlan think he is, hanging a murder rap on my wife?" Heston cries when he hears the news. But all is not lost. Pete Menzies, the sergeant who had defended Quinlan, finds his superior's cane in the room where Grandi's body was discovered. He agrees to help Heston capture the inspector.

Quinlan, meanwhile, has gone to see Marlene Dietrich, who owns the local nightclub. It is this same club in which Heston's wife had been deposited. "C'mon," he urges her, "read my future for me." Miss Dietrich is immobile. "You haven't got any," she informs Quinlan.

Outside the club, wired and recording, Menzies confronts his boss. The two walk into the night. "Watch out," Quinlan informs his trusted aide, "Vargas'll turn you into one of those starry-eyed idealists!" Heston follows them getting every word on tape. It is then that the subject of Grandi's death is broached. Menzies says, "I guess you were thinking about your wife . . . the way she was strangled." Then Menzies accuses Welles of "faking evidence." "Aiding justice,

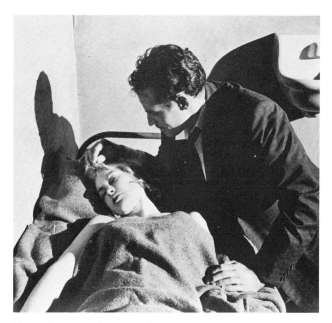

Heston finds his wife in jail, up for a murder rap.

partner!" Welles corrects him. At this, the inspector shoots Menzies, who falls into the mire below. Heston gets this, too, on tape. He then shows himself to Quinlan who, through some sixth sense, had known all along he was there.

"Well, Captain," Heston informs him, "I'm afraid this is finally something you can't talk your way out of." Desperate, Quinlan prepares to shoot Heston, but is, himself, shot by Menzies, who had not yet expired. Evidence in hand, Heston turns it over to one of the Quinlan aides he knows he can trust, and with his wife—smuggled out of the Mexican prison—they leave the country. But there's one final irony: Heston is informed that Sanchez confessed to the crime; that he was, indeed, guilty after all.

Heston has some thoughts on the film.

"*Touch of Evil*, of course, was made by one of the great directors. If it is not *Citizen Kane*, it has been listed not far behind *Kane* in the list of Welles' films. It was a remarkable experience for me, a great learning experience; one of the most valuable I've had in my whole film career. I probably learned more about acting from Welles than from any other film director I've worked for, which is not necessarily to say that I gave my best film performance for him. But he is, himself, an actor, and an incredibly resourceful communica-

Reunited with his wife (Janet Leigh), Heston prepares to drive her from Mexico in *Touch of Evil*.

tor. He understands actors and can communicate to them. He did so to me in great detail, and very valuably.

"The film itself is brilliant; flawed, I suppose. It was probably a little ahead of its time. That is a glib rationale to explain any book or poem or painting or performance or composition whose author is disappointed with its reception. But it may be true about *Touch of Evil*. Although the film was not successful at all at the time, it has remained more or less constantly in art house release ever since. Partly, of course, because it is one of Welles' not-long list of films. But it also is one of his better films.

"The camera work, for which Russ Metty deserves a lot of credit, is incredible; brilliant work. Some of the performances are interesting; some of them remarkable. I don't think Joe Calleia did a better job of acting in his life. Orson is extremely good.

"The main criticism I would make of the film—perhaps Orson didn't think this through, though I rather doubt that; he's a very, very bright man—is he seemed to feel the necessity of concealing from me the fact that he had the central role, and this imposed on him the necessity of putting in a couple of scenes for

me that were not necessary. My part is that of the observer. The film is really the decline and destruction of Captain Quinlan. And I am a horrified and involved observer. Vargas, in the first place, was interesting for me to play because Welles made him a Mexican. And that gave a point of view, an added dimension, to work for. In the second place, he is a good man, and thus a contrast to Quinlan's corrupt man. An interesting character but, nevertheless, basically an observer to Quinlan's destruction.

"Of course, Vargas is not cynical; he's committed. He is newly married and deeply in love with his wife, cares about showing her Mexico, and so on. He's very much alive, and I don't think is corrupted by the criminal world which is his environment.

"At the time it was released, *Touch of Evil* was widely criticized in terms of its non-sequential story line. That kind of film structure was not fashionable then; God knows, it is fashionable now. We see whole films that have an almost abstract time concept, and audiences are prepared to work a little harder, even if they come up empty-handed at the end. If you were willing to work that hard with Welles' films, you didn't come up empty-handed."

THE BIG COUNTRY

United Artists
1958

Produced by William Wyler and Gregory Peck. *Direct-ed* by William Wyler. *Script* by James R. Webb, Sy Bartlett, and Robert Wilder, from the novel by David Hamilton. *Photography* by Franz F. Planer. *Music* by Jerome Moross. 163 minutes. *Starring* Gregory Peck (James McKay), Jean Simmons (Julie Maragon), Carroll Baker (Patricia Terrill), Charlton Heston (Steve Leech), Burl Ives (Rufus Hannassey), Charles Bickford (Major Terrill).

Beyond the action and sweep of *The Big Country* is a story of profound cinematic symbols. It is the sort of picture one might expect from one of film's great directors, William Wyler.

Jim McKay (Gregory Peck) has come to the vast area of the old west, referred to by its inhabitants as *The Big Country*. He has given up his trade as a ship's captain to marry Pat Terrill and live on her father's huge ranch. From the moment he steps off the stagecoach, McKay is exposed to a new and savage set of values.

His first contact with these alien standards comes in the person of Steve Leech (Heston), Major Terrill's foreman. From the time they first meet, it is evident that they grate on each other.

McKay learns of a blood feud between the Terrills and a mountain-dwelling family, the Hannasseys. Intense hatred has driven the humanity from old Major Terrill, and his counterpart, Rufus Hannassey. Unfortunately, McKay discovers it has also done the same to Pat. Because of this, McKay grows apart from Pat and falls in love with her friend, schoolteacher Julie Maragon.

Julie is an involuntary and strategic factor in the feud, for she owns the only body of water for miles around. Both Terrill and Hannassey have tried to get her to sell her land, but she has refused.

When Julie is kidnapped, McKay follows her trail into the mountain stronghold of the Hannassey clan. There he wins the respect of old Rufus. But even he

Original ad-art for *The Big Country*. Pictured are Gregory Peck, Heston, Carroll Baker, and Jean Simmons.

Heston and Charles Bickford in *The Big Country*.

Heston and Charles Bickford in *The Big Country*.

Heston and Carroll Baker.

Artwork that will appear in a poster is often sketched from actual stills, as this shot from *The Big Country* illustrates.

can't stop the confrontation between the Major and old Hannassey, who eventually shoot it out and kill each other.

McKay and Julie are now free to live on her ranch, while Heston and Pat run the huge Terrill operation.

The Big Country is a tale of land—of vast land—and its effect on human beings. The film is a symphony of cinema and music that effectively captures the taste of fresh air and the dominant presence of *The Big Country*. In every way, it is a film about people. We begin with human skeletons and end with massive human icons.

The film achieves its effect through visual means. We see our characters in varied postures of hope, frustration, despair, and understanding. Yet in all of this, the focal point of these images is not Gregory Peck, who is the film's star. He has already been shaped by the sea; he represents an objectivity that enters the tapestry of *The Big Country*. Nor is Major Terrill (Charles Bickford) unique; he has a counterpart in the crafty and craggy Rufus Hannassey (Burl Ives). The characters of Pat Terrill (Jean Simmons) and Julie Maragon (Carroll Baker) are in evidence only to furnish us with emotional springboards, i.e. an eventual choice of companions for Jim McKay. Therefore, only one character in the film merits a focal symbolic interest.

In *The Big Country*, Charlton Heston is as strong and steadfast as the land. He has come from out of nowhere, evolving from a young saddle tramp to be the strong right arm of Major Terrill. In eliminating all mention of Heston's origin, his roots thus seem to emanate from, and therefore reflect, the land itself. He stands tall and, like the land, is manipulated by powers beyond his control. His life and values have been formed by Major Terrill as surely as the forces of nature sculpted the awesome mountains that form the boundaries of *The Big Country*.

During the course of the film, McKay engages in fisticuffs with Heston. The pair fight to a draw, each having broken the other into a state of mutual understanding, proving that each is indestructible in his own right. McKay, of course, gains his omnipotence due simply to his having the coveted position as the film's hero. So by challenging Heston and fighting to the point where both are on their knees, the hero has acknowledged Heston's character to be a personification of the timeless terrain that surrounds them.

As Leech, Heston is superb. For, apart from the tinge of illiteracy that taints Leech, the two are one and the same. As directed by Wyler, *The Big Country*—featuring superb photography, solid performances, and a now classic score by Jerome Moross—brought to Heston a film worthy of his talents. His performance so impressed Wyler that the director starred him in his next production, a film that would win Heston an Oscar.

THE BUCCANEER

Paramount
1958

Produced by Henry Wilcoxon for Cecil B. DeMille. *Directed* by Anthony Quinn. *Script* by Jesse L. Lasky, Jr. and Berenice Mosk. *Photography* by Loyal Griggs. *Music* by Elmer Bernstein. 120 minutes. *Starring* Yul Brynner (Jean Lafitte), Charlton Heston (Andrew Jackson), Claire Bloom (Bonnie Brown), Charles Boyer (Dominique You), Inger Stevens (Annette Claiborne), Henry Hull (Ezra Peavey), E. G. Marshall (Gov. Claiborne), Lorne Greene (Mercier).

The Buccaneer is a disappointment in every conceivable way. Yul Brynner stars as the pirate Jean La-Fitte who aided the American cause during the War of 1812. The film was directed by Anthony Quinn when his father-in-law, Cecil B. DeMille, became sick.

"I found Tony Quinn a stimulating director, a talented man, and a very sincere artist," Heston says, "even though the film didn't turn out well. I believe it was difficult for him to work for DeMille, as it was probably difficult for DeMille not to direct a picture that he had planned from the start. A close associate of DeMille's, Henry Wilcoxon, produced it, and even though DeMille functioned as executive producer, he meticulously stayed out of it. He was hardly ever on the set. I don't think Tony could complain about his interfering in the picture's direction. The cutting, however, was under DeMille's supervision."

The film has a free-wheeling air about it that doesn't quite work. In trying to recapture the swashbuckling grandeur of *Sea Hawk*, DeMille fostered an anachronism—a silly picture that even then was considered "camp." Brynner is fine—when is he not?—even with a full head of hair. Heston is wooden and suffers beneath heavy makeup. Nonetheless, his elderly Jackson, forced to rely upon the assistance of scoundrels to defeat the British, is the most interesting part in the film. For, though stiff of body, Heston's Old Hickory is supple of mind. He personifies human depth with a mere glance; a gentle tilt of the head. And since Jackson is so mighty an historical figure, he understandably dominates all the scenes in which he appears.

As with *The President's Lady*, the story is fictionalized history, and is of little aesthetic worth. The battles are poorly staged and the action weak. It is big and splashy, but it is poor DeMille.

An interesting aside, best mentioned here: Although Heston has portrayed two American presidents (Thomas Jefferson on television and Jackson), and an American patriot (James Otis in the 1951 Studio One presentation of *A Bolt of Lightning*), it has been said his face most resembles that of Abraham Lincoln. When pressed, Heston admits that he would like to play the sixteenth president; he notes, however, that "there have been several good Lincoln films, and I doubt it'll come up again." If it did, Heston, who well fills Lincoln's 6'4" frame, would shine.

An older Andrew Jackson (Heston, second from right) listens to Jean LaFitte's (Yul Brynner) military advice in *The Buccaneer*.

BEN-HUR

MGM
1959

Produced by Sam Zimbalist. *Directed* by William Wyler. *Script* by Karl Tunberg from the novel by Lew Wallace. *Photography* by Robert L. Surtees. *Music* by Miklos Rozsa. 217 minutes. *Starring* Charlton Heston (Judah Ben-Hur), Stephen Boyd (Messala), Jack Hawkins (Quintus Arrius), Hugh Griffith (Sheik Ilderim), Martha Scott (Miriam), Cathy O'Donnell (Tirzah), Haya Harareet (Esther).

Ben-Hur is one of film history's great crowd-pleasers. In terms of size, it is one of the world's biggest films, surpassing *The Ten Commandments, Spartacus, King of Kings,* and others, though falling short of *El Cid, Fall of the Roman Empire, Cleopatra,* and *Tora! Tora! Tora!.* And it features perhaps the finest action sequence ever filmed: the famous chariot race. *Ben-Hur* is filled with symbolism and irony as it skillfully interweaves many different stories into a single, moving tapestry.

MGM was in troubled financial waters when they undertook *Ben-Hur,* a film which would either sink or save them. And Charlton Heston was not the studio's first choice to act the coveted role of Judah Ben-Hur. Burt Lancaster had been offered the role. Considering his athletic work in such films as *Trapeze* and *Crimson Pirate,* and his intense acting style, the selection would have been a wise one. Rock Hudson, too, was pencilled in as *Ben-Hur,* with Heston as Messala. But this, too, fell through. Finally, Cesare Danova was cast, but the studio decided his English would not be expert enough by the time the cameras were ready to roll.

Although Heston was highly recommended for the part by Cecil DeMille, the actor believes this support had little to do with Director William Wyler's final decision. The two had just worked together on *The Big Country,* and their respect was mutual. So Heston became Ben-Hur. And the portrayal, the finest of his career, gave the film more humanity and depth than it might have had with another in the title role. It also gave Heston the Best Actor Oscar.

Charlton Heston as Ben-Hur.

Stephen Boyd as Messala.

Heston and Boyd argue over their respective loyalties to Judea and Rome. The life-long friends part enemies.

The movie cost MGM $12,500,000, which is a healthy sum. "It would probably cost over $20,000,000 today," Heston notes. And it saved MGM from bankruptcy, their gamble paying off, by becoming the third top-grossing film in history, led only by *Gone With the Wind* and *Birth of a Nation*.

Among the first characters we meet are Roman soldiers who arrive in Judea, led by the Tribune Messala. He is a young man, second in command only to the new governor who will arrive in a few days. Leaving his troops, Messala retires to discuss the province with Sextus, the man he is replacing. "The Emperor is displeased," Messala begins. "He wishes Judea made into a more obedient and disciplined province. I intend to carry out his command," Messala asserts. Sextus is annoyed. "Yes, but how, Messala? You can break a man's skull, you can arrest him, you can throw him into a dungeon, but how do you control what's up here?" he asks. "How do you fight an idea? Especially a new idea?" As Messala prepares to answer, he is interrupted by a centurion who says that a Prince Judah Ben-Hur awaits the Tribune's pleasure. Messala says he will meet Judah in short order. As he leaves, Messala turns to his companion and says, "Sextus, you asked how to fight an idea. Well I'll tell you how. With another idea." After a pregnant pause, he leaves.

The reunion between Judah and Messala is a happy one. They were friends as boys. As a symbol of their closeness, they each toss spears at a crossbeam over the door. The two shafts hit close together. "Still close!" Messala exclaims. "In every way," Judah echoes. They retire to the Roman's chamber.

As they speak, it becomes obvious that irreparable ideological differences will separate the men. Messala

The new governor enters Judea, with Messala at his side. A tile from Ben-Hur's roof strikes the potentate and nearly kills him. For this, Ben-Hur is sent to jail.

Imprisoned, Ben-Hur escapes and threatens Messala's life. Drusus (Terence Langdon) intercedes.

is very proud of his Roman legions; Judah, in turn, loves his people. And the two groups just happen to be at war. "I'm a Jew," Judah reminds Messala during their discussion. Messala scoffs. "What have you in common with the rabble that makes trouble here?" he asks. "Rabble?" Judah returns, shocked. "They're my people. I'm one of them."

The next day, Messala comes to Judah's house for lunch. He asks Judah for the names of Jewish resistance leaders. "Would I retain your friendship if I became an informer?" Judah asks, shocked. "To tell me the names of criminals is hardly informing," Messala argues, but Judah remains appalled. "Criminals? They're not criminals, Messala! They're patriots!"

Messala, however, is desperate and begs for Judah's assistance. Judah refuses. The men part enemies.

A few days later, the new governor enters Jerusalem with two more Roman legions. Judah and his sister, Tirzah, watch the procession from the roof of their home. Tirzah, who leans over the roof just as the potentate passes by their house, rests her hand on a tile edging the roof. The stone falls, alarming the governor's horse. The official is thrown against a wall, seriously injured, and soldiers rush madly into the house of Hur. Judah claims he did it, but that it was an accident. He is bound, just as Messala enters. The tribune tells his men to take Judah, his mother, and his sister away. Though Judah begs that he leave his family out of it, that it was his fault, Messala will hear none of it. "I wanted your help; now you've given it to me. By making this example of you, I discourage treason. By condemning, without hesitation, an old friend, I shall be feared."

Judah is taken away. En route to Tyrus, Judah and some three dozen other prisoners pass through the town of Nazareth. The soldiers and horses are given water first; then, what few prisoners the townspeople can aid are given drink. A woman is about to sate Judah's thirst, but a soldier pulls her away. "No water for that one," he yells. Judah's mouth is burning; his lips are white from the desert heat. Slowly, against even his iron will, Judah falls to his knees, then to his face. He lies on the ground, chained to other slaves, and begs God for His help. Moments later, a stranger touches Judah's face, wetting it with cooling water. The helping hand then gives Judah a ladle filled with refreshment. He drinks thirstily. But a centurion, seeing this, runs over. "You!" he cries. "I said no water for him!" The figure by Judah's side stands up and faces the soldier. The Roman stops in his tracks. He stares for a minute, then slowly backs away. Once again the Nazarene turns his attention to Judah. Judah looks into the face of the man, his savior, and is struck by an ethereal light. He begins to walk again, his life and strength renewed.

When next we see Ben-Hur, he has been a galley slave for three years. And on the boat of Roman Commander Quintus Arrius, he so impresses the Roman with his desire to live that when the ship goes into battle, Judah is not chained to his oar. This was a practice used to keep men from abandoning their posts in the heat of battle.

The fleet enters into vicious combat with Macedonian pirates, and in the midst of frenzy, Judah's ship is rammed by another. It begins to sink and Judah unshackles as many prisoners as he is able before running to the deck. As he reaches the battleground, Judah sees Arrius knocked overboard by a pirate. Laden with armor, the Roman will surely sink. Judah jumps in after him. Grabbing the officer, the slave takes hold

Heston is overcome and escorted to Tyrus, where he is made a galley slave.

On the way, however, he is given water by a carpenter's son, in the town of Nazareth.

Judah Ben-Hur spends three years as a galley slave, until his ship is sunk during a battle.

Judah returns to Judea where, one day, he hears a young rabbi from Nazareth deliver a sermon.

The only way Judah can get back at Messala is to race him in the great chariot contest held in Judea. Here, he practices for the big day.

Before the cheering throngs, the race gets underway.

The first lap goes well. . . .

of some floating wreckage. Hidden from the attackers, the unconscious Arrius and the exhausted Judah float from the scene of the battle.

The two return to Rome. Again, years pass. Judah races chariots in the great Circus and becomes adept in the manners of Roman life. At a party one night, Arrius announces that Judah will henceforth be his legally adopted son, and heir to his property. Judah is moved, but knows it is time to return to Judea.

On the way home, Judah meets Sheik Ilderim. Ilderim, impressed by Judah's success in the Circus, invites him to stay for dinner. There they discuss the upcoming chariot race in Judea. The Sheik's people are praying for victory and he needs only a man to race his strong Arabian team. "When they race in Jerusalem, they will challenge the finest teams in the world," the Arab announces, "not to mention the champion of the east, the Tribune Messala with his black devils. He stops at nothing to win!" Judah is stunned, but he will not be turned from his purpose which is to find his mother and sister and "deal with Messala my own way."

Judah arrives in Judea to find his house deserted. Or so he thinks. Living there, still, are two of his faithful servants: Esther and Simonides, her father. Simo-

Messala chews an opponent's spokes apart and sends him flying.

In a desperate maneuver, Ben-Hur pilots his chariot over the wreckage and lands safely on the other side.

The match continues as the
entrants near the final lap.

Realizing he must win, Messala whips his hated enemy.

nides was Judah's steward and keeper of the Hur fortune. His daughter, with whom Judah fell in love before he was taken away, has remained behind to take care of her father who was tortured, his legs destroyed, by Romans searching for Judah's wealth. The reunion is a happy one. Then Judah asks where his mother and sister are. Esther does not know, so Judah prepares to visit Messala.

The following day, Messala and an aide are relaxing in Messala's new, marble-decked quarters, when the former receives a gift from the son of Arrius. "For the Tribune," explains a centurion, handing Messala a package. "With the compliments of Quintus Arrius." "The Counsel?" Messala asks, "Here?" "It is Quintus Arrius, the Younger," the soldier replies. Messala is honored. "Show him in." Messala opens the box; in it is a dagger. "It's magnificent!" Messala cries. "And from a man I've never met!" From the doorway comes a voice. "You're wrong, Messala." Messala's jaw drops. "Judah! By what magic do you bear the name of a Counsel of Rome?" Judah smiles. "You were the magician, Messala. You condemned me to the galleys. When my ship was sunk, I saved the Counsel's life.

Judah manages to grab hold of the Roman's lash. . . .

Massala, yanked from his chariot by Hur is trampled by pursuing chariots, and lies a bloodied heap in the track.

My mother and sister, Messala, restore them to me and I'll forget what I vowed with every stroke of that oar you chained me to."

Messala tells him he will try to find them. That night, the women return home where they beg Esther that Judah be told they are dead. After five years in the dungeons they have become lepers. Esther promises and the pair go to live in the Valley of the Lepers.

Esther tells Judah that Messala had his mother and sister killed years ago. Judah erupts and cannot be calmed. In a rage, he goes to the Sheik and agrees to race his team against that of Messala.

The day for the Circus arrives. A new governor sits on the throne of Judea, Pontius Pilate, a man whom Judah had met at Arrius' home in Rome. Before the race gets underway, however, it is pointed out to Judah that Messala races a Greek chariot; one with spiked bayonets on the wheel hubs. Their purpose is to chew the spokes from chariots near that of Messala's. The charioteers parade about the arena, and eight of them line up for the starting horns. Pilate drops a white handkerchief; the trumpets sound; and the racers are off. For ten minutes they round the courses, Messala slowly eliminating competition by slicing their wheels and carriages to splinters. Ruined chariots litter the track. Attendants move the wreckage and carry wounded drivers to the sides. But one formidable smack-up cannot be cleared in time for the charioteers rounding the arena. Seeing this, Messala paces Judah's chariot, forcing him into the wreckage. In an incredible maneuver, Judah jumps his horses over the destroyed chariots and is nearly thrown from the carriage; clinging to one side, he pulls himself back in. The race is down to five contenders, and the end is near. Messala and Judah ride neck and neck. Then, the underdog makes a deadly move. Messala's spikes are chewing into Judah's chariot and scraping his wheel. Pieces of Ben-Hur's vehicle go flying. Judah locks his own wheel behind Messala's, between the axle pivot and chariot. Then he pulls quickly away, taking Messala's wheel with him. The Roman's carriage falls apart, but Messala holds fast to his reins. He is dragged around the arena. Bruised and broken, he lets go and is trampled under by a pursuing chariot, left a bloody pulp of a human being in the sand of the stadium. Judah coasts on to victory. And after the

To Judah goes the victor's wreath.

After the race, Judah returns the ring of his "new" father to Pontius Pilate; this, a complete renouncing of Rome.

race, wearing his laurel wreath of victory, Judah goes beneath the coliseum to see his beaten foe.

"Triumph complete, Judah?" Messala coughs. "The race won? The enemy destroyed?" But Judah is forgiving. "I see no enemy," he speaks softly. Messala, however, is still arrogant. "What do you think you see? The smashed body of a wretched animal? There's enough of a man still left here for you to hate! You think your mother and sister are dead? And the race over? It isn't over, Judah. They're not dead." Hearing this, Judah grows tense with anger. He collars the splintered form. "Where are they?" he demands. Messala sneers. "Look for them," he gibes, "in the Valley of the Lepers. If you can recognize them! The race," he gasps, "is not over!" With that, Messala dies.

Judah has now become a militant, ready to lift arms against Rome. Esther tries to dissuade him, tells of Jesus, a man from Nazareth, who preaches love and peace; that God is in every man. Judah, however, doesn't listen. He goes off to be with his fellow militants.

The next day, Esther goes to the Valley of Lepers to try and convince Miriam and Tirzah to come with her to see this man Jesus. Unbeknown to her, Judah follows. As Esther approaches, Miriam meets her and says, "No further!" "I was here last night waiting for you," Esther says. "I waited for you all night. What has happened? Where's Tirzah?" "Leave the food," Miriam begs. "No, I'm coming closer," Esther responds. "Don't be afraid. I've heard him again, the man from Nazareth. If ever words were from God they are in everything he says." But Miriam refuses to go. Esther speaks quietly to her. "I cannot bear that you should never have known this hand of quiet reaching towards us. He's going to Jerusalem. Bring Tirzah, and we can go together to find him." Miriam begins to cry. "Tirzah is dying," she says. Hearing this, Judah comes forth. His mother screams to Esther, "Why did you tell him?" But Judah hugs his mother close, despite her protestations. "Mother," he says, "let me see Tirzah." "Tirzah is dying," Esther informs him. "If they would see Jesus of Nazareth, they will know that life is everlasting, and death is nothing to fear if you have faith," she says. Judah crawls deep into the labyrinths of the cave, which is only four feet tall in spots. There he finds Tirzah and carries her from the cave. Together, all four go to Jerusalem.

When they arrive the city is deserted. Inquiring, they find that all have gone to the trial of the young rabbi from Nazareth. The four head for the trial which is just ending. Jesus is given his cross and is lead down a Via Dolorosa lined with crowds. Some people cry; others cheer; many are indifferent. But Judah sees Jesus, and a responsive chord is struck. "I know that man," he declares to Esther, recalling his time of burning thirst in the desert.

Ben-Hur pushes his way through the crowd. Esther is heartbroken. "I brought you here to this, when I had hoped. . . ." But Miriam interrupts. "You haven't failed, Esther."

Reaching Jesus' side, Judah is pushed away by a centurion and lands against a well. He picks up a ladle. Jesus has fallen beneath the burden of the cross, and Judah runs to his side with water. A soldier kicks him away, but Jesus has recognized this man as the one he himself had saved.

Esther, Miriam, and Tirzah, meanwhile, have fled the city. A thunderstorm is brewing and they take sanctuary in a cave. Soon, the rains pour heavily from the sky. Shaded from the storm, Miriam reflects, "It's as though he were carrying in that cross the pain of the world. It was so fearful." "Yet," Tirzah asks, "why is it I'm not afraid anymore?" Lightning strikes all about them. "What a strange darkness," Miriam says. Then, "His life is over," she concludes. All is dark save for that which is lit by flashes of lightning. Between the flashes, we can see that Miriam and Tirzah are lepers no more. "Miriam!" Esther shouts. "Do you see your hand?" They remove their hoods; they are normal. The three rejoice.

The storm ends. Judah walks, his head down, to his old home and into the ruined courtyard. There he is met by Esther. Atop the stairs, he sees his mother and sister. Cured! He runs to greet them; they hug; and the next thing we see is the cross.

It is empty.

A shepherd walks his flock before it, and the film ends.

Before analyzing the various components that went into the film's creation, we will look first at its size and at the incredible statistics that underline *Ben-Hur*.

In the movie, more than three hundred sets are seen. For the building of these over fifteen thousand sketches were rendered. In all, the sets covered a full hundred and forty-eight acres. The arena in which the chariot race was shot accounted for eighteen of those acres, making it one of the largest sets in film history. Into the creation of this arena went 1,000,000 feet of lumber, 250 miles of metal tubing, 1,000,000 pounds of plaster, and 40,000 tons of sand imported from nearby Mediterranean beaches. The stands reached five stories high, every inch of them covered with a special fire-proofing material. And for the race, 8,000 extras were employed to fill the stands. Seventy-eight horses were imported from Yugoslavia. Three months of filming were invested in the twenty-minute sequence. Overall, the construction of the accurate reproduction of an ancient circus in Jerusalem kept 1,000 workmen busy for a solid year.

Props for the film numbered over a million. These included: 3,400 pairs of shoes, 2,000 leather belts, 1,000 spears, 3,000 spears, 3,000 swords, 2,600 shields, 5,500 articles of jewelry, 52,400 yards of fabric, 15,000 pairs of sandals, and 20,000 yards of fine drapery and carpet fabric. And here's an interesting statistic: Charlton Heston appeared in all but a mere twelve scenes throughout the entire four-hour film.

Cinecitta Studios in Rome, where the picture was shot, was an incredible sight to see. Over 25,500 tourists visited the studio during *Ben-Hur's* production.

Months before the cameras and cast arrived in Rome, the studio was changed to fit the film. Cinecitta was built in 1936, and had been used as a factory for Italian war machines during World War II, as a barracks for German soldiers, and later as a compound for thirty thousand persons displaced by the war. For *Ben-Hur,* one of the studio's largest sound stages was converted into a warehouse to store costumes; another sound-stage was transformed into a dry-cleaning plant, laundry, and a shoe repair shop, as well as a gallery where sculptors created the two hundred pieces of statuary needed for the sets in the film.

Even the cameras were unique. *Ben-Hur* was shot in Camera 65, which was then unique in wide-screen motion pictures. As the name implies, the film was 65 millimeters wide (as opposed to the normal 35), and provided greater clarity of image than ever before. The cost of each Camera 65 was $100,000.

Impressive statistics. But what do they all mean in the long run? Was *Ben-Hur* worth the expenditure of $12,500,000? For MGM it was. *Ben-Hur* grossed close to $40,000,000, and made the studio once more solvent. Most critics reacted favorably to the film, though many maligned its pandering to the public. The leprosy, for example, one critic cited as being no worse than a mild sunburn; that *Ben-Hur* was mass-oriented rather than a work of art.

"Well," Heston feels, "obviously, any film that cost $12,000,000 has to appeal to a large audience. This is inevitably the basic fact in making any film. The unique characteristic of film, as an art form, as opposed to all other arts, is the cost of the raw material. Unlike a painter who can work in a gas station and buy his own paints and paint on Sunday, or a writer who, when he gets right down to it, needs only a soft pencil and some yellow paper, a filmmaker has to somehow convince someone to give him, at minimum a million dollars to buy raw stock, booms, and to pay the actors, and so forth. This means he has to attract enough people to see the films or they won't give him any more electric trains to play with. Now you can expand on this. If you're spending $12,500,000 on a film, which is what MGM spent on *Ben-Hur,* obviously you have to tailor it to appeal to a much larger audience. This aspect of film has annoyed critics for a long time, but there's no escaping it. There's also no escaping that while they could've made *Ben-Hur* for less than $12,500,000, it couldn't have been made for $1,000,000. There's no way to do a film with a chariot race for under a million."

Another criticism leveled against *Ben-Hur* was Wyler's handling of the film's more spectacular elements. The epic film was territory into which he had never before journeyed, certainly not in films such as *Mrs. Miniver* and *The Best Years of Our Lives.* One critic went so far as to say the crowd scenes reminded him of a formless cocktail party. Again, Heston takes issue.

"Wyler is a meticulously individualistic director. Every frame is hand-clipped, practically. Besides," he continues, "the only real crowd scene is the chariot race, in which the crowd doesn't move; they're just sitting there.

"I would say, while I take second place to none in my admiration for Wyler, certainly the handling of crowds was not his forte. *Ben-Hur* is the only film he made that had huge masses of people; a scene like the governor's entry into Jerusalem. I suppose it would be fair comment to say he didn't have the instinct for photographing crowds that DeMille did. It's a special kind of capacity to see a mass of people as an entity

Yakima Canutt (in chariot) smiles as Heston (right) looks on. Note padded interior of chariot. Glenn Randall, a horse trainer, is on the left.

and photograph them as a character. I think, however, the prime creative achievement Wyler brought off in *Ben-Hur*, which was surely the reason they hired him, is that he made it a personal film. *Ben-Hur* is, in fact, quite an old-fashioned melodrama in which Christ is a peripheral character. Which is an awkward thing to do. Because how can you make Christ a peripheral character in a story? The love story with the girl is totally implausible, primarily because it's unimportant; you don't care about it. It has no structural function, as we realized even when we were shooting it. We finally came to realize that the story of *Ben-Hur* is not really a story of the Christ, no matter what Lew Wallace says, and it's certainly not a story of Ben-Hur and Esther: It's a love story between Ben-Hur and Messala, and the destruction of that love; turning to hate and revenge; it's a vendetta story, if you like.

"So given those weaknesses in the original piece, I think Wyler did an incredible thing in making the film work as a personal story. He has some dimension in the characters—which was a problem with, for example, *El Cid*. You believe in most of the characters; you care about them. You don't care about Ben-Hur and Esther for the reasons stated, but you care about Ben-Hur and Messala.

"In the chariot race—for which second-unit director Yakima Canutt deserves enormous credit, among other things for teaching me to drive a chariot—the match is personalized. Only Wyler would have realized that you could make that race not just the spectacle it could otherwise have been, but a conflict between the two men. We had this huge set, running a total screen time of something less than a minute. Contrarily, there are dozens of extreme head close-ups of Messala and Ben-Hur, and he makes it a race between the two men. And that's why it is the best action sequence ever filmed. The unique combination of Wyler's contribution and Canutt's contribution did, perhaps, what no other man, individually, could have done. I admire Yak beyond measure. I should. He's contributed a great deal to a half-dozen of my films. Yet if he had shot the chariot race all by himself, it would not be what it is. Obviously, neither could Wyler have shot the chariot race. But between them it's incredible." Heston's appreciation of Yak Canutt runs to a strong friendship. Over Yak's fireplace there sits a horse's head sculpted by Heston. On the base of it is this inscription: *To Yak, for making a half-assed horseman out of a horse's ass!*

Heston saw the role of Ben-Hur as a challenging one. For Judah was not a real person. So, unlike the case of historical characters, Heston was able to build a personality from scratch, which is both a creative blessing and a curse. "Ben-Hur is a nice man of courage and fortitude," Heston explains. "So you're not faced with the problem of saying, 'What did he really think?' But the greatest plus in *Ben-Hur* was Willy Wyler."

Wyler worked his people hard. Most difficult to pin down was the Ben-Hur/Messala relationship; specifically, the scene wherein the two men meet after their many years apart. The actors worked four long days on the comparatively short sequence. The entire segment was shot, and then shot again; "Wyler just worked us to the bone," Heston says. At one point, the actor recalls, he said, "Willy, I don't see what more we can get out of this; I'm really at a loss." To which Wyler responded, "I know. But this is our only chance to show these two men as friends. If you don't believe they love each other, then the fact that they hate each other is not going to interest the audience."

Stephen Boyd is an excellent Messala. After *Ben-Hur*, he went on to star in *Fall of the Roman Empire* for Sam Bronston, and was cast as Marc Antony in the Taylor *Cleopatra*. Contractual difficulties and delays in filming the latter prevented his participation in *Cleopatra*. And though his costumes were not remade for Richard Burton (who inherited the role), Boyd went on to star in *The Oscar, Fantastic Voyage*, and a horde of foreign films. Boyd is a determined, square-jawed Messala; a volatile, one-track-minded human being. His distinguished counterparts are Jack Hawkins (who, as Arrius, was in the film only briefly, and yet received second billing to Heston), Martha Scott (Miriam), Sam Jaffe (Simonides), and Hugh Griffith as the Sheik (for which he won an Oscar as Best Supporting Actor). The only real weak spot, due partially to the reasons cited by Heston, is his leading lady, Haya Harareet, as Esther. She is not convincing as a character or an actress. She merely speaks her lines without conviction. When she feels pain, we don't see it in her eyes; her performance is all too practiced. She got the lead after Wyler remembered having met her at the Cannes film festival.

Action aside, technically, *Ben-Hur* is nearly impeccable. There are a few unconvincing special effects—especially the sea battle between Romans and Macedonian pirates. The ships were all miniatures, floating against a painted backdrop in a studio tank. Due to the clarity of the Camera 65 lens, we can see people on deck, for example, miniature props all; and the effectiveness of the scene falls apart, because these figures don't move. Too, when the water sprays, it is not the beading of a vast ocean but that of a small studio tank. The scenes that take place on the ship's surface were shot in a studio, with the model background superimposed; again, as with *The Ten Commandments*, faulty matte lines run rampant. And when Judah and Arrius sail away on Judah's makeshift raft after the battle, the painted canvas backing is painfully obvious.

The most successful miniature, and one of which most people are unaware, is the city of Rome. Judah and Arrius pull themselves away from a party in Ben-Hur's honor; they talk by a window with Rome spread out behind them. In the dark it is impossible to tell that these are, in fact, just miniatures a few feet from where the actors stood.

Most successful of all, however, was the awesome chariot race, the high point of the film. Throughout, save for one scene, Heston drove his own chariot. It is, according to the actor, not unlike skiing, the stance one must assume. And since second unit man Canutt had only two months in which to educate his racers, he designed a special two-rein harness which made for easy control. Back in ancient Rome, each of the four horses had its own bridle.

In any event, the one scene in which Heston did not pilot his own vehicle was the famous jump over the wreckage of two fallen chariots. It was a risky leap even after elaborate stunt-accommodations were made. Joe Canutt, Yak's son, and one of Heston's close personal friends, took the ride for Heston. A long ramp was set out of camera range, and it was up this runway Canutt ran his carriage. Hitting it too fast, however, Joe was thrown over the front of his chariot, but somehow managed to hold on until out of frame. This was not a planned film element, so improvisation

was necessary. After viewing the rushes, it was decided Heston would, in a close-up, pull himself back into the chariot. It comes off looking great on film.

There are also rumors of many deaths having occurred during the filming of the race; of a spectator having fallen before a screaming racer; of an attendant clearing away a charioteer who had been trampled; but none of these, Heston explains, is true.

Ben-Hur is an inspiring film. It is flecked throughout with simple, religious symbols. When a patron enters Joseph's shop, in the beginning of the film, he nonchalantly kisses a *mezuzah*, a small but effective "throw-away." Then there is the irony of Heston's receiving water from Christ and, subsequently, the reverse taking place. Later, the quick-cut from a crucified hand of Christ to the now-cured hand of Miriam serves to emphasize the Messianic grandeur of Jesus. There is very little verbal trickery such as we saw in *The Ten Commandments* ("Have the days of darkness made you see the light?" spake Moses unto Pharaoh). Though far less reverent, *Ben-Hur* is genuinely more religious.

The music, too, adds much to the overall effect. Composed by Miklos Rosza, the score won an Oscar, one of the record eleven the picture snared. Rosza's music contains themes, separate and distinct, for each of the major scenes and characters. There are five marches in the film, each unique and distinctive: The Roman soldiers passing through Nazareth have one theme; Judah and Arrius' entry into Rome is quite another. The new governor's entry into Jerusalem is still another. Then there's the arrival of the chariots into the Judean arena; the parade of these charioteers is altogether different. There is a love theme for Ben-Hur and Esther; for Ben-Hur and Messala; for Ben-Hur and his mother. There are two melodies to emphasize a different emptiness in Judah's heart; one a longing for home; another, a longing for his family. There are two themes of physical distress: that of Judah's burning trek through the desert to the galleys; and that of Jesus' burdened walk to his crucifixion. And then there is the Christ theme, the most effective piece in the entire film. It is the title music; lightly from an organ it underlines Christ's giving water to Ben-Hur in the desert; later, more majestically, with full orchestra and choir, it highlights Jesus' death and resurrection.

And Ben-Hur is authentic. Much of it was filmed on location in Egypt and, as an historical footnote, in Anzio, one of the bloodiest sites of World War II. The picture was also shot in Rome where, as we have said, it was a great tourist attraction.

Heston and Haya Harareet between takes.

WRECK OF THE MARY DEARE

MGM
1959

Produced by Julian Blaustein. *Directed* by Michael Anderson. *Script* by Eric Ambler based on the novel by Hammond Innes. *Photography* by Joseph Ruttenberg and Fred Young. *Music* by George Duning. 104 minutes. *Starring* Gary Cooper (Gideon Patch), Charlton Heston (John Sands), Michael Redgrave (Nyland), Emlyn Williams (Sir Wilfred Falcett), Cecil Parker (Chairman), Alexander Knox (Petrie), Virginia McKenna (Janet Taggart), Richard Harris (Higgins).

After *Ben-Hur*, Heston took a second-billing spot behind Gary Cooper in *Wreck of the Mary Deare*. Based on a novel by adventure-master Hammond Innes, *Mary Deare* is a good film in which Cooper and Heston are the only characters we come to know.

Heston is in the ship salvaging business and runs a tug called the Sea Witch. Piloting his vessel through a storm one night, he finds a large boat sailing adrift. The ship is smouldering and there's only one tugboat left on board. Although the seas are rough, Heston hauls himself onto the ship's deck. To obtain salvage rights on a boat like this would be quite a financial boon. Heston explores this unusual derelict and finds a man, and a very gruff one at that. He tells Heston to leave the Mary Deare; that although he is alone, the ship is not adrift. Heston is upset, but climbs back to the Sea Witch via his rope. Unfortunately, the tug cannot get close enough to retrieve him. As Heston begins to lose his grip and slip into the sea, Cooper pulls Heston back on board.

Heston soon finds that mysterious events occur on this boat. Besides the absence of a crew, Cooper, who plays Captain Patch, is steering the ship straight for reefs in the English Channel known as the Minquiers. Although Patch tells Heston that the Mary Deare will miss these rocks, he shoots the craft right into their midst. Heston is upset, but wants to know if he'll get the contract to refloat her. Patch is evasive and asks Heston not to tell the investigators that the ship is grounded. Heston asks, "Give me one reason I should trust you?" and Patch answers desperately, "When you were dangling on the end of a rope over the side of the ship, you trusted me. Now," he continues, "I'm on the end of a rope. Do I have to beg you, Mr. Sands?" Hes-

Heston decks Gary Cooper as the latter tries to escape.

119

ton says nothing, and when Mr. Petrie, the owners' investigator (played by Alexander Knox) starts asking questions, all Heston will say is that the forward bulkhead went and the ship could not be saved. He hedges on the issue of the sinking, and Petrie sees through this immediately. Heston is uncomfortable having lied. But Patch insists that the ship's location be kept a secret until the court of inquiry has had a chance to examine the wreck. Patch won't tell Heston why he asks this favor.

The ship is subsequently found by a French salvaging organization, and Patch's plan is scuttled, as well as Heston's dreams of salvaging the ship. Patch's plan for secrecy ruined, the Captain comes clean. He tells the court that the cargo the ship was allegedly carrying had been dropped off on a four-day layover in Rangoon; that a fire was started on the Mary Deare and the crew went overboard; that he, in the name of justice, was only trying to prevent the owners from unlawfully collecting millions of dollars of insurance money on a non-existent cargo. The court agrees to search the ship.

Naturally, the boat is being refloated by the French company in cahoots with the owners. Once this resailing is accomplished, the ship would be led to deep water and sunk. Patch learns of this when he

hears that one of the owners' employees is supervising the salvage operation. He and Heston sail out to the ship and, in scuba gear, go underwater and sneak on board to witness the devious operation. There they overcome a youthful Richard Harris and put a stop to the plot. Patch's name is cleared, and he gives Heston the insurance company's generous reward.

Wreck of the Mary Deare is really Cooper's film. His performance is wooden but is possessed of a fanatic determination that carries through and works. Heston's role, that of the Devil's Advocate, is well played, although there is little to work with in terms of character. As opposed to Cooper who is out to redeem his name (lost by the suspicious murder of the ship's original captain), Heston's Mr. Sands is a paper cutout. All he is interested in is getting the salvage rights to shipping wrecks. He becomes embroiled in Cooper's situation but is emotionally impartial, being circumstantially tied to the situation, until he finally realizes that the man may be right. Justice, somehow, at this point overtakes Heston's preoccupation with making money and he becomes a more rounded character.

All in all, the film is good. Given the lack of depth found in both the screenplay and direction, it is about the best it could have been.

EL CID

Allied Artists
1961

Produced by Samuel Bronston. *Directed* by Anthony Mann. *Script* by Philip Yordan and Fredric M. Frank. *Photography* by Robert Krasker. *Music* by Miklos Rozsa. 180 minutes. *Starring* Charlton Heston (Rodrigo Diaz de Bivar), Sophia Loren (Chimene), John Fraser (King Alfonso), Raf Vallone (Count Ordonez), Genevieve Page (Queen Urraca), Gary Raymond (King Sancho), Herbert Lom (Ben Yussuf).

Heston, as El Cid, battles the enemy champion Don Martin (Christopher Rhodes) for possession of Calahorra.

When this picture was released, it appeared on most everyone's "Ten Best Pictures of the Year" list. But the agony of *El Cid* is that it could have been a classic.

There have been only two great films about an epic hero. These are *Alexander Nevsky* (1938) and *El Cid*. There have been bad films of this genre—such as *Alexander the Great* and *Knights of the Round Table*. Other pictures, such as *Spartacus* and *Fall of the Roman Empire*, featured good-thinking heroes as their main character. But only the Cid and Alexander Nevsky are demi-gods.

Most of what we know about El Cid comes from the epic saga *Poem of the Cid*, written around 1140, nearly a half-century after the hero's death. The author of the poem is not known, although he is believed to have lived along the Castilian frontier which faced the Moorish kingdom of Valencia; Medinaceli or San Esteban de Gormaz, most likely.

In any event, it is difficult to pick fact from legend. We do know that El Cid—Rodrigo Diaz de Bivar—was born some time around 1043, and that at the age of twenty he had already been dubbed knight. We also know that he killed his wife's father, and that he was exiled from Spain and allied himself with the Moors, refused the crown of Valencia, and gave it to the king who had banished him; these are historical facts. And the events are recounted in *El Cid*, along with the hero's incredible capture of Valencia.

Heston believes, "The Cid was surely one of the remarkable men of the Middle Ages. And he—as is true with almost any such figure from that period where literal documentation is so sparse—has become a mythical figure, a figure of legendary proportions."

The film plays upon his great depth as an heroic figure, if not as a human being. And since it is a history rather than a study—like *The Ten Commandments* or *Ben-Hur*—of what made a man tick, very little of the dialogue is of either great quality or import.

Aroused by a fanatical Moorish warlord, Ben Yussuf, Emirs of Spain attack a Castilian village, where they are routed and captured by Rodrigo. Compelled by a sense of mercy—feelings alien to those of the cruel 11th Century—Rodrigo frees the Emirs on their

The Prince (Gary Raymond), the Princess (Genevieve Page), and the Cid.

Count Ordonez (Raf Vallone) and Heston, in *El Cid*.

In exile, El Cid is joined by Sophia Loren.

After their happy reunion, El Cid and Sophia Loren make love in a barn.

promise never again to attack Castile. The men agree and for this act of kindness, one of the Emirs (Moutamin) honors Rodrigo with the name of Seid, meaning lord or leader, and Rodrigo's countrymen adopt the title to their own tongue: El Cid.

In the court of King Ferdinand, however, El Cid's act of mercy is misinterpreted, and the warrior is accused of treason by his rival Count Ordonez, and Count Gormaz, father of his beloved Chimene. Even Chimene fails to understand the Cid's act. So Rodrigo is brought to trial, during which his aged father, Don Diego, is insulted by Gormaz. El Cid begs an apology; it is refused. A duel ensues and Gormaz is slain. Before he dies, however, he asks his daughter Chimene to avenge his murder. Accordingly, she petitions the king for the court's official revenge. But her appeal is interrupted when a King Ramiro of Aragon challenges King Ferdinand for possession of the border city of Calahorra. El Cid convinces Ferdinand to permit him to fight Don Martin, Champion of Aragon. Thus, according to the custom of trial by combat, God would judge Rodrigo's guilt or innocence in the case of Gormaz's death.

Chimene, torn by conflicting emotions, in turn asks Don Martin to avenge her father's death; thus, King Ferdinand's daughter, Princess Urraca, gives her own colors to El Cid. The two mounted knights fight with shattering violence . . . and Rodrigo kills his opponent.

Later, Count Ordonez visits Chimene, confesses his love for her and promises to kill El Cid. She pledges herself to him in return. On a mission, El Cid's group is waylaid by Ordonez' men, but the attack is beaten off. When it is discovered the ambush was plotted by Chimene and Ordonez, El Cid is upset. But despite the girl's part in the attack, El Cid still wants to marry her, and asks that the king order the wedding. He does so, and Chimene accepts the king's command. But on her bridal night she tells El Cid that marriage will become her means to avenge her father's death, and that she will never live as his wife.

At this time, the royal family of Castile is torn by Ferdinand's death. His two sons, Prince Sancho and Prince Alfonso quarrel over division of the throne. Only the intercession of their sister, Urraca, prevents fratricide.

Immediately, Ben Yussuf schemes to make the most of this quarrel by arranging the assassination of Prince Sancho and making it appear that he was killed by Alfonso. El Cid is suspicious, and Alfonso's coronation is marred when Rodrigo forces the new king to swear before the assembled nobles that he is innocent of his brother's murder. Humiliated and made furious by El Cid's act, the king, in his first decree, orders the champion exiled. He leaves, but on a lonely road near

the border of Alfonso's realm, the warrior-hero is met by Chimene who begs his forgiveness and asks to join him in exile. Together, they venture forth, but are soon met by men who are dissatisfied with Alfonso and want to ride with their Lord. Knowing that Chimene cannot go with him and his little band of followers into Moorish territory, Rodrigo leaves her at a convent.

During the next few years El Cid fights under his own banner, winning many friends among the Spanish Emirs. By now, Ben Yussuf has landed troops on Spanish soil and challenges King Alfonso. Desperate, the king recalls El Cid to help defend the kingdom, but the warrior refuses to help when the king rejects the aid of the Cid's allies, the Spanish Emirs.

El Cid now visits Chimene and their two twin daughters, whom he has never seen. He tells Chimene he will fight for Valencia and speaks of the importance of winning that city before all Spaniards may live together in peace. But later, after the Cid leaves, in retreat from Ben Yussuf, King Alfonso finds Chimene. In his hatred for her husband, the king holds her and

One of the incredible armies assembled on the coast of Spain for *El Cid*.

showing himself to the townspeople, he breaks the arrow's shaft and hides his wound. Dying, he realizes that on the morrow a final attack must be made upon the enemy. He makes Chimene promise that, alive or dead, he will lead his men into battle. Now King Alfonso arrives to join the battle, but it is too late; El Cid has died.

The next morning, El Cid, at the side of his king, rides out to fight Ben Yussuf's forces. And frightened by the seeming invincibility of Spain's greatest warrior, the enemy flees toward their ships. Ben Yussuf, himself, is trampled by the Cid's rampaging stallion.

With the enemy driven forever from Spanish soil, El Cid rides across the beach, and a man becomes legend.

El Cid is a good film, even if wristwatches *are* visible on the extras. It's lavish and without doubt the most polished of the epic films, bigger than any in terms of cast and impressive as any in terms of preparation and cost.

To evoke some idea of the sheer size of this production, for the battle of Valencia alone the following statistics are registered: used to portray warriors were 1,700 troops of the Spanish Army, 500 mounted riders of Madrid's Municipal Honor Guard, and 3,500 men from the province; more than thirty-five boats were converted to a Moorish battle fleet. Unlike the sea battle in *Ben-Hur*, no miniature ships were used for *El Cid*.

the children as hostages. But Chimene, knowing the importance of the battle of Valencia, induces Count Ordonez to defy King Alfonso and take her and the children to El Cid.

The following morning after a bloody battle, El Cid captures Valencia and is presented with the crown of the city. Deeply touched, he accepts it, not for himself, but in the name of King Alfonso. This act of fealty moves Alfonso to the realization of El Cid's devotion.

That night inside the walls of Valencia, El Cid watches Ben Yussuf's hordes regroup and set up camp on the beach. Outnumbered, El Cid plans a surprise attack. But leading his knights into the frenzy of battle, he is struck in the chest by an arrow. Barely able to ride his steed, El Cid gallops back to the city. Before

El Cid is struck in the chest with an arrow. . . .

125

Ten thousand new costumes were created for the film, and 7,000 extras were, to a man, armed with weaponry such as battle axes and swords. Forty thousand dollars was spent on jewelry, while $150,000 went to reproducing medieval art objects, such as candelabra, tapestries, crucifixes, etc. Disappointed with the real Cathedral at Burgos because of latter day modifications, Bronston ordered the massive structure entirely rebuilt. There was no expense spared on the production. And it looks it.

But while "It's an enormously impressive film, a beautiful film," Heston admits, "I don't think *El Cid* is a great movie. I think if David Lean or William Wyler had directed it, it would have been a great movie.

"Physically, in visual terms, it's a beautiful film, and I bitterly regret the fact that it fell so short of its potential. And the potential, of course, lies in the dimensions of the character.

"But any great film is largely the work of the director. Therefore, it's fair to lay at least some of the shortcomings of the film on the director.

"Anyway, I, as with any part I've ever played, when I looked at it again, see things—many things, in this case—that I would do differently, that I feel I

could do better. One of the problems with that film, as with any epic film, is that they tend to be rather thin in their character development. They have so many characters to introduce, such a complexity of historical events to get through, that you tend to skim over or eliminate entirely the kind of scene that fills out a character. This is certainly one of the major faults of *El Cid*."

To look at Sergei Eisenstein's classic film *Alexander Nevsky* alongside *El Cid*, is to discuss two very similar works in terms of their subject matter. Their heroes are both incorruptible and wholly righteous. They are brave and lead their men to victory against great odds. Of course, the two films themselves have very little in common except that each ends with a tremendous skirmish. The pictures each have fine musical scores, Prokofiev and Miklos Rozsa respectively, and each is a film of extremes. In both, the good guys are good, and completely so; the bad guys are wicked, and completely so. Thus, all things considered, why does *Nevsky*, despite its age and technical imperfections, come across a better all-around motion picture?

"Well," admits Heston, a fan of *Nevsky*, "I suppose it would be fair to say that Tony Mann was not

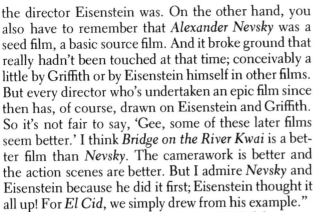
And rides into the fortress, mortally wounded.

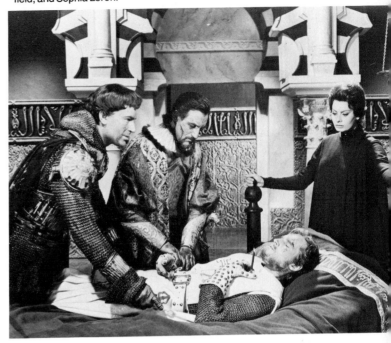
After a night of suffering, the Cid dies. With Douglas Wilmer, Hurd Hatfield, and Sophia Loren.

the director Eisenstein was. On the other hand, you also have to remember that *Alexander Nevsky* was a seed film, a basic source film. And it broke ground that really hadn't been touched at that time; conceivably a little by Griffith or by Eisenstein himself in other films. But every director who's undertaken an epic film since then has, of course, drawn on Eisenstein and Griffith. So it's not fair to say, 'Gee, some of these later films seem better.' I think *Bridge on the River Kwai* is a better film than *Nevsky*. The camerawork is better and the action scenes are better. But I admire *Nevsky* and Eisenstein because he did it first; Eisenstein thought it all up! For *El Cid*, we simply drew from his example."

Still, *Nevsky* has a *panache* that *El Cid* does not. Of course, *El Cid* was made to generate profits and entertain us, as opposed to the propagandistic nature of *Nevsky*. Still, in the process of unfolding, regardless of its failings, *El Cid* gives us the finest, most sturdy image of a hero the world has ever seen. This is what has always made the film a special one for me. But more on this later.

El Cid is a man of honor. He thinks always of his wife, his country, and his king first. Even in death, his thoughts are for others and not himself. He insulted kings and noblemen in the name of justice and honor and did what he knew to be right. He battled the king's living sword in honor of his father; he slew the Champion of Aragon to prove himself innocent of treason. He fought thirteen knights for the safety of his king; he battled not many less in Ordonez's attempt on his life. Obviously, El Cid was not a coward. Yet he was in addition to all of this an extremely principled man. He accepted banishment from the country he loved, and yet brought it on willingly by forcing the king to swear he did not murder his brother. He bore Chimene's initial hatred of him like a man; he asked not for personal quarter. It is no wonder then that El Cid was able to create a lasting impression on the mind of a twelve-year-old.

In terms of a motion picture, *El Cid* has many insurmountable faults. However, there is an incredible amount to recommend the film. For example, the contest for Calahorra, perhaps the most rousing, exciting, one-to-one combat in the history of the film.

It was this scene among the other very strenuous sequences, that put Heston in "the best shape of my entire career."

Daily horseback workouts were only a small part of Heston's physical conditioning program. Each morning under the tutelage of Enzo Musemeci Greco, one of Europe's leading fencing masters, Heston and others went through a rigorous two-hour practice session with broadsword, mace, and other weapons used in the film.

During the afternoon Heston attended a one-hour gym class and then went on a walk, gradually increased in length until he had paced five miles each day. Already lean and muscular he trimmed off twelve pounds during this brutal program. Luckily "the scene was filmed in March," Heston recalls, "so heat wasn't a problem. But it was shot over a five-day period and was very exhaustive with full-day schedules."

To provide a fabulous backdrop for the scene, the Castle of Belmonte, one of Spain's most striking symbols of medieval grandeur, was selected. Before it the full panoply of 11th Century heraldry, bright banners, colorful tents, knights in armor, and ladies in brocades and velvets was arrayed on all sides of the block-long jousting field where the life-and-death contest was staged.

The sequence begins slowly enough with the two helmeted warrior knights jousting in traditional fashion. Finally, El Cid is knocked from his horse, and Don Martin comes galloping after him with mace and shield. Frantic, Heston throws himself under the onrushing horse, kneeling behind the saddle of his own fallen mount, and the other champion runs right over Heston. The horse is unable to maintain its balance and it trips over Heston throwing Don Martin to the ground. The two of them then, for the remainder of the fight, battle it out, Heston eventually overpowering his foe.

The viewer is thoroughly exhausted by the time the battle has run its course. The men bleed and sweat, and the fight is so well staged and edited that it seems entirely real.

Heston and Sophia Loren review Heston's copy of the script with Anthony Mann between takes on *El Cid*.

The battle scenes at Valencia are, too, incredible. Staged by Yakima Canutt, these sequences are a sheer beauty to behold. They move in frenzy, yet one must remember that to film it this tumult had to be choreographed. There are as well enormous hundred-foot-tall siege towers used by marksmen and bowmen that are pulled along by thousands of warriors. These were all life-size, working models, the same sort that would be used in *55 Days at Peking*. And, of course, there were swords and arrows flying about.

Yet, perhaps the most impressive of all was the death and apotheosis of the Cid.

During the flurry of battle, Heston is hit by an arrow. The projectile lodges in his chest right about the heart. After breaking the shaft to hide his wound, El Cid returns to the city. Hiding behind his shield and in great pain, El Cid cuts a path to his residence. The people suspect something is wrong and Heston must appear on his terrace during the night to prove he still lives. This is a tremendous strain and he collapses immediately afterward.

El Cid dies, but his presence at the next day's decisive battle is crucial. He is armored and strapped upright to his horse. His king rides at his side and they lead the hero to the gates of the city. There the camera pauses as El Cid rides to it directly blocking the sun, forming a halo of light around his mounted form. Then, slowly, to the tune of a magnificent organ piece, El Cid and his army ride out, the indestructible warrior not even flinching when hit with arrow after arrow. His immortality is assured.

For the hero is necessary; we all have to look up to someone. Naturally, there are many who insist that the hero is strictly a fantasy figure. Heston, however, sees it as something different.

"I'm not so certain of the validity of the labels hero and anti-hero. Anti-hero has become a fashionable phrase to suggest, in fact, the spurious nature of the identity of the hero. To reject the reality of heroism.

"We do not live, in my judgment, in the time of the anti-hero, as is frequently said. It would be fair to say we live in the time of the victim. We are very much preoccupied with men as victims; group man rather than individual man. The hero, the extraordinary man, is obviously an unusual individual. Most of us don't have the capacities or the endurances required of heroism. I think, therefore, that the example of excellence is always worth emulating. The fact that it is beyond most of our capacities is not significant. No one can paint, for example, like Michelangelo. But that doesn't mean we shouldn't try."

Which, of course, is what El Cid would probably have said were he asked.

And for this student of the hero, now as then, the example of the Cid is well worth emulating. A childish fantasy no more, nor a tribute to empty-headed idealism; rather, El Cid is an acknowledgement of human potential, a nobility lost in the shuffle of modern life—a loss of identity, of individuality, of honor, pride, and grace.

This is the value of *El Cid*. The film is a vehicle for the characterization. For the story in which he played his life. And if not a work of art, for this reason alone the picture is still of greater value than most any other motion picture experience.

THE PIGEON THAT TOOK ROME

Paramount
1962

"Father" Heston drinks a toast. From left to right: Elsa Martinelli, Heston, Baccaloni, Gabriella Pallotta, and Harry Guardino.

Elsa Martinelli, Heston, Gabriella Pallotta, and Harry Guardino in *The Pigeon That Took Rome*.

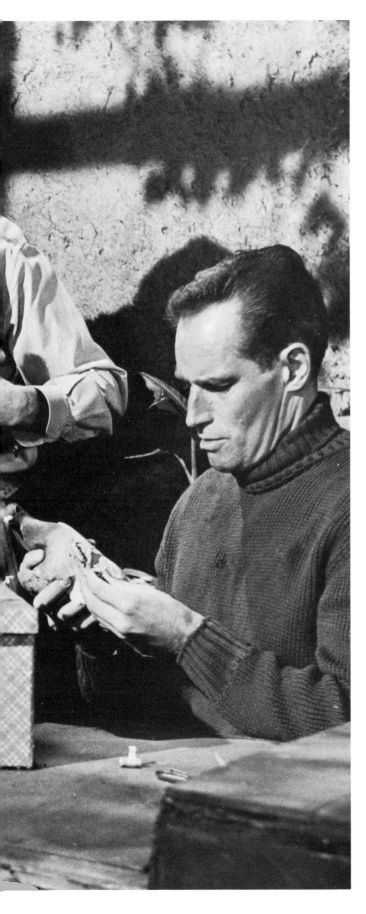

Harry Guardino (center)
helps Heston mark a flock of birds
Baccaloni looks on, suspicious.

Produced, Directed, and Scripted by Melville Shavelson, based on the novel *The Easter Dinner* by Donald Downes. *Photography* by Daniel L. Fapp. *Music* by Alessandro Cicognini. 101 minutes. *Starring* Charlton Heston (Capt. Paul MacDougall), Else Martinelli (Antonella Massimo), Harry Guardino (Sgt. Joseph Contini), Brian Donlevy (Col. Sherman Harrington).

The Pigeon That Took Rome is an extremely poor picture. The trailers for this disaster claimed, "At last! A motion picture that delivers fun!" It did not; at best, it can be said this film is slightly less than a mild diversion.

The plot centers around two allied intelligence agents (Heston and Harry Guardino) who sneak past Nazi lines into Rome on an information and fact-finding mission. They are met, and subsequently housed, by Ciccio and Livio Massimo, a father-and-son team of patriots. Ciccio has two daughters who object to the foreigners involving their family with intrigue and political doings. One daughter is further upset because she is unwed and pregnant. Contini falls in love with the pregnant daughter and they plan to marry. At the wedding feast, however, Ciccio cooks all but one of the carrier pigeons that have been used to send messages from Heston to the allies.

Livio, trying to be helpful, replaces them with German birds. Thus, all the information goes right to the Germans. However, the one vital message that is meant for the Nazis is given to the American bird who takes it to the allies. This enables the allies to attack and liberate Rome, after which Heston marries the other daughter, and the bird is given the Medal of Honor.

Confusing? It's just another of those silly, complicated comedies that came from the 60s, part of the plague begun by the Doris Day school of prudent, pandering lightheartedness.

Through it all, though, Heston is not entirely bad. He is more or less at home with this manner of movie mischief, as he was in *The Private War of Major Benson*, and can handle the genre. The character he plays is once again brave, bold, and just a little bit dense; but somehow, it all holds together until the conclusion.

The Pigeon That Took Rome is based on *The Easter Dinner* by Donald Downes. The book had to be better. Even the title, changed to capitalize on the Heston/Rome mystique, doesn't quite cut it.

DIAMOND HEAD

Columbia
1962

Produced by Jerry Bresler. *Directed* by Guy Green. *Script* by Marguerite Roberts based on the novel by Peter Gilman. *Photography* by Sam Leavitt. *Music* by Johnny Williams. 106 minutes. *Starring* Charlton Heston (Richard "King" Howland), Yvette Mimieux (Sloan Howland), George Chakiris (Dr. Dean Kahana), France Nuyen (Mei Chen), James Darren (Paul Kahana).

In this film Heston made his first of two excursions into pineapple country. Unlike *The Hawaiians* (1970) and his combustible but kindly and fair Whip Hoxworth, Heston's Howland in *Diamond Head* is a ruthless bigot, violently opposed to his sister Sloan marrying a full-blooded Hawaiian native. This, even though he, himself, is having an affair with the local Mei Chen.

At his sister's engagement party, Howland is attacked by Mei Chen's brother, who ends up killing Sloan's fiance, Paul, instead. Sloan blames Howland for the incident and moves off the island to Honolulu. There she finds solace in the bottle. Meanwhile, Paul's brother Dean finds the girl and is upset by her sorry state. He takes her to his mother's house to recuperate.

By this time, Mei is pregnant by Heston. She dies after giving birth to a son. Heston refuses to accept the child. So Sloan and Dean, who now plan to marry, care for the child. Heston finally accepts the half-breed Dean as his brother-in-law, gives his baby the Howland name, which is very generous of him, and all ends with a semblance of happiness.

In *Diamond Head*, Heston, according to the reviews, plays his role in a "haughty and inflexible way," and in the process "etches a swaggering portrait." There is little doubt that the actor's talents could have been put to better use. Howland's lack of dimension was certainly a major stumbling block for the performer.

Although on paper the role is a correct one for the larger-than-life Heston, this vehicle was one that didn't turn out successfully. The directing and script were weak and Heston seemed unusually ill-at-ease among the pineapples. Yvette Mimieux and James Darren were window dressing, although George Chakiris turned in a creditable performance.

Heston as he appears in *Diamond Head.*

Heston and Yvette Mimieux.

James Darren, Yvette Mimieux, and Heston (as Paul, Sloane, and Howland).

55 DAYS
AT PEKING

Allied Artists
1962

Peking, as it looked in 1900. A remarkable reconstruction of the ancient city.

Produced by Samuel Bronston. *Directed* by Nicholas Ray. *Script* by Philip Yordan and Bernard Gordon. *Photography* by Jack Hildyard. *Music* by Dimitri Tiomkin. 154 minutes. *Starring* Charlton Heston (Major Matt Lewis), David Niven (Sir Arthur Robertson), Ava Gardner (Baroness Natalie Ivanoff), Robert Helpmann (Prince Tuan), Flora Robson (Dowager Empress Tzu Hsi), Leo Genn (General Jung-Lu), John Ireland (Sgt. Harry), Paul Lukas (Dr. Steinfeldt), Harry Andrews (Father de Bearn), Nicholas Ray (American Ambassador).

As with all of Samuel Bronston's films *(El Cid, King of Kings, Fall of the Roman Empire, Circus World), 55 Days at Peking* is a pictorially stunning, technically impressive achievement. Unfortunately, as is also the case with most Bronston films, the drama is slim and the characters are two-dimensional.

Until *55 Days at Peking*, Bronston had a fine box office track record; with this production, his empire began to crumble. After having several Hollywood-based films to his credit—such as *Jack London* and *A Walk in the Sun*—Bronston moved his operation to Spain citing the need for "creative freedom." The fact that production costs and tax bills in Spain were impressively lower than in the States must have also been a consideration in the move.

Overseas, Bronston's first production was the Robert Stack film *John Paul Jones*, a big empty-headed epic about one of our great naval heroes. It did well enough at the box office to make Bronston's next effort possible: an epic remake of the DeMille classic, *King of Kings*. *King of Kings* made a handsome profit, even

Heston as Major Matt Lewis.

Heston threatens the Russian Ambassador Kurt Kasznar as Ava
Gardner looks on.

after considering its multi-million dollar budget. Following this Bronston had his biggest money-maker of all, *El Cid*, which grossed some $30,000,000. He followed this with *55 Days at Peking*, which lost money. His next film, *Fall of the Roman Empire*, cost some $15,000,000 to make and dropped every penny of it; John Wayne's *Circus World* followed, also losing Bronston—or more accurately his backer, the DuPont family—a vast fortune. Failure of this film pushed Bronston's next project, *Brave New World*, into limbo.

55 Days at Peking is a story of the Boxer Rebellion in China, circa 1900, which aimed at getting all foreigners out of the land. In it Heston portrays a tough U.S. Marine; David Niven a British ambassador; and Ava Gardner a Russian baroness.

Heston and the marines arrive at their respective dwellings, Heston to the hotel, the others to barracks. Since rooms in Peking are at a premium, Heston is given the room of Baroness Natalie, whose brother-in-law Sergei is after her diamond necklace. Since Natalie won't turn it over, the ambassador revokes her visa. In a fit of generosity, Heston allows her to stay in his room. She accepts. With that, Heston is summoned by a British orderly who asks that he go to see the British ambassador.

Before the meeting, Niven explains the situation to his wife. "In a nutshell, if I encourage a policy that the great powers should be tough with China, that will bring about a situation where China becomes just another battleground for the great powers to fight over," he explains. "So I think it's wise to accept this temporary humiliation at the hands of the Boxers (i.e. let them take power) and hope that by dampening

Heston, dressed to infiltrate Chinese lines, comforts a young girl (Lynne Sue Moon) in *55 Days at Peking*.

down the fire, the kettle won't boil over." This is, of course, what most of the other envoys don't want. They want China, not diplomacy. But Niven is a man of sense, not greed. And now that the audience understands what the movie is all about, Heston enters. He is promptly admonished for having shot a Boxer. "You're not in the wild west now, Major. You don't go around shooting Chinese the way you do Red Indians. And I want to warn you. Any repetition of your irresponsible behavior may well involve the last remaining members of the human race in a conflagration of considerable proportions." As if this dressing down were not enough, Heston is subsequently informed that his men are no longer needed in Peking. But "Look," Heston informs him, "I suppose you know all Hell's going to break loose here." He goes on to explain how the Boxers are killing every white missionary and Chinese Christian they can find. "And I know this much," he concludes, "If the Boxers get as far as Peking you're going to wish there were more soldiers in this compound and less women and children."

Later that day, riding through Peking, the German ambassador is killed. Watching from afar, Heston sees that the killing is done under the watchful eyes of Prince Tuan, who is allegedly on the side of the imperial government which opposes the Boxers. Although the Queen orders the actual assassins killed, Heston protests, insisting that Tuan was behind it all. But the grand lady scoffs, telling Heston that Tuan is a patriot and has just, in fact, been appointed head of the foreign office. The ambassadors realizing now they cannot stop Tuan, vote on whether or not to leave

China. Ten nations vote to leave; only Britain elects to stay. The others realize that they will look ridiculous if they allow only England to remain. Hence they pressure Niven, who remains adamant, explaining that Admiral Sydney is on his way to Peking and should arrive soon. Niven, for one, will not let the Boxers chase him away. So they all stay.

The next day, after Heston sets up the foreign compound defenses, the Boxers attack. The battle is brief and bloody, but the guerrillas are defeated and retreat. Fortifications are built; the soldiers prepare for another onslaught which comes soon thereafter. Underfortified, the legation battles on, setting carts on fire, loading them with straw, and dumping them off city walls onto the Boxers. All the while, Peking's imperial troops do not intercede.

Considering this an act of foreign aggression, the Chinese Imperial Government now side officially with the Boxers. It orders the foreign troops to withdraw or the government will use its own forces to help attack the encroaching governments. Heston decides he must try and get word to Sydney and the reinforcements who must surely imagine that all foreigners in Peking are dead. After much hiding and clandestine crawling, Heston and his men get out of Peking, but they are ambushed and only Heston escapes back to Peking.

Meanwhile, the Baroness, working as a nurse, has been shot while riding into the city and dies. Simultaneously, the Boxers attack the troops in Peking with

Heston first meets Ava Gardner in *55 Days at Peking*.

enormous rocket-launching towers several stories in height. Thinking quickly, Heston builds a catapult which fires Molotov cocktails at the approaching monoliths, setting them afire. There is spectacle and death galore, and now the Queen is really miffed; she sends, in addition to the Boxers, her Royal Imperial Troops against the outsiders. It looks like the end, but as one might expect the cavalry arrives in the nick of time. The armies of several different nations march miraculously into Peking, frightening the Boxers and the army away and averting a final siege.

Seeing this, "The dynasty is finished," the Queen says to herself.

The next morning all armies sound reveille, and Niven complains, "Listen to them. They're all playing different tunes!" Heston smiles. "Well, for fifty-five days we played the same tune. Fifty-five days," Heston comments, amazed. Then, "Will you be staying on in China?" Niven asks Heston. "I'll go where they send me," he answers. "And what about you?" "Oh," Niven admits with a tinge of regret, "I'll be going home to England. Retired to private life, I suppose. A little place in the country with a dog and a few good books. Every Englishman's dream, really. And you?" he asks. "What's home for you?" "I don't know," Heston answers. "I may have to make one yet."

As he prepares to ride out, Heston's jest becomes prophesy. He spots the young adopted child of a friend recently killed in the war. The girl has no one. And as Heston rides out at the head of his army he stops, looks down at the girl, and says, "Here. Take my hand." He pulls her upon his horse and they ride out of Peking.

I can think, off-hand, of about two or three people who distinguish themselves in this film. The art directors for one. On a plain in Spain the entire city of Peking was reconstructed as it looked in 1900. When a building blows up it's a real building and not a minia-

ture. The same goes for the siege towers that attack Peking. Real men are thrown from the tops, and real men fall into the fires, off walls, and are bludgeoned and stabbed through the course of the film. The action sequences, particularly, stand out as well staged and directed by Yakima Canutt. Another fellow who does well for himself is composer Dimitri Tiomkin, whose score is vibrant and exciting, and a multiple Oscar nominee. He takes the national anthems of different countries and weaves an intricate and beautiful tapestry of sound. Indeed, his work on the Bronston films, *Fall of the Roman Empire* and *Circus World*

One of Heston's men (John Ireland) tells the Major that reinforcements are needed for a besieged wall.

are, similarly, highlights of those productions.

The actors are all mediocre, with the exception of Niven. Heston was stiff, while "Ava Gardner moves one step closer to retirement," as one rather cutting critic noted. *The New York Times* offered, "The characters remain largely one-dimensional, though Charlton Heston is satisfactorily tough and stalwart as the U.S. Marine Major"; *Cue* was impressed with the film only from the standpoint that it seemed "Huge . . . spectacularly exciting."

Samuel Bronston is one of the few producers who has managed to assemble exquisite casts and crews, build lavish and exciting sets, and then have his films fall flat, largely due to the directors. Dubbed "The Last of the Big-Time Spenders," Bronston relied on the likes of Nicholas Ray and Anthony Mann to helm his big films, men who were better suited to other genres. As Heston has suggested, had William Wyler or David Lean worked with Bronston, the productions would have been classic.

But in Bronston's favor his films were never dull although they were sometimes ponderous. And *55 Days at Peking* just about epitomizes this type of production.

Heston and David Niven watch as reinforcements arrive at the conclusion of *55 Days at Peking.*

THE GREATEST STORY EVER TOLD

United Artists
1965

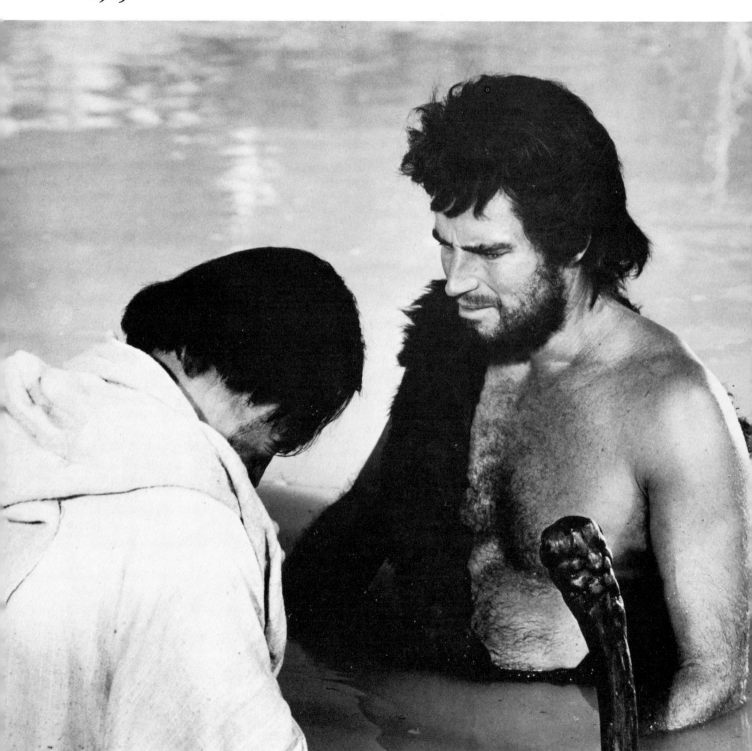

Produced and *directed* by George Stevens. *Script* by James Lee Barrett and George Stevens, with Carl Sandburg. *Photography* by William C. Mellor and Loyal Griggs. *Music* by Alfred Newman. 225 minutes. *Starring* Max von Sydow (Jesus), Dorothy McGuire (Mary), Robert Loggia (Joseph), Charlton Heston (John the Baptist), Michael Anderson, Jr. (James the Younger), Robert Blake (Simon the Zealot), David Hedison (Philip), David McCallum (Judas Iscariot), Roddy McDowall (Matthew), Sidney Poitier (Simon of Cyrene), Carroll Baker (Veronica), Pat Boone (Young Man at the Tomb), Van Heflin (Bar Amend), Sal Mineo (Uriah), Shelley Winters (Woman of No Name), Ed Wynn (Old Aram), John Wayne (The Centurion), Telly Savalas (Pontius Pilate), Angela Lansbury (Claudia), Martin Landau (Caiaphas), Claude Rains (Herod the Great), Donald Pleasance (The Dark Hermit), Jose Ferrer (Herod).

The Greatest Story Ever Told is one of the two films Heston made in which his role is limited to a "cameo" appearance. "It's not the fellah the film's about," as Heston explains.

In this film, Heston's role is that of John the Baptist. Ironically, this is one of the three biblical characters Heston has played in his over forty films (Moses and Ben-Hur being the others), although he's been type-cast as king of the genre.

The performance is a good one, better than that of Robert Ryan in the 1961 Bronston film, *King of Kings*, but still too reverent, as is the rest of the film. Many critics found director George Stevens' style too measured, too fully steeped in pontifical respect to be effective, while others ignored this and likened the film's visual beauty instead to that of a Renaissance painting.

No matter, the film is impressive, inspired; and, if one can empathize with Steven's reverential intent, a moving experience. For non-believers, it's a bore. And, in microcosm, this is how one must react to Heston's portrayal.

The Greatest Story Ever Told did rather poorly at the box office, which is a fate it hardly deserved. The film was originally presented in Cinerama. Many viewers objected to the film's representing the Grand Canyon—where many of the scenes were shot—as the Holy Land, while others objected to a guess-the-star game the production seemed to play. John Wayne, for instance, plays the centurion who follows Jesus to his death and, during the ensuing thunderstorm, voices, "Truly, this was the son of God." It doesn't work, any more than having Telly Savalas as Pilate, Jose Ferrer as Herod, David McCallum as Judas, Martin Landau as Caiaphas, or Donald Pleasance, Sal Mineo, Ed Wynn, Sidney Poitier, Shelly Winters, Harold J. Stone, Van Heflin, or Victor Buono in supporting roles helped the film's artistic standing. Indeed, this serves only to strain tolerance for the more devoutly religious aspects of the film.

There was hope, at the onset, that this would be the definitive film on the life of Jesus. Pictorially, it is certainly this and more. But the emotional pull is one that is more a matter of personal taste than aesthetic appreciation. Which, unfortunately, is something most critics failed to consider when they ripped *The Greatest Story Ever Told* to shreds. It is a pompous attitude, an aspect of film criticism that is both outrageous and unfair.

Heston as John the Baptist in a reverent scene from *The Greatest Story Ever Told*.

THE AGONY AND THE ECSTASY

20th Century-Fox
1965

In the opening moments of *The Agony and the Ecstasy*.

Produced and *Directed* by Carol Reed. *Script* by Philip Dunne based on the novel by Irving Stone. *Photography* by Leon Shamroy. *Music* by Alex North. 139 minutes. *Starring* Charlton Heston (Michelangelo), Rex Harrison (Pope Julius II), Diane Cilento (Contessina de 'Medici), Harry Andrews (Bramante).

This one promised to be a box office colossus, but it fell flat on its face.

What could have been more "right"? Heston as the larger-than-life Michelangelo; Rex Harrison as Pope Julius; Carol Reed directing. Nine million dollars to rebuild the Sistine Chapel as the biggest indoor set ever created. What, then, went wrong? Why was this *good* film not a great film? To understand this we must evaluate the composite elements of the film.

The story, based on the Irving Stone best-seller, tells of that period during Michelangelo's life when he painted the ceiling of the Sistine Chapel. The picture relates, along the way, the artist's struggle with the Pope who commissioned this monumental work.

"If I had not taken up the sword, if I had not become a conqueror, there would be no church, no pontiff, no hope for peace for mankind and, I might add, no patrons for sculpture, painting, and architecture," Harrison tells Heston at one point in the film. And it is just this manner of verbal swordplay that burdens the film, strained, wearisome repartee between the Pope and Michelangelo, that greatly burdens the film. It's as if the men realize they are performing for posterity, and the result is a visually stunning, entirely pretentious motion picture—spiced, of course, with acres of torment by the long-suffering Michelangelo, love interest supplied by Diane Cilento as Contessina Ridolfi de Medici (who prods the painter to search his heart for wise paths of activity), and similar cinematic devices, including a spectacular battle scene.

In essence, though, the film can be boiled down to two lines of dialogue. "He will paint the ceiling or

Striking study of Heston as Michelangelo

A sickly Michelangelo looks on as Contessina de Medici (Diane Cilento) studies proposed sketches for the Sistine Chapel ceiling. Note statue of Moses in lower right-hand corner.

he will hang," says Julius, as contrast with Michelangelo's "It troubles me that princes and tyrants should have the right to order the lives of artists." Unfortunately, it never really gets any deeper than that.

Director Reed saw his picture as "The study of a genius, and not a hero. What interests me most is that Michelangelo was a man tormented by self-criticism; anxious about the work still left to do; a man who thought of his art as an act of self-confession." Heston, however, is a little more practical about the film.

"Michelangelo was the first genius I ever played who was also a great artist," he begins, adding, "I had only played one genius before: Thomas Jefferson. But I know from my own failures as an actor the kind of frustrations involved. I'm sure that when Michelangelo finished his great sculpture of Moses, he must have stepped back and raged at it. I'm sure he said something like, 'Why can't you speak?'"

Preparing for the role, Heston had to watch and study marble sculptors at work, learning the technique of wielding chisel and hammer; then he spent hours upon hours practicing. He also read everything he could find about the artist and boned up on the techniques of fresco painting. And Heston's great regard

Heston plans his scaffolding setup to paint the Sistine Chapel ceiling.

Heston is ushered into the presence of the Pope.

Harry Andrews discusses the chapel ceiling with Rex Harrison and Heston during a take on *The Agony and the Ecstasy*. Note photographer on floor as he tries to shoot both the stars and the ceiling for publicity shot.

Heston slaves away on the Sistine Chapel ceiling in *The Agony and the Ecstasy*.

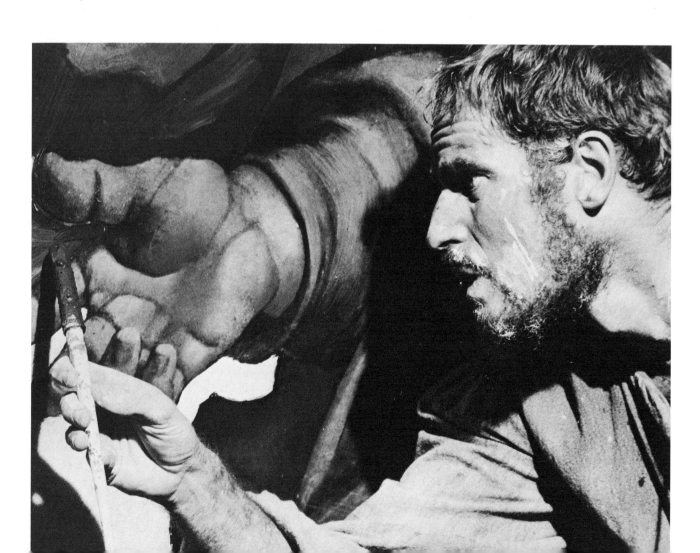

Heston visits Pope Julius (Rex Harrison) during a battle, to beg that the pontiff issue an order preventing the destruction of the Sistine scaffolding, which is being splintered for firewood.

for the artist can be summed up in the following observation: "The Da Vinci 'Last Judgment' is technically deteriorated, whereas the Sistine Chapel ceiling and the Last Judgment, painted in the same period, still survive." Truly, when Heston stepped into character and essayed the job of painting the studio set, he both felt *and* looked the part.

The set of the chapel itself was unique. It was reconstructed completely to scale in the Dino de Laurentiis Studios in Rome. To permit for ventilation, shooting, and lighting, it was designed like an enormous jigsaw puzzle with interlocking sections; some sliding, some hinged, and all of which could be assembled and dismantled as camera angles dictated.

More impressive, however, was the process used to transfer the original art to this bogus chapel ceiling. Over sixty technicians were employed to recreate these paintings in the same vivid colors that were present when the original was rendered over four hundred years earlier. Too, special color photographic processes were used in transferring the basic images from the chapel to the set.

As for the film itself, the acting is melodramatic. Heston is alternately eccentric, indignant, or pious as Michelangelo, while Rex Harrison, as Julius, takes only himself seriously. The two dichotomous characters are well suited to one another, providing interesting, if eventually redundant conflict.

The only breathtaking aspects of the film are those scenes that deal with what goes on inside Michelangelo; specifically, his inspiration for the Sistine subject matter, and his choosing of faces for that chapel. Finally, his discussion of God's image with Julius. For the "inspiration" scene, Heston, hiding from Harrison's men after initially refusing to paint the ceiling, climbs high atop a mountain by a marble quarry. It is sunset, and as day wanes the sky becomes the ceiling and the clouds form God, Adam, and the other focal points of the mural while Heston recites Genesis. It is perhaps a bit *too* reverent, but effective nonetheless.

In the "searching-for-faces" sequence, Heston journeys to a local tavern and therein sees a man's head that is perfect for one of his figures. Sketching hurriedly amidst the dogs and human refuse of that inn, Heston renders a face that has come down to us as a figure of divinity; in real life, he was just a simple peasant going about his life when he unknowingly became an immortal. In the "discussion" scene, Heston and Harrison mount the scaffolding beneath the newly completed masterpiece, and Harrison asks the artist if this is how he envisions God. The two men carry on a weighty discussion, after which Heston asks that the work speak for itself.

Still, though technically superb and with a strong supporting cast headed by Harry Andrews—who also appeared with Heston in *55 Days at Peking*—*Agony and the Ecstasy* is not what it could, and should, have been. It is big and empty rather than grand and sensitive. Heston was able to sum up the entire film in a single sentence: "Michelangelo hated painting. But Pope Julius said paint the ceiling, and you didn't argue with Popes then!"

MAJOR DUNDEE

Columbia
1965

Produced by Jerry Bresler. *Directed* by Sam Peckinpah. *Script* by Harry Julian Fink, Oscar Saul, and Sam Peckinpah. *Photography* by Sam Leavitt. *Music* by Daniele Amfitheatrof and Ned Washington. 134 minutes. *Starring* Charlton Heston (Major Amos Dundee), Richard Harris (Capt. Benjamin Tyreen), Jim Hutton (Lt. Graham), James Coburn (Sam Potts), Senta Berger (Teresa Santiago), Warren Oates (O. W. Hadley), Ben Johnson (Sgt. Chillum).

This is one of the more unusual Heston films. Unusual in that it makes very little sense but more so in that Heston did the film for free. After an argument with the heads at Universal, the actor returned his entire salary of $300,000.

During the final months of the Civil War, the Apache tribe of one Sierra Charriba massacres a cavalry post in New Mexico. Immediately thereafter, the Indians escape into Mexico. Coming upon the slaughter, Major Dundee, who is nothing more than a warden to deserters, Confederate prisoners, murderers, and thieves, takes off in pursuit. But feeling his force not properly mustered for the expedition, he adds the men of Captain Ben Tyreen to his party. Tyreen is an old enemy of Dundee's and vows to kill him at the end of the mission.

As the men enter Mexico, tension increases and dissension grows. Dundee's ability to command falters. In spite of this, however, the Americans free a small Mexican town from the occupying French forces. Here, Dundee and Tyreen compete for the attention of beautiful Teresa Santiago.

Charriba backs a vicious ambush, after which Dundee leads his men in a victorious battle against the savages. During the strife, Charriba is killed, and after the mission Dundee and Tyreen prepare to settle their quarrel. Before they can get to it, the French attack. After a bloody battle, during which Tyreen is killed, Dundee leads the eleven survivors back across the border.

"One of the mistakes I hope I learned not to make again in the preparation of *Major Dundee*," Heston says, "is never, never, never start shooting without a complete script. Part of this was the fault of a very inadequate writer who was on at first and worked for several months and was unable to produce anything even remotely shootable. This forced the studio into a five-month postponement, after which they told Sam Peckinpah to write it. So he finally undertook it and did his best, but we still weren't ready when the second shooting date came up. Also, we all had different films

in mind: The studio's, Sam's, and mine. I was very interested, and remained interested in making a film about the American Civil War. It demonstrated the strength and flexibility of the Union, in that the United States could survive the bloody trauma. For a variety of reasons, this has never been successfully explored in a film.

"As for the picture itself, we shot entirely in Mexico, which gave it some saving virtues. Other than that, the film in its current shape is terribly mutilated. I'm not convinced that if Sam had had the control he wanted over the final cut that he would have had a vastly better picture. But it certainly would have been better than the film we have.

"One of the great problems with *Dundee* was that as the shooting schedule neared completion, the studio began to apply pressure that we somehow curtail the shooting, to eliminate this scene or that, to somehow cut the mounting costs. And I don't and can't criticize them for this. The producers felt that they didn't want a picture budgeted at three million dollars to come in at double that amount. The chances of success which inspired the making of the film in the first place was no longer applicable. But I also recognized Sam's creative needs, and although I detest actors who throw their weight around, frankly, I had more muscle than Sam. I found myself *using* my position to guarantee that we would be able to shoot all the scenes in the script that we hadn't yet shot. We felt

nta Berger

they were necessary to the story we wanted to tell. Ironically, none of these scenes ended up in the final print. Eventually, after the most agonizing kind of daily quarrels with the studio, these scenes were, in fact, shot. By this time the studio had sent executives to the location to get things back under control. We'd spend our lunches or the time between the setting up of lights and cameras to listen to their pleas. Then we'd shoot and, at the end of the day, drive for a half-hour to a hot, dusty Mexican village where we were staying. And then the executives would start on us again. We would have drinks, dinner, and then argue, coming to no agreement whatsoever. This would go on until 2 or 3 o'clock in the morning, and we would find ourselves facing a 5 o'clock call for the next morning.

"Finally, we had the film in the can, but I was concerned about the way I had acted during that period. So I called my agent and told him that I was the one who was always bitching about actors who caused trouble on sets. And while *they* were rebelling *against* the director, and I was *for* him, the principle was still the same. I told him that I thought I should return my fee for the picture, although I didn't think they would take it. He advised me against it. This picture was made under an old contract; I wasn't getting a percentage of the film. The flat salary had been it. But I decided to make the offer just the same. I called and they said that they appreciated my offer, but that it wasn't

necessary. They knew I had worked hard on the film and said it was a hell of a nice thing to do but that I should forget about it. They thanked me for acting in good faith. So I put it out of my mind until two days later when my agent called. 'Chuck,' he said, 'you remember that offer you made? Well, they've changed their minds and have decided to accept it.' Anyway, the story attracted the attention of the press, and I was called by a reporter for one of the wire services. He asked me if I felt that what I had done would establish some sort of trend for other actors. I said, 'Hell, no! It sure isn't establishing any trend with me!'"

Nonetheless, Heston received good notices for his performance in the film. Not surprisingly, however, he is somewhat less than enthusiastic and perhaps too bitterly subjective about the film to review it in detail.

"You quite often get good reviews in a bad film. Actually, the individual scenes in *Major Dundee* work okay, and the relationships also work. But the piece as a whole has no structure. So it's difficult for me to comment on it with any authority."

During the making of the film Heston and Peckinpah got along well—all things considered—having only one out-in-the-open disagreement. Heston was leading a cavalry troop from across a hill and riding past the camera. Peckinpah asked Heston to bring the men in at a trot; Heston did as the director had asked. Angered after the take Peckinpah yelled 'Cut'. "It's too slow, Chuck," he hollered. "I asked you to bring 'em in at a canter." Hearing this, Heston pulled away from the men and rode up to Peckinpah. "I'll bring them in any way you want, but damn it, you said trot, not canter!" Other than that, the men had a viable relationship. For apart from the ordeal of the salary, Heston further proved himself to be an unusual personage. As one writer on location said of him, "Heston is complete unto himself. He is confident and strong. He orders his life."

In fact, harking back to the days of *The Ten Commandments*, Heston did all of his own lighting tests, an unheard of practice for stars and, as always, was available for actors to "talk-at" him, even though he may have had no lines and was off-camera. This is a tribute to Heston's professionalism. He also paid close attention to every aspect of this film, as he does with all others. Indeed, when the studio wanted to cut an opening Indian massacre from the film (again, for budgetary reasons), Heston sided with Peckinpah to the end. As another critic noted, "Heston does not conspire to get his opponents into any of the fixes they may get into. He simply tries to do what he thinks is the most honest and the most selfless thing he can do, and it only makes him stronger. He's really kind of marvelous."

It is only unfortunate that a film with Heston, Peckinpah, Richard Harris, Ben Johnson, James Coburn, Warren Oates, and Jim Hutton wasn't able to realize its full potential.

THE WARLORD

Universal
1965

Heston, Guy Stockwell, and two aides make their way
through the barbarian infested woods of *The Warlord*.

Produced by Walter Seltzer. *Directed* by Franklin J. Schaffner. *Script* by John Collier and Millard Kaufman, based on the play *The Lovers* by Leslie Stevens. *Photography* by Russell Metty. *Music* by Jerome Moross. 122 minutes. *Starring* Charlton Heston (Chrysagon), Richard Boone (Bors), Rosemary Forsyth (Bronwyn), Maurice Evans (Priest), Guy Stockwell (Draco), Niall MacGinnis (Odins), Henry Wilcoxon (Frisian King), James Farentino (Marc).

The Warlord is another Heston spectacle and one that, like *Major Dundee,* suffered merciless post-production shredding at the hands of Universal Pictures' powers-that-be.

Briefly, it is an atmospheric, intelligent film based on a play *The Lovers* by Leslie Stevens. Set in the 11th Century, the film takes place on what is now the coast of Belgium, between Ghent and Ostend.

Chrysagon, a Norman knight in the service of the Duke of Normandy, becomes ruler of a village on the shores of the North Sea. Here, after a battle with barbarians, Heston falls in love with the peasant girl Bronwyn whom he sees bathing in a stream. The lord, of course, doesn't care that she is about to marry her childhood sweetheart; he's got to have the girl.

Conveniently, one of this era's customs gave nobles *le droit du seigneur,* or the right of a lord to spend the wedding night with any bride of his domain. In accordance with this custom, Heston claims the "right of the first night" with Bronwyn. This custom also decrees the girl be returned to her husband the following sunrise.

Naturally, after sleeping with Bronwyn Heston doesn't want her to go. This upsets her spouse but not the girl, who has fallen in love with the Warlord. The local peasants, in support of the lady's husband, storm the castle. This revolt comes at a time when the Warlord needs his serfs to combat barbarian forces that have gathered in preparation for a mammoth attack. In the end Heston triumphs over the invaders, is wounded by his own people, and flees his castle with Bronwyn.

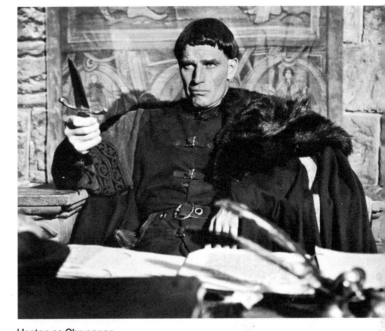

Heston as Chrysagon

Heston and Rosemary Forsyth

That's really Heston, doing his own brutal battle acts, in an action sequence from *The Warlord*.

Heston, as the Warlord, plays Solomon with local peasants settling petty strife.

Maurice Evans, Heston, Guy Stockwell, and Richard Boone in *The Warlord*.

Richard Boone cauterizes a bloody wound as Rosemary Forsyth looks on, and Heston grins and bears it. From *The Warlord*.

Atop his lofty tower, Heston staves off invading and rebellious serfs in *The Warlord*.

The Warlord was directed by Franklin J. Schaffner, who would later guide Heston about the *Planet of the Apes*. The two had previously worked together on the forty-six minute version of *Macbeth* for TV's "Studio One." Heston had recommended Schaffner for this job. Unfortunately, much of Schaffner's original cut of the film was altered by Universal. These scenes, left on the cutting room floor, are those that Schaffner refers to as "the color: Those fragile but always terribly consequential subtleties that you put in a film, so important to character, motivation, and reaction."

Regardless, the film did very well in Europe but was slaughtered in the United States. So much of the costume epic genre had been tripe that *The Warlord* was lumped among them.

Still, the action scenes and castle-storming visuals are magnificent. The frenzy of battle is vivid and gut-ripping; the sword-play is violent. Indeed, a battle between Heston and Joe Canutt—Yak's son—atop the burning tower of Chrysagon, is the best scene of this type ever filmed.

Heston, in his best bowl haircut, is superb. Viewers were invariably disappointed that Heston had shed his long, flowing *El Cid* locks for the Middle Ages look but, historically, it's all very accurate. Supporting players Richard Boone, Rosemary Forsyth, and Guy Stockwell are all fine, Boone in particular. His role as Heston's cynical right-hand man is a fine contrast to the noble's hard, embittered personality.

The sets are superb and the photography most effectively invokes a feel for the lakeside terrain, a misty land that was home for the Warlord.

Sadly, in retrospect, all we can do is treasure what substance remains of *The Warlord* and regret that we were denied a potential showpiece of the genre because of short-sighted studio executives.

Even a castle-top fire is unable to stop Charlton Heston in *The Warlord*.

KHARTOUM

**United Artists
1966**

Produced by Julian Blaustein. *Directed* by Basil Dearden. *Script* by Robert Ardrey. *Photography* by Edward Scaife. *Music* by Frank Cordell. 128 minutes. *Starring* Charlton Heston (General Charles 'Chinese' Gordon), Laurence Olivier (The Mahdi), Richard Johnson (Col. J. D. H. Stewart), Ralph Richardson (Mr. Gladstone), Alexander Knox (Sir Evelyn Baring), Nigel Green (Gen. Wolseley), Zia Mohyeddin (Zobeir Pasha).

Original ad-art showing Heston and Laurence Olivier in *Khartoum*.

Heston, Richard Johnson visit Zobeir, a potential ally, in *Khartoum*. Alexander Knox as Sir Evelyn Baring.

Khartoum is another of Heston's superior films, although one that did rather poorly at the box office. In the picture Heston portrays General Charles "Chinese" Gordon, one of the great military men of British history and one of that country's most admired heroes.

"Gordon is one of those cross-grained kind of men the English seem to produce at intervals," Heston explains, "the soldier fanatic like Lawrence of Arabia, who was such an example, although not really a professional soldier. Or the general who was killed in the war in Burma; or Clive, who was another example; also Montgomery. They were all a curious kind of deeply religious professional soldier, as I said, that you seem to find among the English and nowhere else."

Although there were "practically mobs in the streets" when it was announced that an American actor was to portray one of the great Britons, the filmed results more than pleased English critics; Heston received better notices than did his co-star, the very British Laurence Olivier.

The story of *Khartoum* begins with a bloody and brutal massacre. The army of Colonel William Hicks' 8,000 men, moving from the river of El Dueim one hundred miles beyond Khartoum, is utterly and randomly chopped to pieces by 80,000 Sudanese warriors belonging to the mysterious Mahdi.

The British government is enraged. In a report by Colonel Hugh-Stewart, sent to Khartoum to assess the strength of allied forces, it is explained to members of the Gladstone cabinet that the Mahdi is fighting a Jihad. In other words, a Holy War bent on throwing all infidels from the realm. And the defeat of Khartoum will be the Mahdi's example to the world of his prophet Mohammed's power.

Now the British realize that they must hold on to Khartoum, the key to the Suez. The government realizes also that the empire cannot afford to overextend itself. So Gladstone decides not to send troops to the trouble spot: Instead, he will send General Charles Gordon. It was he who abolished slavery in China (hence, the nickname); he is revered by the British, as well as most foreigners. Gladstone realizes if Gordon is sent to Khartoum and fails to prevent a massacre, it is he who will be blamed; not the British government. For heroes are *supposed* to perform miracles. "In other words," the Prime Minister notes, "since world opinion will not permit us to send out an army, we send out the one man who might reasonably be expected to succeed, all the while knowing that he'll probably fail." The proposal is made to Gordon who, seeing through the sham, accepts the assignment nonetheless. For he is a patriot as well as a man who thrives on challenge.

En route to Khartoum, Gordon discovers that most of Britain's allies and fans of his former exploits have turned against Gordon. They now support this self-proclaimed, right-hand of the prophet Mo-

Heston as General Charles Gordon

Heston is presented with the severed hand of Richard Johnson by
Laurence Olivier in *Khartoum*.

hammed, the Mahdi. But when Gordon with Hugh-Stewart finally reach Khartoum, the people give him a God's welcome. They feel their problems must soon be over now that Gordon Pasha has arrived.

Things, however, do not go as planned. Food supplies run low. The Mahdi's men infiltrate the city. And Gordon, his Bible constantly under arm, seeks a plan. He journeys out into the desert with but one companion, his faithful Khartoumese servant Kahlil, and is eventually ushered into the Great One's tent. "Gordon Pasha," the Mahdi bows slightly in greeting. "Mohammed Ahmed," acknowledges Gordon. "Mohammed el Mahdi," the Sudanese messiah corrects. Ignoring the correction, "We have much to talk about," Gordon says. "I do not often meet with a Christian, Gordon Pasha. Is it because you are a Christian that I feel myself in the presence of evil?" the Mahdi asks. "I think not," Gordon replies affably, "for I smell the same evil on your own person, and yet

you are not a Christian. So it cannot be that, can it?" Stung, the Mahdi observes, "I have at the moment 30,000 warriors in my camp. Is it because you are so brave or so foolish that you come here alone and unarmed?" Gordon lets the remark pass, and the Mahdi continues. "Your meeting with Zobeir Pasha (a former British ally) was not so happy, I believe. How much you must regret today that you killed his son." "Killed him? No, I executed him. I was fighting slave trade, and the execution of Zobeir's son was an object lesson. Because of it I brought peace to the Sudan." The men change to a more pressing discussion of the affairs in Khartoum.

"I have been instructed by the Lord Mohammed, Peace be upon Him, to worship in the Khartoum mosque," the Mahdi explains. "Therefore, I must take Khartoum by the sword."

Gordon is upset by this. "When I first came to the Sudan seven years ago, its body was sick and stricken and abused. I am not a loving man, Mohammed Ahmed, but this land became the only thing I have ever truly loved. I cannot, under *my* God, leave it to the misery and the sickness of which I once cured it."

Heston fights off the enemy in a cattle raid performed to feed the hungry of *Khartoum*.

"I respect you for your thoughts, Gordon Pasha," the Mahdi says. "And on you, personally, I will make no war." "Then make no war on your own people," Gordon replies. "I'll take the Egyptian army away and leave the Sudan to the Sudanese. Nothing will make me happier. But if I am to leave Khartoum to misery and death. . . ." here Gordon is interrupted by the Mahdi. "No. The Egyptian army must stay in Khartoum," he demands.

Gordon is puzzled, and the Mahdi explains. "When you killed Zobeir Pasha's son, an object lesson I think you said?" the Mahdi says. "Well I, too, need an object lesson, Gordon Pasha, as strongly and as urgently as you needed yours. The Lord Mohammed has instructed me to pray not only in the mosque of Khartoum, but in the mosques of Cairo and Mecca and Baghdad, and Constantinople as well. He has commanded me to make Holy War until all of Islam returns to the purity of his teachings. And for this great task I have the need of a great miracle. The Egyptians must remain in Khartoum, for I shall take it in blood, and the streets must flow with blood; the Nile must taste of blood for a thousand miles downstream so that the whole of Islam will learn that my miracle is

a great and terrible thing, and no man will stand against me.

"Without this miracle, Gordon Pasha, the people will not fear me. You have described your object lesson to me: You have told me you slaughtered the sons of slavers that others might learn. Whisper to me the difference, Gordon Pasha. I will slaughter the Egyptians in Khartoum and reduce the city to blood and ruins. And then I shall proceed in peace to the mosques, and the lives of many millions will be spared because they will have understood my miracle. Is there a difference?" A weighty pause.

"That is how it will be?" asks Gordon.

"That is how it will be," the Mahdi assures him.

Gordon returns to Khartoum aware that its 35,000 inhabitants will soon be dead. He orders that Hugh-Stewart send a message to Gladstone saying, "Aside from all humane considerations, I don't see how any British government could survive such a catastrophe if they made no attempt to forestall this coming massacre." Unfortunately, Hugh-Stewart informs Gordon that all telegraph lines have been cut by the Mahdi. The aide leaves Khartoum to send his message. In the meantime, Gordon prepares a defense.

162

He has a deep ditch dug around the city allowing the high-flowing Nile to effectively moat the city. In England, Gladstone orders a small detachment of soldiers to move toward Khartoum only to reopen communications—nothing more. Once this is done the soldiers are instructed to sit tight.

At about this time, Khartoum runs out of food, so Gordon organizes a raid on the Mahdi's own supplies. That night with six hundred men, he moves out. On the return trip, however, at dawn, Heston meets the followers of the Mahdi and they are many in number. Not surprisingly, the Egyptians are slaughtered, but the stolen cattle without loss of a single head are railroaded into Khartoum. There Gordon gets some bad news. Gladstone feels the danger faced by Khartoum has been exaggerated. Gordon demands that Hugh-Stewart return to England and tell them in person what is going on. For if Gordon leaves, Britain will not allow him to return to face certain death, and the people in Khartoum will lose all hope.

While all this is going on, the Nile has fallen low. Breeching it will, in a few weeks, be a simple matter for the Mahdi. By this time, Hugh-Stewart has returned to Khartoum and Gordon assigns him the task of escorting all foreigners and Europeans out of the city. They set sail on board the Abbas, a frail old craft.

In Khartoum Gordon is hopeful. Then word from the English troops show that they are very near. At about this time the Mahdi sends for Gordon, who goes to the conqueror's tent.

"Why did you invite me here, Mohammed Ahmed?" Gordon asks.

"Because the time has come to attack Khartoum with fire and sword. Yet, Gordon Pasha, I should prefer that your blood not sweeten the Nile, for you are not my enemy. I urge you then to leave before I strike the city and destroy it."

"What you are saying, Mohammed Ahmed, is this," Gordon says calmly. "So long as I am in Khartoum you fear to attack. For you know that a British army is nearby."

"Oh, that?" The Mahdi is amused. "*I* sent that message. There is no British army. The troops are still over the border in Egypt." He continues, "No, my friend. You are alone. Quite alone."

"Then," Gordon questions, "if this is so, what difference does it make to you whether I stay or leave?" "Because I am a man of mercy, Gordon Pasha," the Mahdi smiles. "No, Mohammed Ahmed," Gordon corrects, "You are not a man of mercy. And so I ask again. Why do you do this thing?"

"Because you are not my enemy," the Mahdi asserts.

"But I am!" Gordon says, "and you want me to leave, flee the city, because you must have your mira-

cle! And if there is one man, one man in whose heart you do not strike terror, then your miracle has failed. And that is why you want me to leave. So that the world may say, 'Even Gordon Pasha, in fear of the Mahdi's miracle, left the city.' If I stay, your followers will doubt you," he continued. "Islam will doubt you. They will say, 'The Nile tastes of blood, but there was one man who was not afraid, and why was that?'"

The Mahdi orders silence, but Gordon continues. "You should understand, Mohammed Ahmed, for we are so alike, you and I! You would welcome death, would you not, if death could be servant to your life. Well, know that I, too, welcome death! Saved, my life will help your miracle. You give me no choice, Mohammed Ahmed."

In response, the Mahdi tries to frighten Gordon by producing the heads, shrunken and wet with brine, of all those who had been on board the Abbas, which we see now didn't make it to safety. Finally, he produces the hand of Hugh-Stewart with a ring of Gordon's still upon it.

"There were children—children on board the Abbas!" Gordon cries. "They were children of infidels," the Mahdi sneers.

Behind Heston and his camel is the moat dug to ward off the men of the Mahdi in *Khartoum*.

163

Gordon turns to leave. "I will not leave Khartoum, Mohammed Ahmed. For I, too, perform miracles. And you shall witness one. While I may die for your miracle, you will certainly die of mine." With that, Gordon returns to the city.

The next morning, by the tens of thousands, with guns captured from Hicks, the men of the Mahdi level Khartoum. Gordon is killed by a tossed spear, his head subsequently hoisted aloft on the end of a spike, and the city is utterly devastated. But it is not the end, although fear has filled the land as the Mahdi prophesied. For the rats and vultures that feed on the dead of Khartoum carry plague to the tents of the Mahdi. In five months, the Mahdi, himself, is dead. The Expected One is now a memory.

Khartoum is a fine and powerful motion picture. It features incredible color photography, rivaling that of *Lawrence of Arabia,* and is, as well, a showcase for exquisite sets and costumes. Olivier is superb as the Mahdi. Richard Johnson is sturdy as Hugh-Stewart, and Heston is excellent as Gordon.

The only non-historic element of the film is the meeting of the two principals which, in fact, never took place. Indeed, prior to shooting *Khartoum,* the screen play was sent to the present Mahdi, grandson of the warrior Mahdi. The filmmakers were anxious while awaiting the prince's reaction to the work. But he wrote, "It's an extremely fine script." Julian Blaustein, the producer, noted, "We're pleased to hear that. I regret that the only anachronism in the script has to do with your great grandfather and the fact that he and Gordon never did meet." But the present-day Mahdi noted generously, "Ah, but Mr. Blaustein, they should have!" Which is the entire point of poetic license and the validity of poetic truth in film as opposed to the reality of life itself. For everything in film, be it a Disney cartoon or an historical epic, is done to evoke a certain response; the fact that nothing in film is real does not weaken the point of view of the filmmaker. The addition of the Gordon/Mahdi meetings contributed tremendously to the overall dramatic effect of the picture.

Heston enjoyed the challenge of Gordon, of whom one of the Egyptians under Gordon once noted, "When Gordon Pasha look into your eyes you feel that you are a child and cannot tell a lie."

"Now there's no way to act that," Heston admits, "and yet it clearly was part of the dimension of the man. The exploits, the single-handed capacity Gordon displayed again and again to control large groups of people quite unarmed and alone, is almost magical; quite scary, in fact.

"Gordon was a fantastic man. A little mad, I think, but fascinating. He had a serenity of nature, along with a somewhat irrational temper. He was

something of a martinet as well, and a lot of other complicated things. But he did not have that curious neuroticism that, say, Lawrence had, though they both had a sort of soldier mysticism."

The fact that *Khartoum* was not the success it could have been can be attributed to the time of its release. It came more or less at the end of the epic cycle, begun roughly with *Samson and Delilah,* and ending with Samuel Bronston's *Fall of the Roman Empire. Khartoum,* an excellent film, was caught up in this, as was *The Greatest Story Ever Told, The Warlord,* and, to a lesser extent, *The Agony and the Ecstasy.*

tween takes, Heston
ves Joe Canutt a lift.
hind them is the ship
bas used to evacuate
izens from the besieged Khartoum.

A helicopter at the
battle of *Khartoum*?
Not really. . . .

. . . Nor is this man an extra! The helicopter is busy filming the battle from the air, while a second-unit director, disguised as an Egyptian should he accidentally get within camera range, stays in touch
with the pilot.

COUNTERPOINT

Universal
1967

Produced by Dick Berg. *Directed* by Ralph Nelson. *Script* by James Lee and Joel Oliansky, based on the novel *The General* by Alan Sillitoe. *Photography* by Russell Metty. *Music* by Bronislau Kaper. 107 minutes. *Starring* Charlton Heston (Lionel Evans), Maximillian Schell (Gen. Schiller), Kathryn Hays (Annabelle Rice), Anton Diffring (Col. Arndt).

Counterpoint was originally known as *Battle Horns*, either title a rather transparent play on the war/musical aspects of this motion picture.

The film pits Charlton Heston, as orchestra conductor Lionel Evans, against German General Schiller, played with Wagnerian sweep by Maximillian Schell. Their cat-and-mouse game centers around Heston's group having been captured by the Nazis.

The film opens with a concert in a small European town. The time is December of 1944. The orchestra begins with Beethoven's *Fifth*. Soon thereafter, the town is bombed; everyone must be evacuated. "Ladies and gentlemen," Heston announces to his people, "it seems we are involved in a mass exodus. Each of you will be responsible for his instrument, music, and yourselves, in that order." And upon boarding the bus, Heston notes in rather cruel fashion that none will get on until all are ready. "It will be the first time in this tour that the orchestra will finish together," he adds.

After a brief journey, the bus is stopped by German officers. They have orders to let no one pass. "I don't care what your orders say," an angered Heston berates Colonel Arndt. "They don't apply to us!" But the Colonel disagrees. He transports all his prisoners to the castle retreat of the army, where he plans to kill the musicians. "If you make the mistake of shooting us," Heston warns him, "you'll be a lieutenant for the rest of your life . . . lieutenant!" Arndt is unmoved by Heston's grasping at straws, but the orchestra is saved by the intrusion of General Schiller. He orders the execution cancelled. His reasons, explained to Heston privately, are that "a concert by you and your orchestra can serve to relieve the boredom." He tosses a Louis XVI chair into a fireplace. As with everything else, Schiller can see only its "utilitarian purpose."

Heston refuses to play the concert. "I'm not a whore," he declares. Surprised but intrigued, the officer toys with a piano. He plays in a fashion that upsets the meticulous Heston. Aesthetics forces the orches-

tra leader to render the piece properly. "Prostitution," he notes, "isn't the only profession that has been ruined by amateurs." A minor victory for Schiller: Heston's careful professional pride is his weakness.

Meanwhile, Heston returns to his orchestra imprisoned in a cold, barn-like structure in the compound. "We've all toured with corrupt concert managers," he states, "so this should be a familiar experience." His levity is largely effective, although associate, Leslie Nielson confides "That was a nice tune, Lionel. But it sounded a bit like you were whistling in the dark." Afterward, Heston discusses the situation with Nielson's wife, who used to be his girl. She is to dine with Schiller that night. Concerned, Heston warns her Schiller is an "arrogant, egotistical martinet with a God complex," to which she responds, pointedly, "That should be a familiar experience."

As it happens, Schiller's seduction of the girl doesn't come off, and the game between Heston and Schiller continues. Heston realizes that once he plays Schiller's concert they are doomed. Schiller will have won their little game of wits leaving the orchestra non-utilitarian. He calls this to Schiller's attention. "You know," he says, "for a product of a democratic society you are an outrageous autocrat." Of course, Heston is on the musicians' most unfavorite persons list. For he will not bend even to the players who ask that the concert be given in return for the promise of better living conditions. Heston turns a deaf ear. He is accused of being cold. "No, I'll bet he's as warm as toast," his ex-girlfriend comments. "He's got his burning ego to keep him company." To Heston she says, "If I were up there in that rarefied atmosphere, I wouldn't be able to breathe!"

Meanwhile, Heston plots. He agrees more or less to play Schiller's concert at a date not far in the future. While he rehearses the orchestra in a chapel, two soldiers—who joined the orchestra to escape a firing squad—look for a means of summoning aid. They scale the steeple from within, reconnoiter, and obtain an accurate idea of the compound layout.

Several days later the two soldiers try to escape and are killed.

It now develops that Schiller must abandon the complex. He cannot, of course, take the musicians with him. Unknown to the orchestra, a mass grave is dug for them on the fortress grounds. But the musicians refuse to lie down and die. Midway through their concert, they break from within the hall and put up a grand fight. Using the grave as a trench, they battle the Germans. Most return to the bus except Heston, and a few who are killed. Although Heston does a fine job of bringing up the rear, he is soon driven back into the "concert hall." There he is tracked down by the

Heston stands before his orchestra after their arrest by the Nazis.

Heston confronts Col. Arndt (Anton Diffring, left) in *Counterpoint*, a film adaptation of Alan Sillitoe's novel *The General*.

Heston respectfully refuses to play Maximillian Schell's concert in a scene from
Counterpoint

bloodthirsty Arndt who, about to kill Heston, is shot down by Schiller. "Saving the honors for yourself, General?" Heston queries.

Schiller says, "Ours was a conflict of morality," he informs Heston, for whom he has built a great respect. "Each thought his own the greater." He goes on to quote Napoleon—the greater the artillery, the greater the morality—to which Heston responds, "Whatever happened to Napoleon?" and joins his performers.

Counterpoint is a good film, with fine performances by Heston and Schell. Heston is properly eccentric and egomaniacal in his role, stiff-necked and adamant. He is devoid of kindness, and even his heroic stand at the end is precipitated by honor and indefatigable arrogance, as much as concern for his musicians. The Germans have no right to do what they're doing; it's up to Heston, therefore, to teach them a lesson. The only soft spot in his granite mold is his relation with Rice's wife. We learn that at some time in the past he was indeed a human being. But something happened to him; exactly what is not clear. And it is unimportant, really. All that matters is the portrait etched by Heston in his battle against Schell. Schell's Schiller, on the other hand, is more humane and needs this little battle of wits only to relieve the ennui of his lot.

The film's structure is a bit awkward, and the people behind it all are somewhat strained. There is Colonel Arndt, Schiller's butcher, who is always present and ready to kill; he is a two-dimensional figure whose motivation is one of perplexing intensity. Conversely, the two characters that provide the Heston con-

science: Rice, a weak man who cannot keep his wife happy and who wants only to play for Schiller regardless of the consequences, and his wife who serves as Heston's "devil's advocate," always supplying a good reason for Heston not to do whatever it is he's doing.

Stereotypes aside, there are, in fact, some very fine sequences throughout. Foremost among these is the scene wherein Arndt suspects that the orchestra is shielding the escaped American soldiers. Heston has one of them on trumpet, faking it, following the other trumpeters. Arndt asks him to play a solo, and the fellow begins to show fear and collapse. Obviously, he cannot perform. Heston tries to cover for him, but the Colonel insists that he play. Then, in broken notes, the soldier who used to play trumpet in high school, performs a shattered version of "The Star Spangled Banner." It is obviously not the performance of a professional musician, but the song and the tear-filled reaction it gets from his fellow musicians completely crushes Arndt, who must retire in humiliation . . . knowing he is right but has been bested. When, afterwards, the band cheers the solo, it is genuinely inspiring; even Heston smiles!

Generally, though, for the sake of poetic truth and moral commentary, the higher aspects of good storytelling and sensible plot are often put to the side, or ignored entirely. One cannot help but feel that even the soldiers' escape attempt is there only as a token gesture; one expects it from this sort of film. Thus, script and direction leaves us hanging halfway between a war movie and a *Sleuth*-ish game of nerve and mind.

Heston explains why he will not allow his suffering musicians to perform for Maximillian Schell.

Heston prepares to cover the escape of his orchestra in *Counterpoint*, while Leslie Nielsen tries to change his mind.

Mending his clothes after landing a post at the Flatiron spread, Heston is taunted by hired hand Ben Johnson.

WILL PENNY

Paramount
1967

Produced by Fred Engel and Walter Seltzer. *Directed* by Tom Gries. *Script* by Tom Gries. *Photography* by Lucien Ballard. *Music* by David Raksin. 108 minutes. *Starring* Charlton Heston (Will Penny), Joan Hackett (Catherine Allen), Donald Pleasance (Preacher Quint), Lee Majors (Blue), Bruce Dern (Rafe Quint), Ben Johnson (Alex), Slim Pickens (Ike Wallerstein), Anthony Zerbe (Dutchy), Lydia Clarke Heston (Mrs. Fraker).

The picture opens with the last leg of a cattle drive. When it is over, fifty-year-old Will Penny collects his pay and joins his buddies, Blue and Dutchy. None of the men knows where they are going as they face strange terrain and an uncertain future. The men travel for a day, then bunk down. When Blue and Dutchy awaken they go to fetch some water from a nearby stream. An elk happens by and as the men prepare to shoot it, the animal falls dead. Beyond the carcass, across the river, sit four surly figures on horseback.

"Morning," one of the men says politely. "Name's Preacher Quint. And these here are my sons. We can clean the elk ourselves. Brother Rafe here, he handles a knife just fine." Not ones for reckless action, Blue and Dutchy back away. As they retreat, the newcom-

171

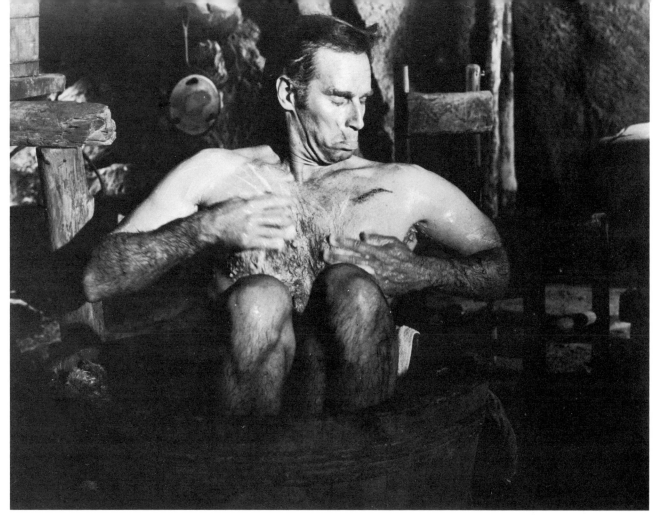

Heston takes his first bath in months.

ers open fire. Just then, from behind a thicket, there's a shot and one of the Quint boys falls dead. Will leaves his cover to join his companions. Preacher Quint roars, "You ain't seen the last of me!" Will and Blue turn to go; Duchy does not move.

"What's wrong?" asks Blue.

"I'm shot," is Dutchy's terse reply. Loading their wounded friend in the wagon, the three ride off. A long trek later they arrive at a road ranch. "Will," Dutchy calls out, "we waited a long time for whiskey. Here is the last place before town. Maybe I don't ever get there." Will agrees to get some liquor. As Will and Blue go inside they spot a woman, clean and dignified, having lunch with her guide, Mr. Bodine. In runs her son, Horace Greeley Allen. He tells his mother that there is a wounded man outside, "and he's cussing something awful!" he adds. Mrs. Allen goes to see the man and asks Dutchy if there is anything she can do.

"If maybe you could hold my hand," is his simple request. He explains what has happened. "Wild Indians they were, lady. Maybe a hundred. They caught us and my friends; them two in there, they ran away and left me." Just then Will comes strutting out. He gives Dutchy his drink.

"Least I could do after all them Injuns you killed," he notes with a wry smile. Hearing this, Mrs. Allen's anger is aroused.

"You call yourself a man?" she asks. She turns to Dutchy. "If I were you I'd never speak to them again." So saying, she returns inside. Will summons Blue and the trio again hit the road. They arrive in the village of Alfred and carry Dutchy in to the doctor's office. The doctor is, as well, the barber and postman. As the good physician and his wife care for the wounded traveler, Will and Blue leave. They bathe, and then Will decides to move on.

"Where will you go?" Blue asks.

"I'll mosey along, see if I can find me a job for the winter." Blue elects to stay, and the two men part. Will rides west into the mountains. After a few days' riding, he comes across a horse whose rider lies dead in the dirt. Placing him upon the mount, Will makes for the nearby Flatiron spread. His reception is far from warm.

"Want to talk about it?" the foreman, Alex, asks Will, pointing to the dead man.

"Found him down in the dirt," Will explains. None of the men believe him. Since the ranch is now short a hand, Will gets his job, but not before partaking in fisticuffs with friends of the dead man who believe Will killed him for the job. Alex breaks it up. He tells Will that he will serve as ranch border guard, watching for stray cattle, poachers, and pilgrims. He will spend the winter in a small shack high in the hills, three days' ride from the ranch proper. As Will rides off he is spotted by Quint and the boys who are just passing through. They decide not to kill him there as that would bring the ranch hands down upon them. They have time and tag behind him.

When Will reaches the shack, he is alarmed to find smoke spiraling from the chimney. Riding up to the small cabin he finds Mrs. Allen and her son within. Their guide who had been leading them to Mr. Allen in California, has deserted them. Will is concerned for the pair, since he cannot allow them to remain in the shack. He tells them to ride on and that he will return in a few days. Heading for the mountains, Will goes about his secondary job of rounding up wild horses. Quint decides that this is the time to spring. That night he and the boys attack Penny, and after a

mighty battle, stab him with a skinning knife. The men take Will's clothes and leave him to freeze in the hostile winter climate. When they've gone Will manages to climb to his feet and stumble back to the cabin. Mrs. Allen and Horace find him and nurse him back to health.

Time passes, and Will grows fond of the woman and her son. Although he knows he is breaking the rules he permits them to stay, and they eke out a living. On Christmas Eve Quint and his boys return. They smash the celebration, assault Mrs. Allen, and bind Will in a corner of the room. Catherine is told she will have to marry one of the two surviving Quint boys.

The next day Will is put to work, a slave of the Preacher. He formulates a plan which he relates to Catherine. He tells her to have each of the Quint boys meet her behind the barn that she may determine which is the best man to be her future husband. The sons, of course, do not know that they have both been told to be there at the same time. Naturally, there is a fight and Quint runs to see what is going on. Will is left

Heston presents Joan Hackett with a ring

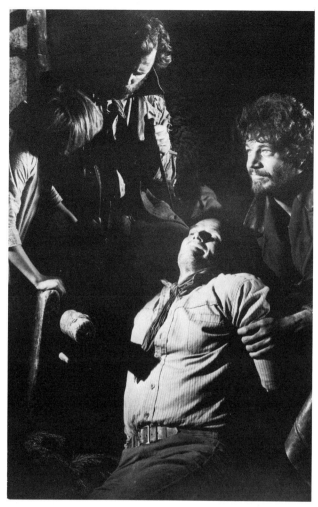

The sons of Preacher Quint prepare to perform some nasty business on Heston after their takeover of his shack. From *Will Penny*. Left to right: Jon Francis, Bruce Dern, Heston, and Gene Rutherford.

Heston as *Will Penny*.

unsupervised, and steals a cart loaded with sulphur. He intends to ride back to the ranch and bring help. As he hurries away, the Quint boys mount up and give chase. When it appears that they will overtake Will, one of the boy's hats is shot to rags. Will comes upon two men: Blue and Dutchy. There is a joyous reunion and they mount a counter-attack. Will sneaks up to the cabin and pours the sulphur into the chimney. Since everyone has holed up inside, they are an easy target. As the Quints run out, they are shot. Just then, Alex and some Flatiron boys ride up.

"A Lazy Bar Seven hand come with the news that our beef was scattered all over their graze with nobody lookin' after them," the foreman explains. For this reason they assumed something was wrong. Will, of course, is out of a job and decides to ride on with Dutchy and Blue. Catherine asks him to take her and her son.

"I'm damn near fifty years old," Will argues. "What am I good for?"

"We could start a farm," Catherine suggests.

"A farm? I don't know nothin' about farmin'. We'd starve. And all the time I'd be thinkin' how I took you from your husband and the boy from his father. I couldn't face it, Cath." Although they are in love, the two part forever.

Will Penny is an extraordinary film. Not only does it feature Heston's most sincere and sensitive performance, it has a fine supporting cast and is one of the most adult western scripts ever written.

Joan Hackett portrays Mrs. Allen with strength and dignity, never collapsing beneath the strain of her tribulations. Donald Pleasance is the most dastardly villain to grace the screen in many long years. He is mean, gritty, and slightly insane. Bruce Dern is equally effective as one of his sons. There is no hoke and no padding in *Will Penny*. It is a straightforward and honest film, a sincere attempt to recreate the old west, and, more important, the people who lived therein. It is truly unfortunate that the film was ignored at the box office. Released at the same time as *Planet of the Apes*, it was eclipsed by this more unique Heston film.

PLANET OF THE APES and
BENEATH THE PLANET OF THE APES

20th Century-Fox
1968, 1969

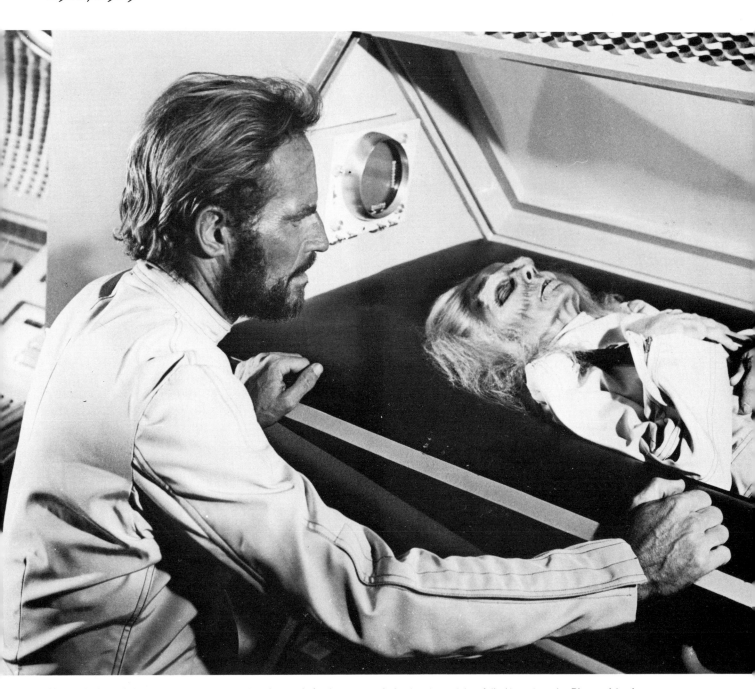

Heston finds his fellow space woman somewhat decayed after her suspended animation unit has failed in a trip to the *Planet of the Apes*.

After his rocketship sinks, Heston tries to plan a course of action

Produced by Arthur P. Jacobs. *Directed* by Franklin J. Schaffner. *Script* by Michael Wilson and Rod Serling based on the novel by Pierre Boulle. *Photography* by Leon Shamroy. *Music* by Jerry Goldsmith. 112 minutes. *Starring* Charlton Heston (George Taylor), Roddy McDowall (Cornelius), Kim Hunter (Zira), Maurice Evans (Dr. Zaius), James Whitmore (President of the Assembly), Linda Harrison (Nova).

Produced by Arthur P. Jacobs. *Directed* by Ted Post. *Script* by Paul Dehn and Mort Abrahams. *Photography* by Milton Krasner. *Music* by Leonard Rosenman. 94 minutes. *Starring* James Franciscus (Brent), Charlton Heston (Taylor), Kim Hunter (Zira), Maurice Evans (Dr. Zaius), Linda Harrison (Nova). (Note: Scenes featuring Heston were used in a flashback sequence for *Escape from the Planet of the Apes* (1971)).

One of the most popular movie series of all time has been the films spawned by *Planet of the Apes*. Four sequels, two television series, and millions upon millions of dollars in merchandising have flowed from the film based on a rather short novel by Pierre Boulle, author of *Bridge Over the River Kwai*. The book, itself, was originally called *Monkey World*.

The film was a long time in coming, and there was a long haul getting it into production. Back in 1963,

Producer Arthur P. Jacobs wanted to make something like *King Kong*. So a literary agent in Paris introduced him to Boulle's novel. Impressed, Jacobs spent the next four years having his property thrown from the executive office of every film studio this side of the *Monkey World* itself. He had sketches made for his presentation, but no one would buy. He added ammunition to his uphill battle by having the late Rod Serling (creator of *Twilight Zone*) write a screenplay. Again, nothing happened. He went to J. Arthur Rank in England and Samuel Bronston in Spain. Nothing.

Next, Jacobs approached Director Franklin J. Schaffner and Charlton Heston. Both were intrigued and agreed to do the movie. Still, the studios turned him down! Finally, Jacobs convinced Richard Zanuck to allow a test film to be made, a scene between Heston and, as an ape, Edward G. Robinson. Upon completion of this segment, a screening room was packed and the scene received a rousing reception. Zanuck gave Jacobs the go-ahead to film *Planet of the Apes*.

The picture was shot under absolute secrecy to prevent anyone from capitalizing on the original concept and ruining it for 20th Century-Fox. Millions of dollars were being spent on the makeup alone and the studio needed a hit. After such bombs as *Hello Dolly* and *Torah! Torah! Torah!*, stockholders were impatient

After roaming for miles, Heston is shocked to find this supposedly uninhabited world populated by gorillas!

Heston and his mate Nova (Linda Harrison) are captured and prepared for scientific experimentation

Heston, unable to speak, is tossed into a jail on the *Planet of the Apes*.

Zira (Kim Hunter, center) shows sympathy for Heston's plight

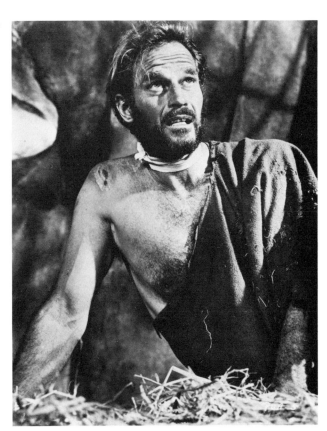

for a success. A heavy promotional campaign was launched by the producers to give the film a fighting chance against MGM's big sci-fi moneymaker, *2001: A Space Odyssey*, and *Planet of the Apes* was released just weeks before the Stanley Kubrick special-effects masterpiece. Both films were box office blockbusters.

The picture is much like the book; heavy in allegory, low on credibility. Serling's script was thoroughly altered, leaving little of the author's original concept or dialogue—which had the apes in a modern rather than primitive setting—replacing them with Michael Wilson's alternately pretentious and witty screenplay. As a result, one is not treated to provocative science fiction film as much as a fable from Aesop.

The picture opens with Heston tape-recording a message on board his incredible spacecraft. "Seen from out here, everything seems different," he says of earth. "It squashes a man's ego. I feel lonely." Time is rocketing by, eighteen months in space being comparable to 2,000 earth years. As we join him, Heston is preparing to step into a booth that will put him to sleep for the duration of a long intergalactic journey. With Heston are Landon and Dodge. The other crew members are already in suspended animation.

What seems like a few moments later arrives with a bang. There is a jolt and Heston awakens. The ship is rushing helter-skelter through space, gauges spinning madly. Dodge and Landon wake as the ship passes through the mountain peaks, valleys, and clouds of some alien planet. At pile-driving speed the ship hits a body of water. Inflating a rubber raft, the men grab whatever rations they can as their ship sinks, and they escape into the (fortunately) breatheable atmosphere of this world. Arriving on shore Heston glibly announces, "Okay. We're here to stay."

The three men walk along and discover plants amidst the arid desert environment, finally coming upon human beings. If, that is, the word is applicable. They are all primitive, inarticulate creatures. "If this is the best they've got around here," Heston observes, "then in six months we'll be running this planet!" However, he is in for a disappointment. There are sounds of galloping horses and guns being fired, and the crew runs from whatever it is that's coming.

What they see is incredible. Apes on horseback.

Fleeing madly, Heston is shot in the throat. Unable to speak he is snared and placed in a cart-cage with other captives. He does not know where his friends are, but turning, he notices a lovely dark-eyed girl beside him. By the time the cage reaches its destination, Heston and the girl, who does not (cannot) speak, are trusting friends.

The strange caravan's destination is an even stranger, grotesquely formed city hewn of rock and stone. Windows and buildings are irregularly shaped

Heston makes a daring escape from ape prison. . . .

. . . only to be pelted by inhabitants of the *Planet of the Apes*.

. . . Heston is put on trial.

He is found guilty of some absurd crime, and is sentenced to die.

indicating a prehistoric orientation. Ushered into a larger outdoor cage, Heston struggles and is clubbed senseless by a gorilla. The girl cuddles him within the metal confines of their new home.

Soon, Heston and Nova, the girl, are taken into a dingy room. Each is placed on operating tables and strapped down. Two chimps come over speaking perfect English; they argue. Zira, the female, swears she can detect intelligence in Heston's eyes. Her husband Cornelius tries to convince her it's just her imagination. But, as is not surprising, Cornelius gives in to his wife. Heston and his mate will not be dissected, but are put in jail cells.

For a long time the apes question Heston. He answers with nods and gestures. The two monkey scientists are impressed. They go to their superior, an orangutan named Dr. Zaius, for permission to maintain their study of the intelligent human they've nicknamed "Brighteyes." Zaius refuses, ordering that Heston be castrated and lobotomized. Argument is futile.

The human prisoner will not submit to this fate. Bursting free, the former astronaut runs through the city. He is pursued by apes—on foot and on horseback—who follow him en masse. During the course of this chase, one of the places to which Heston runs is a museum. There he sees murals and dioramas of stuffed human beings in their native habitat. He is horrified by one stuffed character in particular: his friend Dodge. Heston panics and runs into the street, where he is captured. Pinned by hordes of monkeys, his throat now healed, he cries, "Take your stinking

But Zira, feeling sorry for the human, sets him and his mate free.

Heston Shows an ape-extra how to operate his camera.

From left to right: Maurice Evans as Dr. Zaius, Heston, a crew member, Kim Hunter as Zira, Lou Wagner as Lucius, Linda Harrison as Nova, Roddy McDowall as Cornelius, and Franklin J. Schaffner.

paws off me, you damn dirty apes." These are the first words he has spoken and, needless to say, they cause the simians to recoil in shock.

At this point, Dr. Zaius comes to visit him. Heston assures the fellow that he is not a freak. As proof he asks permission to find Landon, and Zaius orders all males captured that day be brought to the town square for questioning. Sure enough, Landon is there . . . but says nothing. Heston rushes to him only to find a large scar on his forehead. "You cut up his brain," the astronaut shouts in a maddened rage. Still screaming, he is carted off to Zaius' office.

The old ape puffs a cigar and speaks to the bound human. He explains the ape society to Heston and how Heston's presence might upset the structured world of the apes, as well as their ideas of ape supremacy. Therefore, Heston must go on trial. This trial, since Zaius can't simply kill Heston—an intelligent creature—will determine whether or not the human is a blasphemous entity, a mutant violating the apes' sacred right to rule, or whether he should be permitted to live. The verdict was never in doubt. Heston's existence undermines the world structure. The trial is simply a formality.

Gagged, Heston is unable to defend himself, and the court decides that he must be destroyed. Zira and Cornelius are crushed.

Heston is caged again, and as Cornelius speaks with a gorilla guard, Heston reaches out and grabs the simian. Cornelius takes the keys from him and frees Heston. The party of five—Nova, Heston, Zira, Cornelius, and their nephew Lucius—ride out in a cart and head down the coastline, knowing it will be only a matter of time before Zaius and his men come after them.

Cornelius and Zira are now fugitives, and they make for caves in the Forbidden Zone, an area into which the apes are not allowed to go.

When Zaius arrives, the fugitives force him into the ancient caves along scaffolding that Cornelius had been using to excavate the ancient rock shelters.

There, in one of the caves is a living room. Not an ape dwelling but a living room the likes of which Heston recalls from earth. It is fused into solid rock and buried under layers of hardened sediment, but there's no doubt in his mind: it is a human's room. A doll on the floor, a human baby doll when turned upside down, says "mama," and the truth begins to dawn.

Heston and Linda Harrison prepare to ride *Beneath the Planet of the Apes*.

Heston gives Linda his dog tags in *Beneath the Planet of the Apes*.

Once, human beings had been masters of this planet, but they laid waste the world. Apes were not always supreme. Zaius had known this but he had wanted it to remain a secret. He does not want his race to suffer the fate of the humans.

We follow them as they ride along the coastline—and find their destiny, the origin of this world. The loin-clothed Heston falls to the sand of a beach crying, "They finally did it!" We see what has caused him such grief: The Statue of Liberty, wrecked, on the beach. Heston is back home. This is earth of the far future.

This is where the second film, *Beneath the Planet of the Apes*, begins. Heston, recovered from his shock, moves deeper into the Forbidden Zone. He begins to teach Nova speech, and all goes well until a large crack forms in the earth from which a wall of fire shoots. A moment later there is a mountain where, seconds before, there had been no mountain. Heston gives Nova his dogtags and goes to the cliff; he touches it and vanishes into thin air.

The next scene is at the site of a wrecked spaceship, a rescue ship with Astronaut Brent on board. The new arrival's flying partner is dead, and, alone, Brent finds Nova. She cannot speak as yet but gives Franciscus Heston's dogtags. From this point forward, from Brent's capture to escape, the *Planet of the Apes* formula is repeated. The only difference is the apes have by now prepared an expedition into the Forbidden Zone to seek out food and new land. They mount

an "attack force," so named because strange apparitions have been seen in the Zone, and twelve gorilla scouts were inexplicably lost in this locale.

Before the apes head out, however, Brent and Nova find the underground ruins of New York City. They also locate a civilization of mutant humans living under the earth, humans capable of telepathy and far in advance of the apes. Brent is thrown into prison with Heston: it was the mutants' science that teleported Heston beneath the planet of the apes. Meanwhile, the monkeys discover and invade the labyrinths.

These mutant humans worship an atomic warhead, and one of their services is interrupted by the apes' arrival. Preparatory to combat, the humans remove flesh-like masks from their faces, revealing skin that is transparent. The two civilizations clash, Heston and Brent break free, and there is a free-for-all battle. First, Nova is killed. Next, Brent is riddled with machine gun fire and dies. And then, with only Heston and Zaius left, the ape shoots the human in the heart. Before Heston dies, he crawls over to the bomb, detonates the weapon, and the entire planet is destroyed.

Still three more sequels came from this denouement. In *Escape From the Planet of the Apes* (1971), Zira and Cornelius travel to earth of 1973 in one of the astronaut's rockets. In *Conquest of the Planet of the Apes* (1972), their son Caesar leads domesticated monkeys in a revolt against mankind in the year 1990. In *Battle For the Planet of the Apes* (1973), we come full circle, as the apes take over the world, the mutants go underground, and the humans are subjugated.

Heston did *Beneath the Planet of the Apes* as a favor to Richard Zanuck. Twentieth Century-Fox felt that Heston's name would add much box office impetus to the new effort, and indeed, the follow-up film did almost as well as the first. But in terms of quality, there is only the original.

In both films, Heston plays what he considers an "existential" character. He is a cynic who hates mankind enough to make him leave the earth. In the beginning of the film, musing in the spaceship, he wonders, "Does man, that glorious paradox that sent me to the stars, still make war with his brother; keep his neighbor's children starving?" And one of his companions, early in *Planet of the Apes*, says, "You're no seeker; you're negative. You don't like people; you ran out!" All that Heston can answer in his own behalf is that, "There has to be something better than man."

Of course, the irony is that in trying to escape Heston ends up in not only a worse situation but back on his own planet!

Planet of the Apes features one of Heston's strongest, most emotional performances. It was also a physically demanding role. Heston runs, fights, yells, is battered, caged, dragged half-naked, and hosed with powerful jets of water. He runs barefoot through hills, mountains, plains, and an ape city; he is jostled by gorillas, horses, mad ape scientists, and sub-human homosapiens. If the allegory had been as sturdy as its star, the film would have been a masterpiece.

Beneath ape makeup, created by John Chambers (who received an Academy Award for his art), Maurice Evans as Zaius, Kim Hunter as Zira, and Roddy McDowall as Cornelius, are superb. They are recognizable, although the mobility of the ape mouth-appliance is somewhat restricted and plastic. In fact, it's all very plastic makeup, lacking the grit and grime reality of, for example, the classic Universal monster makeups, such as Karloff's *Frankenstein*, or Lon Chaney Sr.'s *Phantom of the Opera*.

But in all, buffered by a magnificent and unusual Jerry Goldsmith musical score, *Planet of the Apes* and, to a lesser extent, its follow-up films, are exciting, provocative entertainment.

Linda has been shot to death; Heston mourns; all of this in *Beneath the Planet of the Apes*.

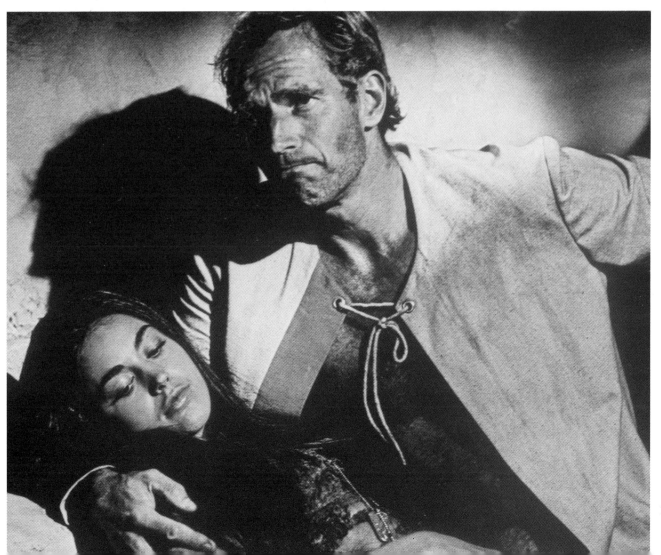

NUMBER ONE

United Artists
1968

A portrait of Heston from 1971.

Flashback scenes to the time when Heston was a star quarterback

(British title: *The Pro*) *Produced* by Walter Seltzer. *Directed* by Tom Gries. *Script* by David Moessinger. *Photography* by Michel Hugo. *Music* by Dominic Frontiere. 105 minutes. *Starring* Charlton Heston (Ron Catlan), Jessica Walter (Julie Catlan), Bruce Dern (Richie Fowler), John Randolph (Coach Jim Southend), Diana Muldaur (Ann Marley), Mike Henrey (Walter Chaffee).

"The most difficult character I've ever played, in physical terms, is the quarterback in *Number One*."

Number One is the story of a football player who doesn't know when to give up. His world collapses about him, the mystique of his divinity crumbles, and the formerly heroic world of New Orleans Saints' quarterback Ron Catlan becomes a sobering reality.

The film opens with a final pre-season loss for the one-time world champion football team. Heston leaves the locker room, signs a few autographs, and bears an insult from an elderly lady: "You're not even worth the price of a ticket anymore!" His wife finally pulls alongside the stadium and picks Heston up.

Finding the company of his wife unsatisfactory,

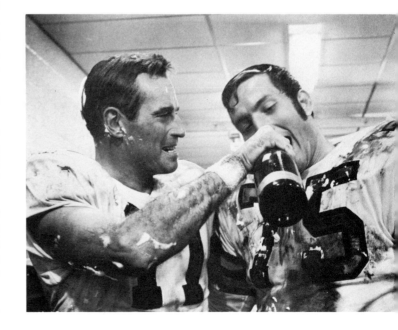

Bruce Dern, football player turned car salesman, tells Heston to give up the game and join him in business.

her interest in her dress shop being greater than in his fading career, Heston goes to a bar. There he receives a call from teammate Richie Fowler, who has moved into a new luxury bachelor pad and is holding open-house. There are young people all about and Heston feels out of place. There is a girl stripping on the bar. Heston strikes up a conversation with the more mature, misty-eyed Ann Marley. Indicating the stripper, Heston says, "You know, I'll never understand what makes a girl do something like that." "Loneliness," Miss Marley responds, leading the quarterback into Richie's plush bedroom. There she lies with him on the bed and talks about her tennis shop. They also discuss Heston's career. "I think you do what you do better than anybody else in the world," she tells him. And although he brushes the compliment aside, the two strike it off well and go for a drive.

Speeding along the highway the pair is stopped by a policeman. For traveling at 95 mph, the officer gives them a ticket. "You look like you might be a football fan," Heston notes. "Ah—I thought I recognized you," the fellow responds. "How would you like two tickets to next Sunday's Dallas game?" the quarterback asks. Pleased, the policeman accepts the bribe. "I'd

like to see you guys win for a change," he adds. "Yeah," Heston agrees, "That'd be nice, wouldn't it?"

After several hours of driving Heston returns home, with nothing serious having transpired between him and Miss Marley. It is late at night and Heston tapes an ice pack to his injured knee as he climbs into bed. His wife is fast asleep.

The next day there's a surprise for the quarterback. Sportswriter Cal Woodward's column declares in part about Heston, ". . . his performance during the exhibition season has been nothing short of embarrassing." The piece further insinuates that the Saints' quarterback is about to retire. When Heston shows up at the training camp his manager comes calling. "When I'm ready to retire," Heston tells the man with finality, "you won't have to read it in the newspaper." "Cat, level with me. Do you want to quit?" the manager asks. Heston says casually, "If I did, I guess I would."

A practice session follows. When a player questions one of Heston's in-huddle calls the quarterback warns him, "Next son of a bitch who opens his mouth I'll stick his helmet in it!"

Driving home Heston passes back-up quarterback

Heston's backup quarterback Kelly Williams gives the old pro some advice: retire.

A scene cut from the final print of *Number One*: The operation on Heston's Joe Namath knee.

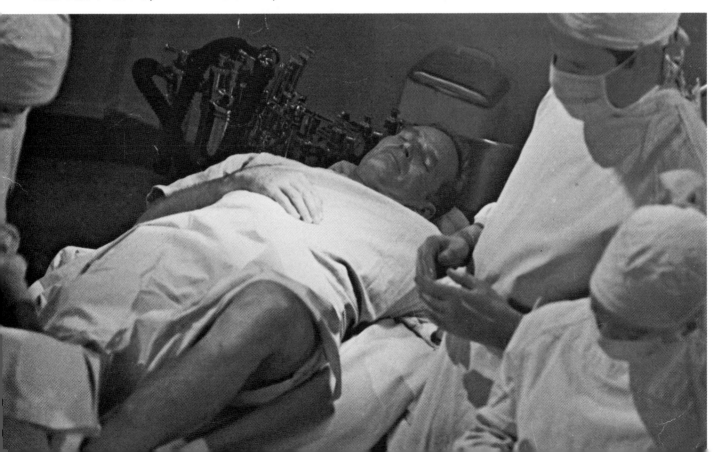

Heston and Diana Muldaur begin a beautiful relationship

Heston prepares to make one final stab at greatness in what turns out to be his final game.

Kelly Williams, who is jogging. Heston offers him a ride but the black player runs on, keeping in shape. He wants the top quarterbacking spot. "You're forty years old, man," he tells Heston. "The party's over. The king is dead."

Heston, of course, is upset by what Kelly says because it is true. Riding on to his wife's shop, the athlete is met by an effeminate designer, who sneers, "I thought they only let you out of your cage on Sundays." "I chewed through the bars," Heston tells him. Once again Heston finds his wife wrapped up in her business. So he goes off on a job interview as a computer company executive, a job into which Heston can retire.

At the office Heston is given a sales pitch. "You're probably the most dynamic leader of men I've met in my life," his contact tells him. "You're a driving perfectionist, accustomed to operating under extreme pressure." But the man understands Heston whose mind is elsewhere. "It isn't easy, is it?" he asks the fallen angel. "No," Heston admits. "But nobody says it's supposed to be. Nothing is." Then he adds that among everything else, "It's pride that keeps him in the game." Heston does not accept the job.

The next day at practice Williams has it in for Heston. The rookie makes a particularly fine play and calls it to Heston's attention. "How'd you like that one, baby?" he asks smiling. Annoyed, Heston heaves a football at Williams' head. "How'd you like *that* one, baby?"

Stung, but realizing he's done well, Williams smirks, "Daddy-Cat, you just blew your cool." Heston is fined by his coach for the intemperate display. He returns home, and once again his wife gives him no attention whatever. Heston talks about retiring. All his wife talks about is bills. "You haven't heard a word I said," Heston finally barks. His wife turns to him surprised. "You're thinking about retiring," she says, "I've heard you saying that for the last five years." Hurt, Heston stalks out and visits Miss Marley's apartment. She starts massaging him and they make love.

Heston returns home and admits his infidelity to his wife. She is upset and Heston asks if she wants a divorce. The answer is no.

But the Heston/Marley affair is a transient one as Heston devotes himself with renewed vigor to the new season. Richie Fowler and Heston's wife go to the game; Heston trots onto the field and he is booed. Richie says to the quarterback's wife, "If you think this is bad, wait'll the game starts."

New Orleans gets the ball and in the huddle Heston announces, "I want you to set those bastards right back on their butts." The team makes a tremendous gain. Another great play and a touch-down is scored. Saints' defense holds and the offence once again takes

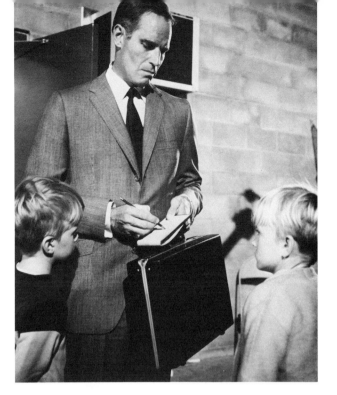

Heston signs autographs for fans in the role of football quarterback Ron Catlan

the field. Riding high Heston sets up; the first down begins and he is hit. Heston falls to the field and does not rise. The camera pans from his inert figure and the film ends.

"As to whether he was killed or not," Heston opines, "that really, of course, isn't very important. Though we took pains to demonstrate that he was not dead by having him move on the field in the last shot. He's not dead but his life is over. All he cares about he can't do any longer."

Number One is a fine film that presents an interesting, often painful, somewhat two-dimensional figure in Ron Catlan, a man who just won't let go. His agonies are vividly represented, identifiable, and empathetic. Heston, of course, strikes a perfect balance between uncertainty and courage, and he receives fine support from Bruce Dern as Richie Fowler, the ex-player who tries to force Heston out of the game and into his business of leasing cars. Jessica Walters as his wife is also good although slightly more intense than her role demands. Diana Muldaur is properly cool and sympathetic. The supporting players and football athletes (real players were used) are all at ease in their parts; ex-Tarzan Mike Henry (once a Los Angeles Ram) does an especially fine bit role.

On the technical side the photography is good, and film from actual games is impressively intercut with the new football sequences.

In all, a solid, professional film, slightly melodramatic, but not without point and poise. In the Heston standings it must be considered a solid win.

THE HAWAIIANS

United Artists

1970

Heston visits the hold of his ship in *The Hawaiians*. Here are Chinese laborers he is importing to the island.

Heston threatens one of his workers—a man drilling for water—in *The Hawaiians*.

(British title: *Master of the Islands*) *Produced* by Walter Mirisch. *Directed* by Tom Gries. *Script* by James R. Webb based on the second half of the novel *Hawaii* by James Michener. *Photography* by Philip Lathrop and Lucien Ballard. *Music* by Henry Mancini. 132 minutes. *Starring* Charlton Heston (Whip Hoxworth), Tina Chen (Nyuk Tsin), Geraldine Chaplin (Purity Hoxworth), John Phillip Law (Noel Hoxworth), Alec McCowen (Micah Hale).

Based on the last hundred pages of James Michener's novel *Hawaii*, *The Hawaiians* details thirty years in the life of Whip Hoxworth, a man who rises from being the black sheep of the family ("The only thing I've ever held against Malama," he tells his brother-in-law, "was marrying you!"; later, he tells the same man, "Frankly, Micah, as prime minister you aren't worth spit in a windstorm.") to become pineap-

Heston and Miko Mayam (as Fumiko)

Heston knocks a leper senseless on the island of Molokai in an effort
to rescue a newborn infant.

Heston amidst the spectacular burning of Honolulu

Tina Chen (as Nyuk Tsin) tries to calm down a panicked crowd during the Honolulu fire, as Heston looks on.

ple monarch of Hawaii. The film begins in 1870 with Whip returning home to the islands with a cargo of Chinese laborers. He becomes particularly attached to one of them, Nyuk Tsin, and before the film has unreeled, he subdues an island of fierce lepers, helps battle a raging fire, introduces American Imperialism to the islands, and becomes the father of a dynasty.

The picture was directed by Tom Gries, Heston's director in *Number One* and *Will Penny*, although neither man is in top form. The screenplay is adequate in terms of dialogue; incomprehensible in terms of continuity. The late James R. Webb (*How the West Was Won*) had seen better days. The music, by Henry Mancini, was the nicest touch to the lumbering film.

The philosophical thrust of *The Hawaiians* is two-

fold. First, it shows how the development of the island's pineapple industry, one of its mainstays, turned the weak monarchy of Queen Liliuokalani into a stable government. Second, it shows how a stubborn man (Heston) can destroy all who disbelieve his divinity. The result is a very shallow, choppy motion picture.

Technically, the movie is eloquent. The town of Honolulu as it looked in 1900 was built and burned for the film, and a fleet of ships was constructed for the port scenes. The Heston plantation is grandiose. And, naturally enough, Heston does his damnedest to personify this grandeur. He is described in the film's publicity notes as a "no-nonsense he-man." Unfortunately, the elements do not make for a satisfactory film.

JULIUS CAESAR American International 1970
and
ANTONY AND CLEOPATRA 1972

Julius Caesar (1970) *Produced* by Peter Snell. *Directed* by Stuart Burge. *Script* by Robert Furnival based on the play by William Shakespeare. *Photography* by Ken Higgins. *Music* by Michael Lewis. 116 minutes. *Starring* Charlton Heston (Mark Antony), Jason Robards (Brutus), John Gielgud (Julius Caesar), Richard Johnson (Cassius), Robert Vaughn (Casca), Richard Chamberlain (Octavius Caesar), Diana Rigg (Portia), Christopher Lee (Artemidorus).

Antony and Cleopatra (1972) (No American release). *Produced* by Peter Snell. *Directed* by Charlton Heston. *Script* by Charlton Heston based on the play by William Shakespeare. *Photography* by Rafael Pacheco. *Music* by John Scott and Augusto Alegero. 160 minutes. *Starring* Charlton Heston (Antony), Hildegard Neil (Cleopatra), Eric Porter (Enobarbus), John Castle (Octavius), Fernando Rey (Lepidus), Juan Luis Galiardo (Alexas), Freddie Jones (Pompey).

Heston as Marc Antony in *Julius Caesar*, both before . . .

Julius Caesar is Peter Snell's adaptation of Shakespeare's play, with weak performances by most of the major players. Heston is a fine Marc Antony, and in supporting roles Chris Lee, Diana Rigg, and Richard Johnson are superb. On the other hand, John Gielgud as Caesar, Jason Robards as Brutus, and co-star Robert Vaughn are ineffectual. Robards, in particular, turns in an embarrassing performance. The film relates the story of the events preceding and following the assassination of Julius Caesar.

The picture did polite box office business, well enough to inspire a sequel, again produced by Snell and this time directed by Heston himself. The film was *Antony and Cleopatra*. And though the story is from Shakespeare, according to those critics who saw Heston's effort, the picture is from hunger.

Antony and Cleopatra was never released in the United States, although it did fine business in England and Japan. Understandably, this is a circumstance which annoys Heston. For what do superficial critics know about a labor of love? If they had looked beyond the mistakes any first-time director is liable to make they would have found a sensitive interpretation of Shakespeare.

Made for $1,600,000, the picture is quite good. It is peopled with quality actors who all turn in strong performances. The production values are excellent and care was taken to preserve as much of the original text as possible. The film is, in fact, about the best that could be done with the subject matter.

Regarding his subject Heston was sincere and quite knowledgeable. "The problem of playing Marc Antony," he begins, "is a far more complex one than playing The Cid or the lead in *55 Days at Peking*.

. . . and after the assassination of Caesar.

Heston as an older Marc Antony in *Antony and Cleopatra*. This photograph was taken by Lydia Clarke, who is Mrs. Heston.

Marc Antony is unique among the great tragic heroes in that he is the only such hero who is explored by Shakespeare in two plays, and who also has so elaborately documented an historical record. So in a sense, you are playing the real Antony, the historic Antony, and Shakespeare's Antony. Which is the man documented: Shakespeare had the same documentation that is available to us, but it was extended by Shakespeare's genius into a figure of genuinely tragic dimensions.

"In the first play you see Antony's rise and triumph in the forum and the defeat of the conspirators. And, of course, *Antony and Cleopatra* explores his decline and destruction in the arms of Cleopatra.

"It's the same man in both plays, but the man changes, of course. In *Julius Caesar* he was young and confident and sure of what he was doing, sure that he will win. And he does win. In *Antony and Cleopatra* he is an older man who feels the cold breath of disaster on the back of his neck. And who knows that his life with Cleopatra will destroy him. And yet, he's not afraid of death. No Roman was afraid to die. They almost welcome death, in a certain sense. Rather, he's afraid of defeat. To die could be the crown of your life. It can serve your life, as many men have recognized. But to be defeated, to be destroyed, to have all you've worked for go for nothing, that Antony is afraid of.

"To put things into simpler, currently fashionable

terms, in one play Antony's a winner, and in the other he's a loser. His personality in *Julius Caesar* is sanguine, confident, full of *hubris*—or *chutzpah*, if you like—and this he retains until the end. And he dominates *Julius Caesar* partly because he is this winner. He knows that he is the best soldier alive, that he can defeat Brutus and Cassius, and they know it too. This is not only true of Shakespeare's play but of history as well.

"In addition to the profoundity of the character, you have the play *Antony and Cleopatra* itself. It is what amounts to Shakespeare's first screenplay. Shakespeare was the first screenwriter; he instinctively understood the whole medium of film that would not be invented for four centuries, just as he understood the entire essentials of psychoanalysis four centuries before Freud was born. He was, of course, the universal genius. Everything about the human condition was familiar to Shakespeare instinctively.

"*Antony and Cleopatra* has never been an overwhelming success on the stage, for reasons that no one has understood. I appeared in the longest run the play has ever had, with Katharine Cornell. And critics have never had a satisfactory answer to why this play, which they concede ranks with *Hamlet, Othello, Lear,* and *Macbeth* as one of the great tragedies of Shakespeare—which means of the world—has never quite worked on the stage. I think it is because it needs a camera.

"*Hamlet* takes place in a castle in Denmark; it could be a castle in England; it really takes place inside Hamlet's head and in his heart, which is a country difficult to explore with a camera. But *Antony and Cleopatra* not only takes place in Egypt, Sicily, Athens, Greece, and so forth, it is about these places. And you must be able to project the difference in these places; also the distance between them. This, I suggest, is something you can't really do on the stage. Again, to use the analogy of *Hamlet*, all you've got to have is a castle. Any stage designer can give you some kind of castle. Where it is is not that important. You can do it in modern dress. But you can't do *Antony and Cleopatra* in modern dress. It needs the other. And I hope we will have found things with a camera that they have never found on the stage in the play."

This goal was, in fact, achieved by Heston, but fell upon unresponsive viewers. It was "in" to support the Olivier Shakespeare adaptations, but some fifteen years later the classics were out. This was the era of generic film art, and Heston's fine film was a victim of this intellectual snobbery. As one particularly irresponsible critic noted, "Heston's back in a toga playing with swords." If that's all a critic could find to say about the production then one must wonder if it ever really had a chance in the first place.

THE OMEGA MAN

Warner Bros.
1971

Produced by Walter Seltzer. *Directed* by Boris Sagal. *Script* by John William Corrington and Joyce H. Corrington based on the novel *I Am Legend* by Richard Matheson. *Photography* by Russell Metty. *Music* by Ron Grainer. 98 minutes. *Starring* Charlton Heston (Robert Neville), Anthony Zerbe (Matthias), Rosalind Cash (Lisa), Paul Koslo (Dutch).

Heston as Robert Neville, *The Omega Man.*

Heston machine guns a vampire nest

Heston, in his mansion, contemplates how best to combat vampires

Because of the success of *Planet of the Apes*, Heston became very briefly type-cast as a science fiction hero. In this vein he did *The Omega Man* and *Soylent Green*, both solid moneymakers.

The Omega Man is the second film version of Richard Matheson's novel, *I Am Legend*. And as an adaptation it's rather poor; it does, in fact, prostitute a great film property. The book is a well-written science fiction classic that details a biological, war-spawned plague; conversely, the film replaces science fiction with social awareness. And although in and of itself it is good, sturdy entertainment, *The Omega Man* too often lapses into self-indulgent "relevancy" that is simply awful.

The plot tells of a biological war that turns everyone on earth, except for Heston, as Robert Neville, into vampires. Not really vampires in the Draculanian sense: rather, albino creatures whose dilated eyes and minds cannot bear the light.

The picture opens with Heston driving through the deserted and disarrayed streets of Los Angeles. Accidentally wrecking his car, Heston's first words after five minutes of film have gone by are, "Damn. There's never a cop around when you need one."

Taking his spare gas container, Heston walks into an auto showroom. Long-rotted corpses litter the place. He walks over and asks a dead salesman sarcastically, "How much? Can't say I'm crazy about the paint job." Taking the keys to a car, "How long to get an order from the factory?" he queries. "All right. But how much ya give me in trade for my Ford? Oh really? Thanks a lot."

Driving his new vehicle straight through the store window, our hero, bored, pulls up to a movie theatre that screens the film *Woodstock*. "Great show," he mutters. "Held over for a third straight year!" In the cinema we get the feeling that Heston's been here before as he mouths words simultaneously with the on-screen images.

Coming from the theatre, Heston realizes he's stayed longer than he should have. "My God!" he cries. "It's almost dark. They'll be waking up soon." Of course, the audience has no idea about what it is. Pulling onto the expressway he rushes home. But it is dark by the time Heston arrives and, speeding for his garage, he is descended upon by several murderous, hooded figures. Heston navigates into the far wall of the garage interior, tossing one of the characters off. He quickly shuts the door on the others. Though their torches have begun a blaze, Heston has little difficulty getting it under control. He next slams a generator switch. The darkness surrounding his home turns to daylight as powerful beams shatter the night. The other figures run off, blinded. Locking up behind him

Heston prepares to plug a vampire

Heston takes the elevator from his garage to the second floor. There he is secure.

Dressed in a fancy dressing gown, Heston eats dinner. Drinking, he addresses his companion, a plaster bust of Julius Caesar. Outside, the vampires start a fire, whoop and holler, and generally make Heston edgy. "At it again?" he asks pensively, his expression blank. "What'll it be tonight? The museum of science? Some library?" Flashback. Heston recalls how this devastation came about. How a Sino-Russian border war flared into a biological conflagration of international import.

Returning to the present we see a different vantage point. Outside the mansion Matthias, leader of this vampire "family," speaks with Brother Zachary, a once-black man who still bears some malice for the world that was. "Neville can't see in the dark," Matthias begins, "anymore than we can see in the light. He has nothing to live for but his memories. And yet the entire family can't bring him from that. . . ." He is interrupted by Zachary who gazes at the ornate dwelling that was Heston's house even before the holocaust. "From that honky paradise?" he flares.

Another flashback. We see the once-normal Matthias on television. Heston looks on from behind his laboratory desk. "Now the question is survival," the newscaster intones. "Is this the end of technological man? We were warned of judgment. Well, here it is. Now." Heston sits quietly, his face in his hands. He has just discovered an antidote to this plague unleashed by the war. Hence, soon after, Heston is flown to where his cure may do the most good. In mid-flight, however, his pilot is stricken with "vampirism." He dies immediately, and the copter plummets to earth. As it falls, Heston, too, falls prey to the disease. When the copter has crashed, Heston crawls from the wreckage and in a moment of great awareness injects himself with the untested antidote. It works.

At this point Heston's reverie is interrupted. Matthias calls to him. "We have purified all that lives with our zeal," he speaks to Heston. "And nothing quite cleanses like fire." So shouting, he unleashes flaming fireballs at Heston's terrace, from a huge catapult. The scientist excuses himself from Caesar, nonchalantly picks up a machine gun, and mows down several of the family members, thus ending the threat. He returns to Caesar with whom he was playing chess.

The next day Heston returns to downtown Los Angeles. He has been searching for the daylight resting place of the vampires in the hope of destroying Matthias. "Speedy Bob Neville, his great legs churn-

Rosalind Cash, as Lisa, keeps a bead on Heston

ing, goes speeding across the finish mark," he notes sardonically. He has just completed jogging about the city. We see that the date is August 5, 1977.

His mission aside, Heston goes to a clothing store. Dropping unwanted selections on the floor ("Nah! Not my color!"), he sees someone move. It is a black girl. A *human* being. She runs and Heston gives chase, but loses her in a park.

Distressed, "Is this how it starts?" he asks. "A trip to the laughing academy?" Thinking the girl to be a vision, he returns to the city. In a store he finds an empty sardine can from which *he* hadn't eaten. Following up on it, Heston locates an old wine cellar into which he ventures. Which is a mistake. When his back is turned, a rack of bottles falls upon it, and Heston is taken prisoner by a horde of monsters.

The scientist awakens strapped to a table in a room. Matthias and the others stand about him. "I ask you, oh brothers and sisters, does he have the marks?" the scarred leader asks. Then, joyfully, "You see here the last of the scientists, of bankers, of users of the wheel." It looks as if Heston's number is up.

After the speech Matthias says to Heston scornfully, "You are the refuse of the past." Heston responds, "Tell me something, will you? Are you fellows really with the internal revenue?" Matthias ignores Heston's levity. "You are the angel of death, Doctor," he accuses. "Not us. We were chosen for just this work, to bury what was evil. When you die the last living reminder of hell will be gone."

After this encounter the prisoner is brought to the center of what used to be the Colosseum in Los Angeles. He is crucified on a large wooden stake, a pyre spread beneath his suspended form. As the vampires prepare to immolate Heston all the lights go on. Someone runs from the sidelines, frees Heston, and the pair leaves. It's the girl he saw earlier in the day! They mount a waiting motorcycle and ride into the country. Not, however, before a wild chase in the stadium ensues, with Heston and his companion piloting their bike up the arena steps, over car-tops, and running down vampires by the dozen.

Once in the country the girl explains that she, a few children, and a one-time medical student named Dutch are all that's left of humanity . . . or so they suspect. For, though all on earth contracted the plague and eventually die from it, transformation from human to humonster may be rapid . . . or may take weeks. And this group is "going over" slowly. Their only hope is that Heston can help them. Indeed, the girl's own brother is almost completely trans-

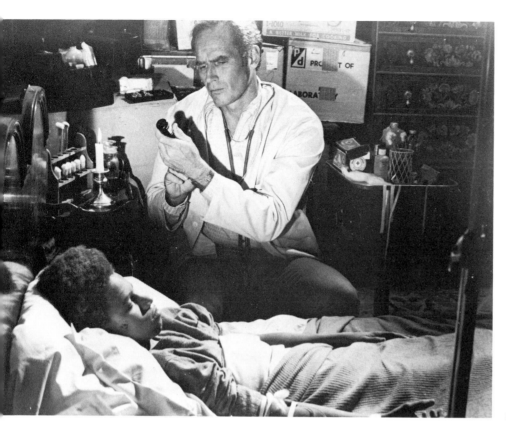

formed. Thinking quickly, "My blood might be a serum," he gives the boy transfusions.

When the blood exchange proves effective, Heston decides to inoculate the half-dozen survivors with it. But he needs tools from his lab to synthesize the cure.

Heston and the girl return to town to his apartment. Relaxing after the ride and rather innocuously, Heston goes up to Caesar and moves a chess piece. "Your move," he says innocently to the statue. "I just made my move," the girl answers, dressed seductively, and the two prepare to make love. As they go to it, however, the lights inside and outside the house go out. It is night and Heston has forgotten to recharge the generator in his garage. He leaves the girl alone, grabs his machine gun, and goes to refuel the engine. As he does, Matthias' black aide takes a gun and goes after Heston. But "Beware, Brother Zachary," he is warned. "Neville has the luck of a devil."

Zachary scales the wall. He reaches the second floor balcony just outside Heston's room as the lights go back on, but he does not turn back.

Meanwhile, Heston comes strutting from the elevator. He does a double-take, brings his machine gun to rapid-fire life, and the girl thinks that Heston has gone mad. Not so. Behind her Zachary goes flying out the window and over the balcony, his body riddled with lead. Alone now and safe, the pair take up where they left off.

"Can I borrow your credit cards?" is the next pressing question answered by the film, as Lisa goes shopping for things they may need. Heston, meanwhile, packs up his tools and the two return to the country.

Ready now to survive any contingency, they ready the children and prepare to move far into the country, beyond Los Angeles. Before they go, however, Lisa wants to pick up some more items in town. Heston warns her to be home before nightfall. Unfortunately, she has not yet been inoculated, and upon reaching Los Angeles she becomes one of the family. Heston goes after her even though darkness is upon them. On the way he battles vampires, loses his car, braves firebombs, and empties many different guns many times over. Finally, however, he discovers Lisa in his room. Unfortunately, Matthias and his people are also there waiting for Heston. They hold him and proceed to destroy his home, smashing paintings, the walls, Caesar, and everything else in sight. Pleased with the carnage, "None of it was real," Matthias says. "It was all an illusion." Still, Heston is not about to give up. He manages to free himself and grabs the girl. Together they rush to the elevator leaving the vampires without transport to the ground.

Heston runs toward his jeep, but Matthias will not be so easily beaten. He calls to Lisa, who hesitates. Heston turns to grab her and leaves himself wide open: seizing this opportunity Matthias plunges a spear deep

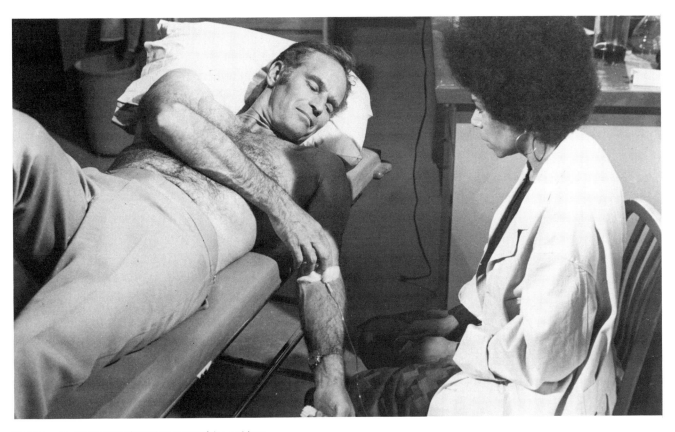

Heston uses his blood to formulate more of the antidote

Heston has just rescued Rosalind Cash from death

Heston tries to get Rosalind Cash to return to his hideaway after she has been stricken with the vampire disease.

into Heston's shoulder. The scientist falls backward into a pool, up against a statue in the midst of the water.

It is near dawn now and the vampires disappear. Dutch and the children come riding along as Lisa cowers within the shadow of the sculpture. Heston lies "crucified" in the pool. In his vest, however, is a pint of his blood; the serum to cure the plague. Taking the girl and the children, Dutch says, "Let's move, kids, we got a long way to go." There is hope for our world.

According to Charlton Heston, "I am deeply interested in science fiction, although films of this type usually require virtually no acting. They fall roughly into two categories: the 'There he comes again' film in which the protagonist is running away from a monster; and the 'Wow, look at that' film in which he is an explorer pointing out fantastic sights never before seen by man." But Heston was impressed with the possibilities of *The Omega Man*. He was particularly stirred by the most intriguing aspect of the film, the vampires' rebellion against technology after an awful science-based catastrophe.

In fact, it was Heston who was responsible for the film's being made, long after the book had been brought to his attention by Orson Welles. As would come as no surprise to a Heston fan, the big change, of course, was the transformation of Neville's character from man to demigod.

"In my opinion—obviously it has to be my opinion, because I was responsible in large part for the changes—the screenplay was better than the novel," Heston declares. "Now I'm not saying that the film was a creative success; I don't think it was. But of the changes we made in the novel, I would defend them, because if I didn't, we wouldn't have made them.

"As for the continuing Christ reference, it was not meant to be taken as seriously as many people took it. There are fragments of the analogy throughout the film. The business of the blood of the redeemer, the survival of the innocent, the crucifixion pose, and all that." But understated or no, the changes and symbolism were unnecessary and they ruined much of the novel's strength. Especially annoying was Rosalind Cash's 'black power' lingo, to which the Heston persona does not relate at all. Indeed, when Heston is called upon for simple, twentieth-century slang (such as in one scene where he addresses Miss Cash as "baby") it falls flat.

Thus—and regrettably—a good portion of the film's impact, as is often the case with science fiction films, is due to the quality of the photography, art direction, and special effects. *The Omega Man* does succeed in conveying Heston's isolation with a constant zooming in and out, leaving our hero truly alone amidst cities, his room, or whatever. There are brutal, impersonal shots of this brave new world: in one instance when Heston chases Miss Cash, he runs over the arm of a years-old corpse. He doesn't even notice this, inured to the bodies and wreckage that dot the landscape.

Technically, however, the most interesting scene in the film is the crash of Heston's helicopter. There is clever trickery here! In a long shot, the craft plunges to earth and explodes. It's a real helicopter and there are real people inside. What the producers did, however, was to fly the copter into a ditch. When, in perspective, it "hit" the ground, a perfectly timed detonation went off between the camera and the bird as the latter slipped behind the wall of the trench. And the effect, with the chopper spiraling down and exploding, is fantastic. Unfortunately, the scene that follows with Heston giving himself the curative injection is ruined by the fact that when he jabs himself, the pad in his leg is painfully visible to the audience. Good followed by bad: in a way, it's really a microcosm of the entire film.

SKYJACKED

MGM
1972

Between takes on *Skyjacked* are Roosevelt Grier (left), Heston, an extra, and James Brolin.

Produced by Walter Seltzer. *Directed* by John Guillermin. *Script* by Stanley R. Greenberg, based on the novel *Hijacked* by David Harper. *Photography* by Harry Stradling, Jr. *Music* by Perry Botkin, Jr. 101 minutes. *Starring* Charlton Heston (Capt. Hank O'Hara), Yvette Mimieux (Angela Thacher), James Brolin (Sgt. Jerome K. Weber/Weller), Claude Akins (Sgt. Ben Puzo), Jeanne Crain (Clara Shaw), Walter Pidgeon (Senator Arne Lindner).

Pilot Henry O'Hara as played by Heston

Charlton Heston has twice taken to the commercial skies. First, it was as pilot of an ill-fated 707 in *Skyjacked*, and then as the man who saves a stricken 747 in the *Airport* sequel, *Airport 1975*.

In *Skyjacked*, James Brolin plays an army officer who goes berserk and hijacks a plane, forcing a flight behind the Iron Curtain. The journey is made interesting by a near collision with a small plane and a stopover in Alaska during a storm. In a tense finale Heston and Brolin fight it out onboard the airplane surrounded by Russian militiamen. Heston is shot by the hijacker and lives; Brolin is shot by the soldiers and their fire sets off hand grenades attached to his belt, blowing him to bits.

The picture has excellent performances, particularly by a low-keyed Heston, as well as absolutely stunning aerial photography. These two extremes make for a slick and exciting thriller. Unlike *The Omega Man* it pretends to do nothing more than entertain. Nonetheless, it still managed to stir up controversy.

"Yes," says Heston, "skyjacking films should be made." This comment came hard on the heels of *Skyjacked* being banned in Australia. The censor there felt that the film too meticulously illustrates the methods whereby one might hijack an airplane. This edict was handed down by the censor despite the fact that the novel *Hijacked*, on which the picture is based, is on sale throughout the country and includes far more detail on how to stage a skyjacking.

"No," Heston continues, "movies should not depict skyjacking as glamorous, funny, exciting, or profitable. So while many people refer to *Skyjacked* as being controversial, I cannot conceive of it being controversial for anybody but hijackers, who surely remain a distinct minority in our society. Had we approached the film carelessly, I can well see the possibility of a controversy arising. When a film examines some public event or recurring situation such as air pirating—hijacking, or our word for it, skyjacking, which seems the most appropriate—the makers of that film undertake, inevitably, a social responsibility that, say, the painter, or the novelist, or the poet doesn't quite have. They cannot either abdicate or forget that responsibility. There are some public controversies in which, though you and I might disagree with the filmmaker's point of view, we can concede the logic of why he holds it. But nobody is going to responsibly argue that hijacking is a good thing, or deserving, or that a hijacker deserves any sympathy. And it's from that point of view, of course, that *Skyjacked* is made. Our hijacker comes to a richly deserved, abrupt unsympathetic end. All through our film it's apparent that he's not a fine fellow; not even a particularly interesting one. I think the communications media has a responsibility which on at least one recent occasion has been avoided. The media covering of a hijacking on Thanksgiving Day with the parachuter presented him as a somewhat glamorous figure. As a result, there

Heston and Roosevelt Grier

A flashback sequence in *Skyjacked* showing a one-time romance between Heston and Yvette Mimieux.

were three more hijackings almost immediately and two people were killed. I can't speak for media responsibility, but I can for this film. It will not encourage anyone to ever hijack a plane."

Heston, even though he sat throughout most of the film, went through a typically Hestonesque training program. He would jog, as he always does at sunup, a full four miles around Mulholland Drive where he lives, in Beverly Hills. This is so he can be back home and make it to the studio by 7:00. "If I don't run before starting work in the morning," he admits, "it's a lead-pipe cinch I'm not going to later at the studio.

"Early each day I slid into a pilot's belt and flew nowhere but on Stage 30. If I was lucky, Director John Guillermin let me take ten for a brisk walk to the bathroom once before he called lunch. Otherwise I was

Two views of the cockpit with Heston and his co-pilot Mike Henry in *Skyjacked*.

strapped right there in the cockpit. The only muscles I could exercise there were my vocal chords."

In all, there are several nice touches to *Skyjacked*. Besides the striking photography there's the way, for example, the skyjacker announces himself: he scrawls on the bathroom mirror, "Bomb on plane . . . no joke . . . no tricks. You will obey my commands!" which is effective, impersonal, and a slightly maniacal presentation. In fact, the film's only major failing—an unnecessary concession to the genre—is the inclusion of a variety of stock characters. There's the elderly senator onboard . . . the pregnant girl . . . the love affair between Heston and Yvette Mimieux that stands in the way of their professional pilot-stewardess relationship, and so forth. Other than that, *Skyjacked* is a much-overlooked entertainment gem.

CALL OF THE WILD

MGM 1972

(No American release). *Produced* by Harry Alan Towers. *Directed* by Ken Annakin. *Script* by Peter Welbeck (Harry Alan Towers), Wyn Wells, and Peter Yeldman, based on the novel by Jack London. *Photography* by John Cabrera. *Music* by Carlo Rustichelli. 105 minutes. *Starring* Charlton Heston (John Thronton), Michele Mercier (Calliope Laurent), Raimund Harmstorf (Pete), George Eastman (Black Burton).

Heston in the foreign film version of *Call of the Wild*.

Call of the Wild is a Charlton Heston film that has disappeared from exhibition. At last report according to George Thomas, Heston's public relations man, "It has vanished from view and none of us knows when, or indeed whether, it will ever be released."

The film was made in 1972, a German, Spanish, Italian, French collaboration, directed, in magnificent color, by Ken Annakin.

Save for striking technical credentials, it's a rather poor film. Based on the Jack London novel *Call of the Wild*, it is strong on realistic dog-fights, exciting sled chases, frozen globs of gore, barroom brawls, and Arctic photography; weak—very weak—on acting. As a

Variety review accurately observed, any film that stars an animal, especially a dog, has a strike against it to begin with. Since dogs cannot act it is up to the humans to let an animal/man relationship come across in realistic fashion. And it is in this respect that *Call of the Wild* fails. Too, there is a lack of punch in its interhuman relationships. Each performer is out to call attention to himself rather than to the film as a whole.

The story concerns a couple of gold-seeking buddies named John and Pete who trek about Alaska's frozen wastelands encountering trouble and adventure in one hundred minutes worth of beautifully photographed landscape.

209

SOYLENT GREEN

MGM
1973

Produced by Walter Seltzer and Russell Thacher. *Directed* by Richard Fleischer. *Script* by Stanley R. Greenberg based on the novel *Make Room! Make Room!* by Harry Harrison. *Photography* by Harry H. Kline. *Music* by Fred Myrow. 97 minutes. *Starring* Charlton Heston (Det. Thorn), Edward G. Robinson (Sol Roth), Leigh Taylor-Young (Shril), Chuck Conners (Tab Fielding), Joseph Cotten (William Simonson).

Edward G. Robinson bicycles up some electric energy as Charlton Heston prepares to go to work in *Soylent Green*.

Heston informs a landlord that he must stop maltreating Leigh Taylor-Young

The best way to describe *Soylent Green* would be to say it does not quite achieve what it set out to do. This is unfortunate, for it could have been a great motion picture.

As with *The Omega Man, Soylent Green* is a bastardized version of an excellent novel, in this case science fiction author Harry Harrison's *Make Room! Make Room!*

The film is set in New York City of 1999, when the population has reached an incredible forty million people. Heston portrays a policeman, sharing a small, dingy apartment with Sol Roth, an elderly walking encyclopedia of information and reference necessary to Heston's investigatory work.

Heston's objective in this film is to discover why Simonsen, an executive of the Soylent Corporation, was murdered in his apartment. Soylent "green" is the world's newest, most plentiful food supply, square wafers made from sea algae, used to feed the masses of people for whom meat, vegetables, and other sustenance is no longer available.

What Heston discovers by the conclusion of the

film is that the Soylent Corporation is no longer using seaweed for their crackers. Instead, they are chemically reducing human beings and recycling them into food. As Heston, stabbed and beaten by Soylent Corporation henchmen, cries out at the end, "Soylent green is people!"

That's the plot. More interesting, strangely enough, is the sub-plot, headed by the late Edward G. Robinson. Robinson is old enough to remember what the world was like way-back-when. And he misses it, so much so that after awhile he decides to take his own life. Since twenty-first century society sanctions euthanasia, the victim is given a pleasant death. Left alone in a large chamber he is permitted twenty minutes of film showing the beauty of a now-dead nature, as well as his favorite music quadrophonically pumped throughout the room. After twenty minutes of this ecstasy, the patient is quietly put to sleep. Heston, of

Heston bandages a wound while Leigh Taylor-Young looks on

Heston beats some information out of Chuck Conners in *Soylent Green.*

course, learns of Robinson's decision and follows him to the auditorium. He literally breaks down and cries when, pushing past the guards, he sees visions of the world that was. As Robinson lies dying on a table, he asks if Heston can now understand how utterly depraved the world has become. "How could I have known?" is all Heston can say from behind a protective window. After this genuinely moving sequence, Heston follows the disposal of Robinson's body, locates the plant that transforms people into food, and the diabolical process is made public. He also learns that Simonson was murdered because of his objection to this sophisticated form of cannibalism.

Soylent Green was Edward G. Robinson's last film, and, ironically, his suicide scene was the final one he shot. Robinson, who knew he was dying, gave this film all he had. Heston, too, was remarkably loose throughout, as were his supporting players, Chuck Conners, Mike Henry, Cotten, and others. Alas, *Soylent Green,* with awful production values, as well as a rambling script, added little lustre to their repertoires.

Nonetheless, the film has several positive qualities beyond the acting. As Heston leaves his second floor apartment and climbs over the impoverished bodies that litter every square inch of free space, there is a credible air of overcrowding. Later, a riot of the populace when soylent wafers are unavailable is effective although the subsequent repression of the uprising, using huge derricks that literally scoop people into dump trucks, is silly. The interior sets of wealthy futuristic apartments, as well as the shabby dwellings of the poor, are well done, but the well decorated sets are few and far between. The Soylent manufacturing site, for example, looks like a Con Edison plant littered with green wafers for effect. And the transports that carry bodies to the place are undisguised garbage trucks. That's either puerile symbolism or lazy art direction.

Too, Heston's love interest with Leigh Taylor-Young is absurd. She is "furniture"; that is, a girl who comes with an apartment. When Heston investigates Simonson's death, she happens to be that apartment's furniture, and he, of course, falls in love with her.

Outside, there is a fine, all-pervading feel of seamy, sweltering heat, many scenes actually tinted yellow-green for effect. And everyone from Heston to his fellow policemen sweat and remain entirely filthy throughout.

This is a picture, as are most of his recent films, that Heston especially wanted to make. The message was one he felt important to bring to the public. To paraphrase Harry Harrison in his dedication to the original novel, "I hope this proves to be a work of fiction."

Not surprisingly, Heston agrees. "If one examines carefully every one of my forty films," he explains, "a central theme runs through the majority of them. Almost all the characters I've played are men with an individual sense of total dedication and responsibility which motivates their triumphs. No one in *Soylent Green* is terribly upset about the human condition at the time. Edward G. Robinson plays a character that laments the lost civilization, but everybody else has a sad sense of acceptance—lethargy—nothing takes on any importance except food and miserable shelter. It's a lethargy we don't need now to avoid it then, if you know what I mean."

We know what he means—but it's a shame the point was lost in the film.

Heston presents a pass that will gain him entry into a euthanasia parlor

THE THREE MUSKETEERS and
THE FOUR MUSKETEERS

20th Century-Fox
1973, 1974

Produced by Alexander Salkind. *Directed* by Richard Lester. *Script* by George MacDonald Fraser based on the novel by Alexandre Dumas. *Photography* by David Watkin. *Music* by Michel Legrand and Lalo Schiffren. 107 minutes each. *Starring* Michael York (d'Artagnan), Oliver Reed (Athos), Raquel Welch (Constance Bonancieux), Richard Chamberlain (Aramis), Frank Finlay (Porthos), Charlton Heston (Cardinal Richelieu), Faye Dunaway (Milady de Winter), Christopher Lee (Rochefort), Geraldine Chaplin (Anne of Austria), Jean-Pierre Cassel (Louis XIII), Simon Ward (The Duke of Buckingham), Spike Milligan (M. Bonancieux).

Although *The Three Musketeers* made a lot of money, there were many disappointed and angry leading players behind the scenes of this film, a spectacular retelling of the classic Dumas tale. Originally produced as a three-and-a-half-hour epic, the picture's producers saw fit to split it in two, making of it two hour-and-three-quarters films—*The Three Musketeers* and *The Four Musketeers*. Since the performers were paid for one film, legal action rocked the post-production environs of this motion picture. The many motions were settled out of court. Nonetheless, the film is a good one, a humorous look at the rowdies known as the Three Musketeers.

Richard Lester, the film's director and the man responsible for the widely acclaimed and popular Beatles' films, *A Hard Day's Night* and *Help* said, "I think Dumas liked his heroes somewhat less than people imagine; the Musketeers are mercenaries; they'll fight if anyone gives them the money to have a pretty horse or a pretty suit, and they're just bully boys. D'Artagnan is illiterate, an innocent who becomes a show-off rather too quickly. I was after the balance of a romantic adventure with some cynical comedy in it, rooted as closely as possible in the 1620s. You should be aware that even though it's a romantic piece, everyone was pretty filthy, that they never washed, and they urinated on all those tapestries that are now in the museums. But all that detail must be there without interfering with the sweep of adventure."

And adventure there is in this first half of the original picture, subtitled "The Queen's Necklace." It relates the story of D'Artagnan's ride from France to England to retrieve Geraldine Chaplin's necklace from Simon Ward. As Queen, Chaplin had given the diamond piece as a token to her lover, Ward, the Duke of Buckingham. Prompted by Heston—who seeks to discredit the Queen and create a scandal that would enable him to take power—the King plans a ball in two weeks' time asking, specifically, that the necklace be worn. Naturally, after much dalliance, the necklace is returned to the Queen in the nick of time, and Heston is foiled. "Milady's Revenge," subtitle for *The Four Musketeers*, features Heston's final defeat.

In both pictures Heston plays Cardinal Richelieu, the man who really ruled France through the King. It is a small part, but it gave the actor a chance to do a tongue-in-cheek character role.

"I did the picture because of Dick Lester," Heston admits. "The director is the most important thing about a film; and then the part itself. Richelieu is the most interesting and intelligent character in the film. He ran France for Louis XIII, and great men are always a little more interesting to play. Of course, I don't look anything like Richelieu; there's the problem of physical bulk for a start, because he was a slight man. I play him with a lighter voice than usual, and also with a limp to try to diminish my size a bit. I have a false nose too. My wife Lydia took one look at the portrait in the National Gallery in London and said, 'He was a migraine sufferer,' because she used to be one too. He was a very driven man."

In terms of the film itself Heston says, "If you ask about Dick Lester's camera style, if he's doing supposedly zany Dick Lester things, I can only say that he shot it very simply; there wasn't even a camera dolly around. I guess I must have been in this business too long," he adds, "because we were shooting a scene by a river a few days ago, and I suddenly realized we'd done a scene there for *El Cid* in 1961. I told Dick and he said, 'Tell me where you put the camera.'"

Heston is most impressive in his wig, moustache and goatee, with priestly red robes causing him to stand out majestically amongst the grime-laden garb of the Musketeers, as well as the pomp and frill of the royalty. Indeed, in his brilliant performance Heston mocks not only the straight-laced epic that *The Three Musketeers* has traditionally been, but parodies himself as well. Once or twice during the course of the film he strikes Moses-like poses that accent the pomposity of his character and, to a lesser extent, poke fun at Heston himself.

Charlton Heston as Cardinal Richelieu in *The Three Musketeers*.

AIRPORT 1975

Universal
1974

Heston and James Gavin radio instructions to a stricken 747 in *Airport 1975*.

Heston (left) and George Kennedy (behind Heston) watch as Ed Nelson prepares to transfer from an air force helicopter to a pilotless 747

Produced by Bill Frye. *Directed* by Jack Smight. *Script* by Don Ingalls from the novel by Arthur Hailey. *Photography* by Philip Lathrop. *Music* by John Cacavas. 107 minutes. *Starring* Charlton Heston (Murdock), Karen Black (Nancy), George Kennedy (Patroni), Efren Zimbalist Jr. (Stacy), Susan Clark (Mrs. Patroni), Helen Reddy (Sr. Ruth), Linda Blair (Janice), Dana Andrews (Scott Freeman), Roy Thinnes (Urias) Sid Caesar (Barney), Myrna Loy (Mrs. Devaney), Ed Nelson (Major Alexander), Nancy Olson (Mrs. Abbott), Larry Storch (Purcell), Martha Scott (Sr. Beatrice), Jerry Stiller (Sam), Guy Stockwell (Col. Moss), Gloria Swanson (herself).

After a lengthy flight from Washington, D.C., to Los Angeles, passengers of a 747 are annoyed that the Los Angeles airport is fogged-in and that their plane will land at Salt Lake City. Worse, is the fact that a private plane flown by a business executive is headed in the same direction. The executive is suddenly stricken with a heart attack. His hands lock on the stick and his plane noses upward climbing higher and higher until it crashes into the nose of the jumbo jet's flight deck. Impact puts a gaping hole in the cockpit of the giant plane. The co-pilot is sucked from his seat and goes flying into space; the navigator is killed by a falling instrument panel. The pilot is blinded and cannot fly the aircraft. Nancy, the head stewardess, scared but cool, takes over the controls as flying instructions come from the tower.

On the ground everyone has been alerted. Joe Patroni, Columbia Airlines' president, and Heston, a former jet pilot who is engaged to Nancy, decide to try and put a pilot into the giant plane as quickly as possible. Heston and Patroni accompany the Air Force rescue team in a jet helicopter, and an Air Force major is lowered on a tether line toward the crippled plane. Unfortunately, as the daredevil nears the craft, a flapping piece of the airplane's torn skin catches his tether release and the fellow plummets to the ground. Heston, against Patroni's orders, attempts the mid-air transfer . . . and succeeds. He lands the plane safely and all ends happily.

Although Heston learned to fly a 747 for the film (he practiced on the American Airlines simulator in Dallas; "I crashed it several times," he admits) and, indeed, flew the real McCoy itself for a total of ninety minutes airtime, plaudits for the box-office giant *Airport 1975* must go to none of the film's superstars but to the photography and to Joe Canutt. First, Mr. Canutt, the man who actually executed the mid-air transfer from helicopter to jumbo jet.

One of the most flamboyant stuntmen in film history, Canutt had hoped to make the first actual completed mid-air transfer in aviation history and have it

Heston, Ed Nelson, and George Kennedy watch as their helicopter pilot lower them toward a gaping hole in a 747. . . .

recorded on film. Despite weeks of begging for airline permission (in which Heston was a vocal participant, realizing how much the stunt meant to Joe), he could not persuade the bigwigs to allow the transfer. Too, for the scene in which the Air Force major attempting the transfer falls to his death, Canutt wanted to wear a lightweight piggy-back parachute which would not be visible from the front, and free-fall into space while the airborne camera crew filmed the action. Again, this bit of derring-do was denied him.

In any event, what Canutt did do, well protected with a flying suit and helmet, was to fly in an Air Force HH-53B helicopter to within ten feet of the 747, which was flying below the helicopter at an altitude of 8,000 feet. Wearing no parachute, the stuntman was required to do the stunt four times at half-hour stints, for the camera to get all of its shots. Talking about the stunt, Canutt said that dangling thus in space produced "an odd sensation" but that he began to enjoy it after a while. He was also surprised to learn how frigid it was out there: spinning around in the sky he found ice forming under his nose!

Another incredible sequence in the film was the landing of the damaged aircraft. The scene required the renting of a jet for six days, at a cost of $52,000 a day! In the story, though its full braking system is inoperative, the plane is forced to land and in so doing crashes through and demolishes a radar shack. For the stunt a break-away structure was erected and a plug placed in the jet's third engine to prevent any real damage. The pilot ran the course once as a dry run, and then proceeded to smash the shack without causing a single scratch to the plane!

So there was hardly a dearth of stunt-courage in this effort. And unlike *Airport*, not a single miniature airplane model was used for the film. All shots of the monster aircraft and of the plane's death-defying flight just yards above the peaks of the Rocky Mountains, were real and breathtaking.

The only false note about the $3,000,000 film were the performances, although the actors are not to blame; in terms of script they had a reworking of *The High and the Mighty* with which to work. And when Helen Reddy, as a nun, picked up a guitar and started singing. . . .

As an historical note, *Airport 1975* marked the fourth happy co-starring of Charlton Heston with Martha Scott. They were together on Broadway, and she played his mother in both *The Ten Commandments* and *Ben-Hur*. However, the bottom line of the film must be somewhat negative. For while *Airport 1975* made a lot of money and brought Heston back into a spectacular, it was a far cry from the distinctive days of Judah Ben-Hur.

. . . Heston and Nelson plan their strategy. . . .

. . . and Heston watches helplessly, as Nelson's umbilical tether tears, sending the Major to his doom.

Heston, himself, finally makes the transfer and, here, brings the 747 down safely.

EARTHQUAKE

Universal
1974

Produced and *Directed* by Mark Robson. *Script* by George Fox and Mario Puzo. *Photography* by Philip Lathrop. *Music* by John Williams. 107 minutes. *Starring* Charlton Heston (Stuart Graff), Ava Gardner (Remy Graff), George Kennedy (Lew), Lorne Green (Sam Royce), Genevieve Bujold (Denise Mitchell), Richard Roundtree (Miles Quade), Marjoe Gortner (Jodie), Victoria Principale (Lisa).

Twenty minutes were cut from *Earthquake* prior to its theatrical release, and it is something for which we can be thankful. These were scenes dealing primarily with the attempt of a 707 to land in Los Angeles while the airport is breaking up beneath it. Since *Earthquake* was released a month after *Airport 1975*, Universal felt that they were being redundant. Someone should have told them that the entire film was redundant.

Earthquake is one of Heston's worst and, paradoxically, most popular films. The special effects are fine, but the drama is almost as poor as the acting. It serves to reinforce the notion that when Charlton Heston plays an "everyday guy," either the character becomes Moses or Heston becomes ill at ease.

Heston is a building executive whose boss Sam is his wife Remy's father. His wife is a bitch and she turns Heston to the arms of a mistress, Denise, whose husband had died in an accident on a building site to which Heston had assigned him. Revolving around this dull narrative core are subplots featuring Lew Slade, a policeman suspended for slugging a fellow officer, Jody, a demented army reservist, a motorcycle daredevil named Miles Quade, and a seismological institute that knows there's an earthquake coming but can't decide what to do about it. In the end, trapped in a flooding storm drain with his wife, Heston chooses to try and save her rather than run up a ladder to the waiting arms of his girlfriend. He drowns for his efforts, along with Remy.

Earthquake like its contemporaries, *The Poseidon Adventure* and *The Towering Inferno*, among others, is a disaster film. "This really isn't a new thing," Heston explains. "It's a pattern that goes back as far as movies. And one reason for the return of the group jeopardy movie—as I prefer to call them—is that filmmakers can once again afford to burn down an office building, or destroy Los Angeles, or rent a 747. The past year (1974) has been a very good one for the industry. And people are willing to invest in multi-million dollar productions. Because when the economy isn't very good people are less likely to be out on vacations, or on skiing trips, or out gambling in Las Vegas.

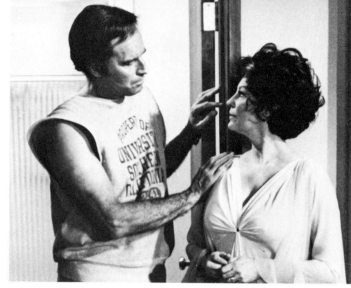

Heston, as construction executive Stewart Graff, has an early morning argument with his wife Remy, played by Ava Gardner, in *Earthquake*.

. . . so Heston visits his new mistress, Genevieve Bujold

And film is an inexpensive form of entertainment. About the least expensive, in fact, if you don't count television. Which you can't, really, because people still want to go out.

"As for *Earthquake*, most of the acting parts are more or less chemical contributions. The audience needs someone they can identify and say to themselves, 'He's going to do something about all of this.' And because people know me as an authoritative presence, there's no problem in featuring me as a person who takes charge of a holocaust. Part of the reason for this is my shadow. No matter how versatile an actor may be or how he strives to widen his range, he must deal with his shadow. And my shadow has been Moses, El Cid, and Michelangelo, not to mention a president or two. If you need a chariot race run, a ceiling painted, or the Red Sea parted, you think of me. So in this film it isn't necessary to explain that my character will be responsible. You don't have to take time out to explain that to the audience. It's built in."

Anyway, so much for generic definitions and an

Los Angeles crumbles around Heston and Miss Gardner as they hide beneath Heston's car

One of the incredible miniature sets constructed for *Earthquake*.

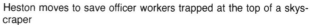

Marjoe Gortner (left) prevents Heston (right) and George Kennedy (second from right) from transporting wounded civilians through a quarantined area

Heston moves to save officer workers trapped at the top of a skyscraper

overview. Regarding *Earthquake*, to quote Universal Studio publicity releases: "Against the canvas of a giant megalopolis *Earthquake* dramatizes the raging fury, the destructive force, and the apocalyptic horror of a temblor that strikes Los Angeles and reduces a great part of the city to rubble. Movies depicting the ravages of nature have been attempted before, but never on the massive scale of *Earthquake*. *Earthquake* is one of the most want-to-see motion picture entertainments in the history of the film industry. It stars Charlton Heston, Ava Gardner, George Kennedy, Lorne Greene, Genevieve Bujold, and Richard Roundtree. Over a thousand actors, atmosphere and extra players, appear with them as personae in the gallery of characters caught up in the quake's devastation. There are spectacular scenes of shaking and crumbling buildings, hundreds of people buried in a hail of debris and rubble, falling elevators crowded with passengers, toppling high tension towers, broken bridges, trapped people, buckling streets, twisting freeways, tumbling vehicles, people hurled from high places, crackling earth, collapsing houses, explosions, fires, and finally the awesome bursting of the Hollywood Dam and the simulated release of three and a half billion gallons of raging flood waters that sweep away people and buildings.

In one hazardous street scene Heston, shielding Miss Gardner, found safety underneath a parked car. A second later, great chunks of concrete slammed down on cue, hitting, as preplanned, within inches of the stars. All around them actors fell to the ground, dodged falling fragments, and were caught in a hail of metal and plaster. While some of the material was fashioned of styrofoam as a safety measure—with steel reinforcing bars inserted to speed descent—large signs, concrete boulders, and cement walls were real. In fact, the broken concrete that crushes two cars within six feet of Heston and Miss Gardner weighed over six tons."

In actuality then it is the special effects, and not the stock characters which are the stars of *Earthquake*. Along, of course, with the new audience-participation process called *Sensurround*. This gimmick is a low-frequency sound system that simulates the effect of earth tremors. It will, according to press sheets, "Thrust each moviegoer into the epicenter of the cataclysmic earthquake."

Whether it does or not is really unimportant. Charlton Heston doesn't need gimmicks to sell his films. When Heston can do work the quality of *Will Penny, Planet of the Apes,* and the historical dramas, the puzzle is not why he does these senseless lemons—he's got to make a living—but why the powers-that-be in Hollywood insist on throwing a distinguished talent into these buzzards!

Heston and George Kennedy argue with soldiers to permit them paasage to a hospital in *Earthquake.*

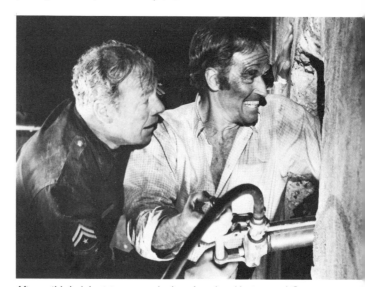
After a third violent tremor rocks Los Angeles, Heston and George Kennedy dig through debris to rescue seventy trapped civilians

Heston and Phil Lathrop

MIDWAY

Produced by Walter Mirisch. *Directed by* Jack Smight.
Script by Donald S. Sanford. *Photography by* Harry
Stradling Jr. *Music by* John Williams. 132 minutes.
Starring Charlton Heston (Capt. Matt Garth), Henry
Fonda (Adm. Chester W. Nimitz), Toshiro Mifune
(Adm. Yamamoto), Edward Albert (Ensign Garth),
Robert Mitchum (Adm. William F. Halsy), James
Shigeta (Vice Admiral Nagumo), Christina Kokubo
(Haruko Sakura), James Coburn (Capt. Maddox),
Glenn Ford (Adm. Spruance), Hal Holbrook (Cdr.
Rochefort), Cliff Robertson (Cdr. Jessop), Ed Nelson
(Adm. Pearson), Robert Wagner (L. Cdr. Blake),
Monte Markham (Cdr. Max Leslie), Kevin Dobson
(Ensign George Gay).

The American victory at the Battle of Midway,
fought in June of 1942, is generally acknowledged to
have been the turning point of the war in the Pacific.
The defeat of the Japanese fleet ended Admiral Yamamoto's plan to use the small island as a stepping stone
for an invasion of the west coast of the United States.

Midway, another presentation in *Sensurround*,
was Heston's first foray into the navy, so it was only
natural that he celebrate the occasion by sinking an
aircraft carrier single-handedly and be martyred in the
process. Unfortunately, portraying the fictitious Captain Matt Garth, Heston served as little other than a
focal point to shuttle the viewer back and forth between the staff of Admiral Chester A. Nimitz (Fonda),
as the navy brass formulated strategy, and the aircraft
carrier on which he served.

Although the second half of the overlong film was
swallowed up whole by the battle—actual and riveting
16mm combat footage cutting with only fair results
into the 70mm film, and stock shots from an uncredit-
ed Japanese film used to represent scenes on the flag-
ship—the first half of the picture managed to work in
some romance and weak social commentary. Matt's
son, Ensign "Tiger" Garth (Albert), is in love with Haruko Sakura (Christina Kokubo), a Japanese-Ameri-
can girl who was arrested with her family and held at a
Hawaiian detention camp, charged by the FBI with
subterfuge. Convinced of her innocence, and in def-
erence to his son, Matt throws his weight around to try
and get her released. He succeeds, of course, and Haruko is on hand at the film's conclusion when her
wounded fiance returns to the base. Given the drama
inherent in such illegal restraints, the subplot is a tremendous letdown. The situation is never presented
from the point of view of the victimized family—its
most potentially effective perspective—and boils down
to a flat study of Matt. His associates warn him that his
sympathy for the Nisei girl will ruin his career, but the
captain accepts it all with righteous determination,
bent on seeing that justice is done.

Given the parameters of the character *Midway*
offered Heston his third dimensionless role in as many
films. Like the *Airport 1975* and *Earthquake* personalities Garth is a colorless, unrounded icon who was tailored to the heroic Heston mystique, rather than vice
versa. Indeed, Heston played his character with such
wooden unflappability that even the few emotional
scenes with his son fell apart. In contrast, Fonda,
Albert, Holbrook (as Commander Rochefort, the
codebreaker), and especially Glenn Ford (as Admiral
Spruance), worked their every scene to highlight the
man beneath the military uniform. Apparently, as
long as Garth did good and noble deeds Heston did
not care to look for his human substratum.

The *Sensurround* gimmick used to rumble the
viewer in varying degrees whenever a plane rose from
a carrier deck, negotiated through flak, or bombed a
target, was well used in *Midway*. It underlined the battle scenes with precision rather than, as in *Earthquake*, served with parity or often dominated the
on-screen action. On the negative side, technically,
the few action sequences shot exclusively for the film
were terribly drab, particularly the strafing of Midway
Island itself, and the decision to have the American
announcer Paul Frees dub Toshiro Mifune's lines
drew a laugh from the audience at every turn. In all,
this was not the film that fans had hoped would ultimately be drawn from one of history's most significant
military encounters.

From left to right: Dabney Coleman as
Commander Murr Arnold, Charlton Hes-
ton as Capt. Matt Garth, and Gregory
Walcott as Capt. Elliott Buckmaster.

221

TWO-MINUTE WARNING

Produced by Edward S. Feldman. *Directed by* Larry Peerce. *Script by* Edward Hume from the novel by George La Fountaine. *Photography by* Gerald Hirschfeld. *Music by* Charles Fox. 115 minutes. *Starring* Charlton Heston (Capt. Peter Holly), John Cassavetes (Sgt. Chris Button), Beau Bridges (Mike Ramsay), Martin Balsam (Sam McKeever), Jack Klugman (Stu Sandman), Gena Rowlands (Janet), David Janssen (Steve), David Groh (Spinner), Joe Kapp (Charlie Tyler), Walter Pidgeon (Pickpocket), Marilyn Hassett (Lucy), Brock Peters (Paul), Mitchell Ryan (Priest), with cameo appearances by Merv Griffin, Howard Cossell, and Frank Gifford as themselves.

A competent suspense film, *Two-Minute Warning* is nonetheless another in a growing list of disappointing vehicles for Charlton Heston. Always ill-at-ease when playing ordinary citizens, Heston stars as a police captain whose job is to stop a sniper from training his sites on a championship football game.

The setting is the Los Angeles Colosseum on the day of a play-off match. Through subjective shots we see the sniper drive to the stadium and sneak into a tower above the stadium score-board, a fateful journey staggered with vignettes featuring the requisite host of supporting players: the gambler who is betting with syndicate money (Jack Klugman), the quarreling lovers (David Janssen and Gena Rowlands), the swinging single (David Groh), the pickpocket (Walter Pidgeon), the tired veteran quarterback (ex-football quarterback Joe Kapp), and, most satisfying of all, a young man recently fired from his job and trying to show his family a good time (Beau Bridges). Since the audience is never told either the sniper's mission or his identity, one assumes that he is waiting for the arrival of the President of the United States. Perched in his cement aerie the sharpshooter sits munching on candy bars, when he is picked up by cameras positioned on the Goodyear Blimp. Heston and a SWAT sergeant, played by John Cassavetes, are called in. They go coolly about their business, secretly positioning men about the stadium, in helicopters, and on park lights, as the game builds to its climax. When it is announced that the President's visit has been canceled and the sniper spots the SWAT team, he opens fire. Several policemen, as well as Klugman, Janssen, and Pidgeon

are killed, Bridges' wife is wounded and, as the killer shoots at random into the crowd, the fans panic. People are trampled in the frenzied exodus from the stadium. Cassavetes is wounded when he tries to broach the tower, and it is up to Heston to finally nail the sniper by braving his fire and drilling him with a handgun.

Two-Minute Warning makes several cogent points about the sorry way in which the media will make the sniper famous, while just as invariably condemning the police by asking if it were *really* necessary to kill what turns out to have been a young and clearly demented individual. The picture takes the SWAT to task for manhandling, beating, torturing, or practicing punting methods on stadium patrons who look like they might be in league with the sniper. Only Heston, of course, is against these shoot-first-ask-questions-later tactics, and stands by them until the sniper actually opens fire. However, on a broader moral scale, *Two-Minute Warning* dramatically points out the insanity of our species by showing us that such creatures as the sniper *do* exist. It makes the sickness much more immediate than when it is shown on the evening news. Indeed, the film's most effective moments are the opening shots. Alone in a hotel room the sniper peers through the telescopic sites of his rifle and casually picks off a bicyclist for target practice. It's a sobering dose of reality that argues persuasively for instituting more careful methods of making arms available to the public.

Two-Minute Warning suggests that Heston is out of his league trying to play a simple, twentieth century human being. He can't utter colloquial oaths with any authority and is terribly awkward in contemporary dress and amidst modern surroundings. In short, he belongs to the spectacular character roles and there is some of this in Heston's future: he is Henry VIII in Richard Fleischer's *The Prince and the Pauper*, and a sheriff in pursuit of the men who raped his daughter in *The Last Hard Men*.

There is no doubt but that Charlton Heston has

Heston and John Cassavetes (left) draw a bead on the sniper.

Heston climbs the clock-tower ladder in a final assault on the sniper.

staying power. Twenty-six years as a movie headliner prove that. And there is no question as to his talent: *Ben-Hur, The Warlord, Will Penny,* and *Planet of the Apes* feature some of the cinema's most thoughtful and evocative performances. He turned down *The Omen* because he felt that the Devil should not triumph in art; he accepted *Two-Minute Warning* because it made social observations which he believes are valid. Realistically, of course, his bearing is more ideally suited to that of the United States Ambassador in *The Omen* than to the policeman in *Two-Minute Warning*. In the fullness of time, we will no doubt have many more classics from the man who was Moses, Andrew Jackson, Thomas Jefferson, Michelangelo, El Cid, et al . . . and even for Charlton Heston that is quite a lot for one lifetime!

APPENDIX

The Stage Plays

Regarding the stage performances outlined in the biographical chapter, Heston has made the following comments about *A Man For All Seasons*, in which he played Thomas More. In fact, it is this role, in the motion picture version of the play, that Heston wanted more than any other role.

"Now there," he offers, "although Scofield's performance was remarkable and enormously effective, oddly enough, More was rather closer to my persona than to Scofield's. Historically, he was fond of hunting, was an affable man with a wide circle of friends, a man who genuinely liked not only people like Erasmus and so forth, but he sincerely liked King Henry, and got on enormously well with the Duke of Norfolk, who was a very different sort of man.

"Anyway, that's the outstanding part I was disappointed in not having. I wasn't busy at the time; they, understandably enough, wanted Scofield for the part. He created the part, he was English, he was very good in it. I don't blame them. But I still would have liked to play it."

One unfortunate play in which Heston starred was the 1960 stage production of Benn Levy's *The Tumbler*. After *Ben-Hur*, Heston turned down a role opposite Marilyn Monroe in *Let's Make Love* to do this play on Broadway, directed by Sir Laurence Olivier and co-starring Martha Scott. The plot was that a young girl returns to her countryside farm in England and there meets and succumbs to a laborer named Kell, whom she later discovers is her stepfather. On top of this is the complication that Kell may have murdered her first father. It's a somewhat bizarre premise,

and the play did not go over at all well with the critics. Although Heston got some good notices, called by *The New York Times* "Massive, masculine, and fluent," and by *The New Yorker* "Wry, verbose, and sexy . . . speaking lines with a leaden thrust." The show closed after only five performances.

One observer, Pete Hamill, felt that Heston's characteristically defensive attitude toward film may have been fostered by his unfortunate experience with the play. "Acting for films is just as important as acting for theatres, if not more so," Heston told him. "This is simply because of the overwhelming numbers of people you can reach."

Regarding *The Tumbler*, Heston said in an interview after the play closed, "I feel I'm the only one who came out of it with a profit. The producers lost money, and the writer lost months of work. Larry Olivier lost out too. But I got out of it precisely what I went in for: a chance to work with Olivier. I learned from him in six weeks things I never would have learned otherwise. I think I ended up a better actor, with more responsibility.

"Of course, poor Benn Levy had his baby chopped into mincemeat. The reviews were just scathing. And Olivier, who was then in the midst of the most agonizing personal situation with his then-wife Vivien Leigh, found it a traumatic and painful experience. I fared slightly better. Since acting is a highly subjective art, I don't think it's a remarkable comment to say critics' area of competence is not in the judgment of acting. And I didn't really expect the play to run like *Barefoot in the Park*."